GEORGIAN & REGENCY ARCHITECTURE

Endpapers: *a section of the very distinctive façade of the Circus, Bath, 1754–66, by John Wood the Elder with John Wood the Younger. It was inspired by the Colosseum in Rome, and each storey is embellished with an independent order of columns*

Facing page: *the Palladian Bridge at Stowe was the second of three nearly-identical bridges that were built in English gardens between 1737–55, and has been attributed to James Gibbs. The first, by Roger Morris with Henry Herbert, ninth Earl of Pembroke, was erected at Wilton, near Salisbury, and the third, thought to have been designed by Thomas Pitt, is at Prior Park, Bath*

Overleaf: *Lewes Crescent, Brighton, c 1825, by Charles Augustus Busby*

GEORGIAN & REGENCY ARCHITECTURE

CHAUCER PRESS
LONDON

First published in Great Britain by
Chaucer Press
an imprint of the
Caxton Publishing Group
20 Bloomsbury Street
London WC1B 3JH

ISBN 1 904449 01 8

Designed and produced by Superlaunch Ltd
P.O. Box 207, Abingdon, Oxfordshire
OX13 6TA, England
Imagesetting by Midsomer Planning
Colour reproduction by IGS
Printed and bound in China by
Sun Fung Offset Binding Company Limited

Contents

Hawksmoor were its chief exponents in England, and they produced titanic compositions in stone and brick that relied upon their heroic proportions to convey the impression of magnificence.

The death of Vanbrugh and Hawksmoor followed that of Wren, coinciding with the demise of this free-enterprise spirit of experiment and invention. The large houses that followed later in the century, although continuing to be laid out on the grand scale, evolved into less generous, more rigorous structures. Their air of aristocratic superiority was conveyed by the 'Palladian' style of features such as doors, windows and mouldings, which was commonly employed from the mid-eighteenth century onwards.

Towns continued to grow rapidly throughout the eighteenth century, especially trading centres such as Norwich, Bristol and Liverpool, fashionable spa resorts such as Bath, and that epicentre of business, the City of London, where the population grew from 490,000 in 1700 to 950,000 in 1800. This pressure to house entrepreneurs close to their businesses resulted in the invention of the terrace, which provided an unparalleled density of housing. The first terraced houses were mostly four storeys high, plus the basement, with a short flight of steps to the front door. The principal rooms were located on the first floor. Their windows were tall and dignified, with sash openings and wooden glazing bars.

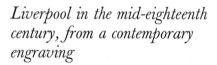

Liverpool in the mid-eighteenth century, from a contemporary engraving

Large tracts of land relatively close to city centres were still in the hands of single landowners. The building of a whole street of houses all run together offered economies of both space and scale, which encouraged it to be treated as an architectural whole. This harmony lent these homes an air of dignity, apparently reflecting the wealth of the occupant, and thus the owners were able to develop these parcels of land so as to attract tenants who would be able and willing to pay high rents for properties they deemed suitable to their own social standing. The terraces appeared in simple straight streets, bordered fine big squares, formed crescents or created circuses with one terrace leading to another, finally terminating in an avenue of trees.

Architects and contractors became responsible for very large mass housing schemes for the first time, and so were able to plan accordingly. For instance, the architects John Wood senior (1705–54) and his son, also John (1728–81), were responsible for developing large areas of Bath; similarly George Dance (1700–68) and his son, also George (1774–1825) for Dublin and somewhat later the Adam brothers for developing large parts of London in a style all of their own. The Adams, whose designs were influenced by ancient Greek details, refined all of the features of the Georgian town house.

Under the influence of the patronage of the Prince of Wales, the Georgian period gave way to the Regency period. The style manifested itself in the building of the Royal Pavilion, Brighton and the remodelling of both Buckingham Palace and Windsor Castle. A scheme devised by John Nash (1752–1835), the Prince Regent's favourite architect and the chief exponent of the Regency style, redeveloped Regent Street to Regent's Park, in London's West End.

During the Regency and the reign of George IV, middle-class homes continued to be in the classical tradition, brick-built and often covered in stucco or painted plaster. The buildings were graced by a delicate Graeco-Italian flavour with their refined proportions and painted surfaces. The fashion for stucco had been imported from Italy, and originally it was colour-washed to imitate stone.

A tendency that had been foreshadowed by the Adam brothers, the enthusiasm for Greek and Graeco-Egyptian motifs, developed under the influence of archaeologists such as Lord Elgin and many other amateur antiquaries. All the richness and refinements of Greek carving, fluted columns and the delicate folds of classical drapery were reproduced in elegant stucco. This elegance is the essence of Regency architecture. The grander buildings of the Nash terraces around Regent's Park continued to be planned in the grand Roman manner, but were tricked out in all of the refinements of contemporary versions of classical Greece.

The smaller and less ostentatious terraces and houses of the Regency, also often in stucco, are simply a less robust version of the Georgian. Almost any town with pretensions to fashion has a number of such buildings, with their refined glazing bars, gossamer-fine iron balconies roofed in curving metal like Chinese pagodas, or curved bay-windows, bay fronts and round-arched front doors. Their wall surfaces are nearly always plain and their roofs often low-pitched with wide projecting eaves, recalling the warm Mediterranean, an effect that was deliberately heightened by the use of painted wooden shutters.

Above: *44 Berkeley Square, London, c. 1745–50, by William Kent; a perfect Georgian terrace house, the splendour of its staircase and saloon were unmatched by those of any terraced London house*

Chapter Two

The Georgian Dynasty

THE HOUSE OF HANOVER took its name from Ernest Augustus, First Elector of Hannover in north-west Germany. He was the father of George I (1660–1727) who inherited the British crown through his mother Sophia, a granddaughter of James I, and a Protestant.

George I (reigned 1714–1727) succeeded to the British throne on 1 August 1714 under the 1701 Act of Settlement. He was then 54, and was to reign for almost 13 years. He appointed a Whig ministry and came to depend upon his powerful ministers, Sir Robert Walpole and Viscount Charles Townsend. He married Sophia Dorothea of Celle (1666–1726), divorcing her in 1694 after he had fathered two children, George II and Sophia Dorothea.

George II ascended to the throne on 11 June 1727, and reigned for over 33 years. He married Caroline of Ansbach (1683–1737) and had eight children. The last British king to lead troops into battle, he was victorious at Dettingen in 1743. His reign saw major agricultural and manufacturing advances which led to social and political change. He was succeeded by his grandson, George III.

George III had been born on 4 June 1734 and became King on 25 October 1760. He reigned for 59 years and 96 days, dying deaf, blind and senile on 29 January 1820. During his lengthy reign Britain's population doubled and the Industrial Revolution gathered momentum, bringing with it new social classes and the shaping of modern party politics. By the time of his death in 1820 Britain was Europe's leading power, with a growing world empire.

George IV, son of George III, effectively had ruled since becoming Prince Regent in 1811. He reigned for ten years until 26 June 1830. Although his lazy, profligate life damaged the monarchy's moral influence, he fostered art and literature. His prolific and enthusiastic patronage of major building projects encouraged a style which became identified as Regency. It brought to an end the Georgian influence which had been advanced and developed under the House of Hanover for more than a century.

Opposite: *a statue of George I in the guise of Emperor Marcus Aurelius, which stands near the front of Stowe House*

Below: *King George IV being crowned at Westminster Abbey*

Chapter Three

Towns: Buildings and Town Planning

IN SEVENTEENTH-CENTURY BRITAIN spasmodic attempts to contain a sprawling and intensively individualistic building system and establish a planned, socially balanced and architecturally coherent urban scheme had already been made; but the eighteenth century was to be an age obsessed by town planning.

These exceptional attempts to create entire architecturally pleasing compositions in the earlier century include Inigo Jones' Palladio-inspired Covent Garden for the Duke of Bedford in 1631; that same Duke's more socially-engineered development of Bloomsbury Square in 1660, and the Duke of St Albans' creation of the 'small town' of regular brick houses at St James' Square, of 1670. From these disjointed beginnings, the ideal of estate development emerged to play a key role in the formation of large-scale town planning and urban development.

The government introduced the Building Act in 1667, following the Great Fire of 1666. This was intended at once to regulate the rebuilding of the city, to influence both the design and the construction of terrace houses, and town planning throughout the country. One of its primary concerns was to ensure the sound construction of buildings, including fireproofing, to which end it specified that party walls as well as external walls should be built of brick.

This Act covering town planning dictated that 'small' houses were to be built in the smaller side-streets, with the largest houses permitted only on the principal roads. The size of the buildings should relate to the width of the street or square in which they stood, and houses within the same street should be constructed more or less to a uniform height. The enactment of this can be seen on the Grosvenor Estate in London and more noticeably in Edinburgh, where the oblong grid of the New Town was laid out in 1766 by James Craig for the City Corporation.

The Great Fire of London

More than two-thirds of the City of London was destroyed by fire between 2 and 6 September 1666. St Paul's Cathedral, 89 parish churches, the Guildhall, 44 livery company halls, the Royal Exchange, the Customs House and 13,200 houses went up in flames in a fire that ravaged the city for five days.

Wren, with others, devised a scheme for the rebuilding of the city but the old street plan was reinstated and a coal duty was levied to help pay for public rebuilding and improvements. These included street widening and the relocation of markets, under the direction of royal commissioners.

Opposite: *Chester Terrace, 1825, part of Nash's Regent's Park development*

James Craig's Edinburgh

The city was laid out in 1766 with the three main streets, Princes Street, George Street and Queen Street, running parallel to each other and terminating with broad squares, Charlotte Square and St Andrew's Square. Three evenly-spaced shorter cross-streets form the main oblong grid, with each plot within the grid being divided by two still smaller streets which run parallel to the three main streets.

The largest and best houses were built in the squares at each end of the grid, secondary houses along the three principal streets, more modest houses in the three cross-streets and more affordable, 'artisan', dwellings in the two long narrow streets.

These two long narrow streets also afforded access to the mews behind the main-street houses. The city commissioned Robert Adam to produce an elevation for Charlotte Square in 1791. The result of this was one of the most spectacular urban compositions in Britain, with Adam indulging in a late-Palladian austerity complemented by bold, simple neoclassical motifs.

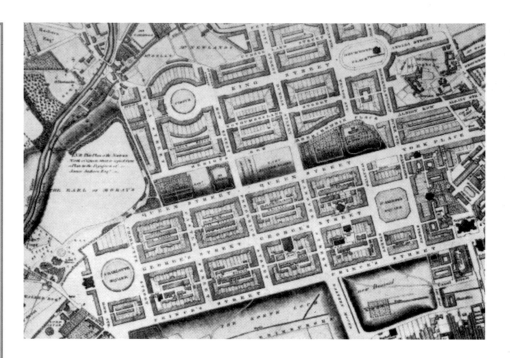

Part of the plans for the New Town, Edinburgh, drawn up by James Craig and published in 1767

Built c. 1720, 12 St Thomas Street, Winchester, shows windows that were bricked up later in the century

Further legislation was soon on the statute books, and in 1707 another Act was passed with the object of preventing fire from spreading through London and the City. It barred the use of decorative wooden eaves and cornices, because of the ease with which fire could spread from house to house along large and exposed timbers. The Act also stipulated that the façade of the house should be extended above the eaves and party walls by at least 450mm (18in) to form a parapet to protect the roof timbers. This was followed in 1709 by further legislation which called for the window sash boxes to be set back at least 100mm (4in) into the façade of the house.

These two Acts of Parliament obviously influenced the appearance of façades, as had the window tax introduced in 1696. This was expanded during the eighteenth century so that by 1766 houses with seven windows or more were liable for tax, as were houses with just six windows from 1784. Inevitably many occupiers bricked in windows to avoid the tax, and thus Georgian façades often feature blank windows.

Finally, an Act passed in 1774 to strengthen the previous London building acts provided for any work not carried out in accordance with them to be demolished or made good, and for the workmen to be liable to a fine or imprisonment. This Act took fire precautions a step further by banning all wooden decoration from façades, while at the same time introducing a scale of rates on buildings according to their volume, expense of construction, use and location. This effectively dictated the form of late Georgian domestic building, laying down standards for both materials and method of construction for external wall thicknesses, façades and party walls.

Initially individual estates were separately planned rather than being an integral part of an overall general town plan, even though as early as 1666 Sir Christopher Wren had promoted a plan for the rebuilding of the City of London. Such ambitious plans invariably fell foul of the individual site owners' vested interests and the lack of Royal or corporate nerve to force through unpopular planning legislation.

It was not until the end of the Georgian period that a large-scale architectural development emerged in Britain, when John Nash engineered the building of Regent Street in the 1820s. Even then it was a private speculation, with individuals undertaking to build sections under Nash's guidance. Many of these builders were under-financed but had been able to convince Nash of their competence to comply with the master plan of a coherent whole.

The construction of Georgian towns and cities depended on a speculative building practice which appears to have been adopted from 1666, with the redevelopment of the City of London. Speculators such as Nicholas Barbon began by acquiring a site from the ground landlord on a building lease. Only a peppercorn rent was payable for the first few months while the site was under construction. Building land was readily available, so over time the length of these leases tended to be negotiated upwards. A traditional 31 years had been granted for Covent Garden in the 1630s, but 150 years later the period of a lease had escalated to 99 years.

The speculator then erected the shell of a building consisting of a floor, roof, external walls and a minimum of rough-plastered internal walling, and sold it on before any ground rent became payable. The first occupier would be responsible for completing the building, which he was permitted to do to his own taste and budget.

Later in the century, as speculators became wealthier and more ambitious, they were to undertake larger scale developments with the potential of even larger profits; by the late eighteenth century the houses were being finished out internally, albeit in a fairly uniform manner, by the speculator.

However not all speculators were successful and many ended their days as bankrupts. Indeed, the Adams brothers were very fortunate in escaping such misfortune. Their Adelphi development was begun in 1768 on a 99-year lease from the Duke of St Albans on a site just south of Covent Garden, but by the time the buildings were ready in 1772 they found it impossible to let them. The brothers were eventually granted permission by Parliament to hold a lottery in which the individual houses would be offered as prizes. The tickets sold well and the brothers were saved from bankruptcy.

One major consequence of such speculation was that building practices had to evolve. The builders were intent on

Sir Christopher Wren 1632–1723

His works and influence spread classicism and gave it firm roots in a very English form. Wren's London buildings made a mark on the City and its surroundings which has not been exceeded by any other architect until modern times. He is known to have designed 70 buildings in and around London, and about ten more have been attributed to him. Nearly 50 of these buildings still exist, including the churches of:

St Benet, Upper Thames Street, 1667–83
St Michael Cornhill, 1670–72
St Mary le Bow, Cheapside, 1670–73
St Mary at Hill, Lovat Lane, 1670–76
St Bride, Fleet Street, 1671–74
St Magnus the Martyr, Lower Thames Street, 1671–76
St Lawrence Jewry, Gresham Street, 1671–79
St Stephen Walbrook, 1672–79
St James Garlickhythe, Garlick Hill, 1676–82
St Peter-upon-Cornhill, 1677–81
St Martin Ludgate, Ludgate Hill, 1677–84
St Mary Aldermary, Bow Lane, 1681–82
St Mary Abchurch, Abchurch Lane, 1681–86
St Margaret Pattens, Rood Lane, 1684–87
St Margaret Lothbury, 1686–90
St Vedast, Foster Lane, 1695–1701.

Part of an Adam drawing, showing the elevation of the Adelphi development towards the wharf

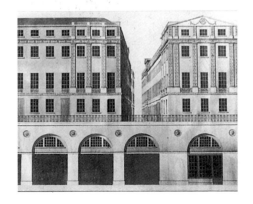

building as cheaply and as quickly as possible, and so tended to use inferior-quality bricks for concealed work. Only the façades were rendered in good-quality face bricks, commonly laid in Flemish bond, and even then in only a single thickness. This led to a lack of structural stability, increased by the use of softwood timber in the brickwork and the mixing of street dirt in the lime mortar.

The development of Bath was another spectacular result of the 1667 Act, although it followed a more picturesque sinuous form, unlike the rectangular grid layout of Edinburgh. However, when development at both Edinburgh and Bath was at its height and the building Acts were beginning to be effective just after the mid-century, standardisation and regimentation were given a further boost by the products of the developing Industrial Revolution.

These included Coade stone and the various iron products from the Carron and Coalbrookdale companies which led to a nationwide availability of mass-produced and uniform products. A further by-product of this trend was the appearance of pattern books and builders' manuals, which promoted house designs based on the rating specifications and the use of the more readily available, and cheaper, standard products.

The Circus, Bath, designed by Wood the Elder with Wood the Younger from 1754–56; it was inspired by the Colosseum, Rome, each storey being embellished with an independent order of columns

Terraced housing

The origins of the terracing phenomenon can be traced back to Inigo Jones's designs of blocks of palatial grandeur for the Covent Garden piazza terraces of 1631. He also designed a block of buildings for Lord Maltravers at Lothbury in the City of London, the first example of a classical uniform astylar urban terrace. During the eighteenth century the unified terrace was the architectural ideal of urban design, and now represents the Georgian period's most important contribution to its development. On the grandest scale the emphasis tended to be on a centrally-placed pediment and end pavilions to create a 'palace' front. A more economical version was the terrace of regimented façades without emphasis.

However, before Jones's terrace re-emerged in the early eighteenth century, a period of architectural baroque was dominated by Wren, Hawksmore and Vanbrugh, so that when the terrace did return it displayed many of these baroque characteristics. An early example appeared in Albury Street, Deptford *c.* 1706–15 that still survives, but is only semi-uniform, consisting of two-storey houses of between $2^1/_2$ and 4 bays but constructed behind a façade, the elevation of which is articulated with recessed vertical window bays set between full-height pilaster strips. The pilasters are without capitals, and the regular rhythm of the bays cleverly disguises the differing widths of the houses.

The first major example of the uniform eighteenth-century astylar terrace was Colen Campbell's 31–34 Old Burlington Street, Westminster, London, that was built between 1718 and 1723. Here the austere elevations, based on Jones's designs for Lothbury, are proportioned according to the Palladian canon. The vista is of an immaculately-proportioned façade with the vertical spacing of the window openings complemented by the embedded reminders of the conceptual temple front on crucial parts of the façade; a cornice marks the top of the temple entablature, a deep string course indicates the base of the columns and the start of the basement level.

In contrast to Campbell's design, Wren employed red dressings to windows, segmental red-brick arches, red brick moulded string courses and façades generally of brown-purple bricks, box sashes were flush and door cases intricately carved.

In 1725 Campbell designed his houses for Grosvenor Square. More confidently handled than his Burlington Street terrace, they were embellished with the full regalia of the Roman temple front; entablature, columns or pilasters, and a rusticated ground floor basement. He also designed the ground floor as the basement of a temple and the first floor as a genuine *piano nobile*. The main entertaining rooms were thus as in the larger Palladian country houses, not susceptible to the noise and dirt of the city street on the ground floor like contemporary baroque homes.

Inigo Jones 1573–1652

The introduction of Italian Renaissance ideas and their establishment in England as the only civilised form of architecture was the completely personal achievement of Inigo Jones. He was the first to establish the Palladian style in this country. His existing buildings are few, and most of them are in London.

Andrea Palladio 1508–1580

Born in Padua, Italy, he was the most significant architect of the later Renaissance. His architecture is concentrated in Venice, where he was responsible for two of the city's greatest churches, San Giorgio Maggiore (begun in 1566) and Il Redentore (begun in 1576); in Vicenza he remodelled the façade of the Basilica in 1549 and designed the Teatro Olimpico (begun in 1580). He also built about 20 villas in the Venetian province of the Veneto.

Meticulously reproduced in book form, his work was enormously influential in Britain where it inspired Inigo Jones and later the 'Palladian' circle of Lord Burlington (1694–1753), and later also in America.

Grosvenor Square, London, 1789, was an attempt to create a London square that was not only the largest but also the most imposing architecturally.

The east side was built as a five-part symmetrical block by John Simmons and comprised a large pedimented house in the centre with large houses at both ends, producing the effect of a single palatial building. It was perhaps the first instance in London of terraced houses being grouped in this way. The rest of the Square was built in a cacophony of different styles by the builder-architect Edward Shepherd, including Nos 19 and 21 on the far left of the illustration, in 1725. Shepherd's attempts to create a co-ordinated whole were thwarted by other interests, and the Square contained many pompous Palladian houses on the north side (the last of which was demolished in 1962) although the typical house was constructed of brown brick with red dressings

Opposite, above: the north side of Queen Square, Bath, which marked the beginning of uniform Palladian development in the city. It united seven houses in a symmetrical 23-bay composition, dressed with pilasters and columns and embellished with a five-bay central pediment

Opposite, below left: The Paragon, Bath, is a long curving uniform terrace, begun in 1768 by Thomas Atwood

Opposite, below right: the rear of houses in the Circus, Bath, 1754–66

Campbell's elevational treatment after 1740 became the standard form for advanced astylar urban terraces in London and leading provincial towns. However, in the majority of provincial towns the Palladian influence on terrace design was less marked in the composition of the elevation than it was in the details.

Long before the end of the century the Campbell-revived austere Jones astylar terrace with all its uniformity had established itself in the builders' vernacular. It may be no better seen than in the Bedford estate in Bloomsbury, where James Burton's bold and well-proportioned façades line entire streets such as Bedford Place or Montague Street. An imposing presence is created by the extremely austere brick façades of equally-spaced windows, stucco ground floors and the third-floor cill courses.

John Wood the Elder first fully developed the palace-fronted terrace, as prefigured in Jones' Covent Garden, on the north side of Queen Square, Bath, in 1729. Although at Covent Garden the development was without central or terminal emphasis in the form of either pediments or pavilions, it was dressed with pilasters and a cornice and had a rusticated arcaded base. Queen Square followed an earlier eighteenth-century scheme for a palace-fronted terrace by John Price in 1720. Unfortunately Price's scheme was never completed and was later demolished. Queen Square preceded further building at Bath which included Wood's Circus, begun in 1754, which also lacked a central emphasis but had instead an elevation with three tiers of attached columns, each with its own appropriate entablature.

The development of the astylar terrace

The following examples help to trace the development of the astylar terrace through the century:

Campbell's elevational style, including
61 Green Street, Westminster, by Roger Morris, 1720;
4 St James's Square, Westminster, by Edward Shepherd, 1726;
36 Sackville Street, Westminster, by Henry Flitcroft, 1732;

9 & 10 St James's Square, Westminster, by Henry Flitcroft, 1735–36;
Grand Parade, Bath, by John Wood the Elder, 1740;
Southampton Place, Bloomsbury, London, thought to have been supervised by Flitcroft, c. 1745;
The Paragon, Bath, by T W Atwood, 1768–71.
Provincial terrace design with Palladian detailing:
16 Market Place, Yarm, Cleveland, c. 1760;

55–63 North Bar, Beverly, Humberside, c. 1760.
The austere astylar uniform terrace:
Abbey Square, Chester, completed in 1780;
Lemon Street, Truro, Cornwall, begun in 1794;
Parliament Street, Kingston-upon-Hull, Humberside, 1796–1800;
Bedford Place, London, by James Burton c. 1800–01;
Montague Street, London by James Burton, c. 1800–01.

The supreme example of the palace-fronted terrace is John Wood the Younger's Royal Crescent, *right*, also at Bath and begun in 1767. Its front is embellished with no fewer than 114 giant Ionic columns that rise from first-floor level, with central emphasis created by the doubling-up of the columns at each side of the central bay. The first-floor window of the centre bay is round-headed.

The palace-fronted terrace changed towards the end of the century, when architects such as Michael Searles worked on developments with smaller budgets and so broke up the continuous brick terrace by introducing separate compositions in the form of articulated linked pavilions. At Gloucester Circus, Greenwich (1790), Searles used semi-detached houses, some pedimented and linked to lower entrance blocks, whereas at Blackheath he produced a crescent of semi-detached houses linked by colonnades. This evolution away from the established palace and astylar terrace was an immediate precursor of the more picturesque and less uniform ideal promoted at the end of the century.

Bath

John Wood the Elder undertook to build Queen Square in the late 1720s; he grouped together seven ordinary terrace houses, treating them so as to suggest that they formed a palace. This echoed Colen Campbell's vision for Grosvenor Square, the north side of Queen Square being built as a Palladian elevation of 23 bays. It has a five-bay central pediment embellished with pilasters and columns and three-bay end pavilions.

Each house in Queen Square (1729–36) was sub-leased to an owner-builder or builder-tradesman who had a free hand in the planning but had to follow Wood's elevations.

The Square was connected by Gay Street (1735–55), also built under Wood's control, to the Circus (1754–66), which should be considered as Wood's greatest urban scheme. It had been conceived earlier and was completed by John Wood the Younger.

The Circus was designed in a particularly idiosyncratic and monumental manner following the general arrangement of a Roman amphitheatre, except that instead of having, as at the Colosseum, a convex façade facing outwards, the façades were concave, facing inwards.

As with the Colosseum, however, superimposed orders were used, with Doric at the bottom, then Ionic, then Corinthian, and between the paired columns were the window and door-openings.

The Circus, which now entered into the language of town planning, and was an important precedent, was connected by the relatively modest Brock Street (1763–67) to the large and splendid Royal Crescent, which was begun in 1767, under Wood the Younger's control, and completed in 1775.

The Royal Crescent was even grander than the Circus, having a giant order of engaged Ionic columns rising from the *piano-nobile* level to the crowning entablature, and sitting on a plain ground storey.

Above, left: *Alfred Street, Bath, c. 1772; a good example of a loosely uniform late-Palladian street*
Above, right: *Bath Street, looking towards Cross Bath*
Right: *Grosvenor Place, London Road, Bath, 1791, by John Eveleigh*

Initially the drive towards the more picturesque took the simple form of replacing the Roman details with Greek, coinciding with the arrival of the vogue for Greek Classicism. Nash's Cumberland Terrace, built in Regent's Park with Thomson between 1826–27, is a refined example compared to the more thorough Greek revival attempt at St Bernard's Crescent, Edinburgh, by James Milne, of 1824. Here the massive two-storey centre is emphasized by massive Greek Doric columns that rise from the ground to support a deep entablature.

The palace-fronted terrace was expanded into an entire palace-fronted street under the development of a single speculator. Its origins were at Bath (Somersetshire Buildings and Great Pulteney Street) and in London (Portland Place) but were never more perfectly executed than by Nash in his development of Regent Street between 1811–33. This development comprised largely individual buildings in a 5.6km (3.5 mile) stretch between Park Crescent with its pedimented end bays (1812) at the northern end, and at the other end, Carlton House Terrace (1827–33).

The impact of the Regent Street development was inspirational. In Brighton, Charles Busby mixed types of houses and flamboyant architecture for Kemp Town, especially at Lewes Crescent; James Burton developed St Leonards-on-Sea in 1828 near Hastings, and at Newcastle-upon-Tyne John Dobson created

Examples of the palace-fronted terrace

Crescent, Buxton, Derbyshire, begun in 1780 by John Carr for the Duke of Devonshire

Somersetshire Buildings, Milsom Street, Bath, 1781–83, by Thomas Baldwin; a 17-bay composition of three storeys with three-bay pediments acting as unconventional terminal features and a three-bay, three-storey curved bow in the centre

Lansdown Crescent, Bath, 1789–93, by John Palmer; a four-bay central pediment, supported on Ionic pilasters, rising from a rusticated ground floor and balanced by a pair of terminal bow-fronted houses

Great Pulteney Street, Bath, begun in 1789 by Thomas Baldwin; long terraces with terminal, intermediate and central pedimented and pilastered features

Lower-budget examples include:
233–291 Kennington Road, London, *c.* 1788;
51–75 Rodney Street, Liverpool, *c.* 1790;
Surrey Square, Southwark, 1795, by Michael Searles; a long brick terrace with arcaded ground floor windows and doors;
32–37 Castle Street, Caernarvon, *c.* 1800.

Left: *Cumberland Terrace, Regent's Park, London; one of two intermediate arches leading to a courtyard and numbers 17–20*

Below: *the façade of Cumberland Terrace, which was built by John Nash with James Thomson in 1826*

Right: *the pedimented, pilastered frontispiece*

Below, right: *Park Crescent, London, 1812–22, which was the northern end of Nash's Regent Street development*

the wonderfully austere ashlar-faced Eldon Square for Richard Grainger in 1825. Dobson also designed Leazes Terrace, which was built by Thomas Oliver in 1829, and Grey Street (1835–40), both in Newcastle-upon-Tyne, which like Lewes Crescent in Brighton has added complications in that it descends a hill. Here the individual blocks are composed with a central emphasis and terminating features.

The now-established terrace house was also built in small uniform groups, in which symmetry was achieved in relation to the size of the composition by whatever means were necessary. For instance, at Market Place, Blandford Forum, Dorset in *c.* 1734, John Bastard gave focus to a small group by using a central one-bay open pediment supported on a pair of pilasters.

In *c.* 1730, at Queen Street, Bath, John Wood the Elder united a seven-bay Palladian country house composition with a three-bay pediment. A similar solution was later employed in 1746 at Caius House, Middleton Street, Wymondham, Norfolk, where a three-bay pediment was embellished at the corners of the seven-bay composition and below the ends of the pediment with four giant Doric pilasters that rise from ground level to the eaves.

At 119–120 St Stephen's Green, Dublin of *c.* 1740–50, the two houses are united by a blank-centred Venetian window. At first-floor level a large round-headed blank window, sited over the

Lewes Crescent, Brighton, built c. 1825; a loosely uniform composition that descends a hill

party wall, is linked by a cornice to the adjoining window of each house to form a tripartite composition.

Perhaps surprisingly, one major type of terrace house is that which, although built independently, almost accidentally found itself forming part of a terrace. For these there is no overriding feature, as they may have merely employed the current local architectural fashion, or have utilised a variety of pleasing devices to display their individuality.

These individuals are far-flung and numerous, but a concise list of the more noteworthy appears *overleaf.* The Palladian designers of individual terrace houses tended to eschew the use of applied orders in favour of merely alluding to the presence of an architectural hierarchy, just as in the composition of large-scale uniform terraces. The most common means of drawing attention to an astylar Palladian terrace house was the crowning pediment, but even with no pediment an astylar terrace house could still be given individuality by the embellishment of the centre bay to produce emphasis. This could take the form of loading the centre window with architraves or a pediment, or of making it a different shape. These, however, are perhaps not nearly so engaging as those terrace houses where the centre bays have been given up to the display of an inventive variety of flamboyant window forms; the garden front of Peckover House, Wisbech, Cambridgeshire of 1727 is an early example.

> ### *Examples of unified groups*
>
> 23–24 Lawrence Street, Chelsea, London, *c.* 1720; these share a triangular pedimented door surround, as at the two following groups:
> 23–24 High Street, Kingston-upon-Hull, Humberside, 1751;
> 127–129 Long Westgate, Scarborough, North Yorkshire, *c.* 1760.
> 66–67 High Street St Martin's, Stamford, Lincolnshire, *c.* 1735; here all of the ground-floor windows have matching Gibbs surrounds
> 5–7 Queen Street, Lancaster, *c.* 1750; a pair of plain three-storey houses sharing a large swan-necked pediment
> 3–5 Downham Road, Ely, *c.* 1750; Cambridgeshire; these are united by the use of Venetian windows and round blank windows
> 59–60 West Stockwell Street, Colchester, Essex, *c.* 1750; these share a three-bay pediment which contains the pedimented front doors of the houses, separated by a Venetian window

Vanbrugh House, Oxford

An alternative method of giving a single house individuality was the abandonment of the central emphasis in favour of an overall exquisite Palladian uniformity, in which the various horizontal levels received the treatment deemed appropriate to their function. Thus the ground floor was rusticated, the first floor *piano nobile* and the top floor attic; the first floor was emphasized with pedimented window surrounds and the top floor with square windows.

Sheer freedom of design has produced many individual oddities. Roger Morris built a large house for himself at 61 Green Street, Mayfair, in 1730. It consists of a centre block of three widely-spaced bays, flanked by two slightly recessed, two-bay three-storey wings. The exterior is perfectly plain except for a first-floor string course. Originally the centre block of the house was two-storey while the flanking wings were three, as now. The unique effect that Morris successfully created was that of a Palladian villa in the language of London street architecture, a town version of the Palladian tower house (*see page 35*).

Windows and bays

One feature that was to remain popular throughout the eighteenth century was the Venetian window. It was promoted by both the Palladian and the baroque designers alike as a device which would give a home some individuality. Edward Shepherd used a hierarchy of Venetian windows in 1736 at 71 South Audley Street, Westminster. On the first-floor this was embellished with columns loaded with rustic blocks. A decade later 18 Low Pavement Street, Nottingham, was built with a three-bay three-storey façade which contains six Venetian windows. By 1768, James Essex was squeezing four Venetian windows into a three-bay, four-storey composition at 74 Trumpington Street, Cambridge. A contemporary single-bay four-storey house at 61 Broad Street, Worcester, has three.

The other single enduring feature of the period was the bay window, available in many guises as fashions changed throughout the century. It was hexagonal *c.* 1750–70, semicircular *c.* 1770–80 and elliptical *c.* 1790–1830. The vogue appears to have originated in Ireland some twenty years before its English popularity, where the windows were most commonly composed as full-height rises on both sides of central single doors. In England they remained more popular in the country house than in the town house designs.

The combination of both Venetian and bay windows was also popular. John Wood the Elder designed a three-storey round bay with Venetian and tripartite windows decorated with rustic blocks at 41 Gay Street, Bath (1740). Later, in 1762, John Carr combined a pair of full-height canted bays flanking a central door and a first-floor Venetian window on the rear elevation of Castlegate House, 26 Castlegate, York.

71 South Audley Street, Westminster

Examples of bay windows

Those with canted bays
Grey Friars House, High Street,
  Colchester, 1755
87 High Pavement, Chesterfield,
  Derbyshire, *c.* 1765
Clavering House, Clavering Place,
  Newcastle-upon-Tyne, 1784
Those with rounded bays
2 Highweek Street, Newton Abbot,
  Devon, *c.* 1790–1800
12 West Street, Builth Wells, Powys,
  c. 1815

By the last quarter of the eighteenth century the application of Greek classicism had begun to gain favour in the London terraces. Initially, Palladian-proportioned houses were detailed with Ionic columns supporting pediments; for example, the Royal Society of Arts building in John Adam Street of 1772 was embellished with neoclassical decoration. A little later, the striking neoclassical composition at 14–16 Castle Street, Cirencester, Gloucester was built with a three-bay, two-storey ashlar façade focused by a one-bay pediment. It contained six Venetian windows set within blank arches in the Palladian Adam manner, all linked horizontally by continuous imposts and cill courses.

As the nineteenth century approached, there were far too many individual and independent buildings to detail here. Some of the more noteworthy are Sir John Soane's buildings at 12–14 Lincoln's Inn Fields, London; number 12 was built for himself between 1792–4. It has a modest façade, three bays wide and three storeys high; a fourth was added later.

An elevation of the House of the Society for the Encouragement of Arts, Manufactures and Commerce (now the Royal Society of Arts), 8 John Adam Street, Adelphi, London, by Adam from his Works in Architecture *vol 1, No 18, Plate IV*

However, in 1812 when Soane rebuilt No 13 as his home, he abandoned all conventions of elevational design. He constructed a three-storey, three-bay house fronted by a three-storey stone loggia. Breaking forward about 1m (3ft) in front of the building line of the neighbouring houses, it has three arched bays on the ground floor, three arched bays on the first floor and just one centrally-placed bay on the second floor, to create a stepped effect. The flanking second floor bays are set back on the same plane as the neighbouring houses, which makes the loggia read very much as a stone screen placed in front of a conventional terrace house. This extraordinary loggia-cum-screen is embellished with characteristic Soanean motifs such as pilaster strips incised with Greek fret-pattern decorations and Coade stone caryatids. The loggia was glazed in 1834. Soane acquired and rebuilt number 14 to match number 12 in 1823–24, thus making number 13 the centrepiece of a tripartite composition.

The neoclassical revolution, apart from introducing Greek Classicism to the town terrace, also encompassed a parallel though less popular fashion for Egyptian manifestations. Such buildings were epitomised by the now long-demolished Egyptian Hall by P F Robinson in Piccadilly, London, 1812, which appeared at the beginning of the vogue, and The Egyptian House, Penzance, Cornwall, *c.* 1830, which with its tapering structure represented a truly flamboyant essay in, and the culmination of, the fashion.

Designed by Sir John Soane, numbers 12, 13 and 14 Lincoln's Inn Fields were built in stages between 1792 and 1824. The projecting stone screen of number 13 represents a break with the traditions of terrace house design

Town terrace houses of the nineteenth century with individual embellishment

224–240 Regent Street, London, 1822, by Samuel Baxter; gigantic crowning acroteria, incised Grecian ornament and long narrow attic windows enclosing Grecian urns set *in antis*
Pelham Crescent, Hastings, East Sussex, 1824–28, by J Kay, where each house is one tripartite window wide and embellished with verandas to the first and second-floor windows
363 Kennington Lane, London, 1825, by J M Gandy, which has a two-storey tripartite bar window set within a three-storey arch

Chapter Four

Rural Buildings

THE COUNTRY HOUSE best represents the architectural movements of the period, because it was free from the constraints that the new regulations were imposing on the design of town buildings. Furthermore, there was still an abundance of money available for the landed gentry and the newly-rich merchant classes to indulge in architectural competitiveness.

The one single composition that was to influence British architecture for more than a quarter of the century was Colen Campbell's Wanstead House of 1713–20 (demolished 1824), for it was the first fully-developed expression of the Palladian style. It directly challenged the established Continental baroque, which had hitherto predominated with such buildings as Vanbrugh's Blenheim, 1705–16, or Thomas Archer's Roehampton House, 1710–12. It offered an interpretation of the doctrines of Palladio, with the components of the elevation limited in number and disposed with great horizontal emphasis, in contrast to the verticality of baroque composition. Campbell's portico had a ridge that continued visibly over the hall and saloon behind it, creating the effect of a Roman temple set within the house.

However, Wanstead House did not just happen, it had

Far left: Vanbrugh's Blenheim Palace, Oxfordshire, 1705–16, was completed by Hawksmoor, 1722–23.
This photograph is reproduced by kind permission of His Grace the Duke of Marlborough

Below: Wanstead, Essex, 1720, by Colen Campbell; the third design, which omitted an earlier planned cupola over the hall but had towers added at each end (these were not built). This was the model for English Palladian country houses for the next century and the composition was the precedent for many buildings

An elevation of Wilbury House, Wiltshire, taken from Vitruvius' Britannicus *of 1715. Its proportions were a radical departure from those of the typical country house of the late seventeenth century; both the hall and saloon were each a cube and a half, while the flanking apartments were cubes*

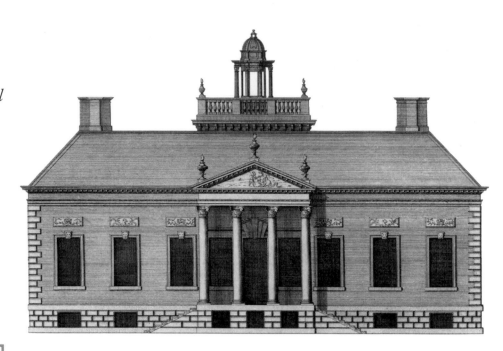

Early-century baroque houses

Those with main rooms on the ground floor and decorative external giant columns which rise from plinths
Seaton Delaval, Northumberland, 1717–29, by Vanbrugh
Buntingsdale, Shropshire, 1721, by Francis Smith

Those with columns rising from squat podiums containing basement windows
Stoneleigh Abbey, Warwickshire, 1714–26, by Francis Smith

Those with columns from ground level
Barnsley Park, Gloucestershire, 1720–21, thought to be by John Price
Sutton Scarsdale, Derbyshire, 1724, by Francis Smith
More Park, Hertfordshire, 1725, by James Thornhill

Newby Park, Yorkshire, 1720, by Colen Campbell

'ancestors'; not the least of which was William Benson's Wilbury House, Wiltshire, *c.* 1708. The latter was raised on a plan inspired by Palladio's Villa Pogliana, with an oblong hall that had its long side to the front elevation leading to an oblong saloon. Placed symmetrically on each side of the saloon are matching stairs, then two pairs of rooms, two of which are square, complete the ground floor plan. This, broadly speaking, was to become the model for countless eighteenth-century houses and Palladian villas.

Wanstead conventionally adopted the above floor plan, but its exterior provided the revolution. Internally Wanstead lacked an architecturally emphasized and formal axis of honour, normally considered essential by the baroque architect; externally, the principle floor was raised to the first floor level like that of a Renaissance *piano nobile*, with a rusticated basement level (known in the eighteenth century as the rustic) at ground level. From this low rugged storey sprang the columns of the portico.

The building boom in country houses took off in about 1715, and between 1720 and 1724 twice as many country houses were begun as in any other five-year period of the eighteenth century. The favoured form was that of the villa, many of which were built for the newly-rich merchant classes who required compact country residences devoid of large estates. At that time the new fashion was Palladian.

Campbell designed Baldersby (originally Newby) Park, North Yorkshire *c.* 1718, and this should be regarded as the first fully-fledged eighteenth-century Palladian villa. It lacks a rustic and is only of two storeys, so that the giant columns of its pedimented frontispiece rise directly from the ground in the baroque manner.

Internally it was designed with a double-height square

entrance hall, separated from a slightly less deep saloon by a pair of stairs which flank a central passage. On each side of the hall-saloon axis were triple-room apartments set in enfilade. This general scheme was repeated on the first floor.

Meanwhile, the Palladian style was on the verge of being established in Scotland. William Adam designed a villa at Mavisbank, Lothian, in 1723 which was an elegant mix of Palladian forms but with baroque detailing. A flush of austere Palladian constructions then followed, before the first major and pure Palladian house was built in Scotland in 1761, albeit in the manner of Wanstead. This was Penicuik House, Lothian, by James Clerk with John Baxter.

In Ireland there was also a Palladian revival, which had its roots in 1709, in a proto-Palladian house by Thomas Burgh called Oldtown at Naas, Co. Kildare. The Florentine architect, Alessandro Galilei, designed the elevation of Castletown, Co. Kildare in 1719, which marks the dramatic arrival of Palladianism in Ireland.

Galilei built in an Italian manner, providing Castletown with a regimented entrance façade with a correctly emphasized *piano nobile*, and an attractive attic below a suitable cornice. He used colonnaded links to the lower pavilions to provide wings in the manner of Palladio's villas in the Veneto. There is, however no proper rustic, which means that the main rooms are on the ground floor.

Castletown also differed from its English contemporaries in its plan. This was heavily influenced by Sir Edward Lovett Pearce, who also designed the double-height entrance hall with its screen of columns carrying a balustraded gallery. Along the ground floor garden front the rooms are arranged in enfilade, in true seventeenth-century baroque tradition, meeting in a central saloon which connects to the entrance hall. This is similar to the layout adopted at Ragley Hall, Warwickshire, 1679–83, by Robert Hooke.

One major difference from the English Palladian plan was that instead of being paired as in England, in Ireland the stairs were sited in a generous hall beside the entrance hall. This formula was repeated at Castle Ward, Co. Down, of 1760–73; Castletown Cox, Piltown, Co. Kilkenny, 1767–71, by Davis Ducart; Lucan House, Lucan, Co. Dublin, *c.* 1775, and at Rokeby, Co. Louth, 1785, by Cooley and Johnson.

Important early English Palladian villas

Stourhead, Wiltshire, designed *c.* 1720 by Colen Campbell but not built until 1741. It has a freestanding portico on a somewhat squat rustic

Mereworth Castle, Kent, 1722, by Colen Campbell. a rendering of Palladio's Villa Rotunda; its elevations are the same on all four fronts

Castle Ward, Co. Down; left, *the Palladian frontage of 1760–73, and* right, *the gothic front*

Other Irish villas with curved bays

Belvedere, Lough Ennell,
Co. Westmeath, c. 1740, by Richard
Castle; full-height semi-circular bays
light oblong drawing rooms on the
side elevations and the stairs are
arranged in a staircase tower placed in
the rear elevation
Drewstown, Athboy, Co. Meath, c. 1745,
thought to be by Francis Bindon; a
curved bay to only one side elevation
Dysart, Delvin, Co. Westmeath, 1757,
by George Pentland

Other major Irish villas of the period

Summerhill, Co. Meath, begun in 1731
by Pearce (destroyed by fire in 1922);
a massive construction with a central
block dominated by a frontispiece of
four inset giant Corinthian columns
and flanked by long, tall two-storey
quadrant wings terminating in
octagonal domed towers
Powerscourt, Enniskerry, Co. Wicklow,
remodelling completed 1740 by
Castle. The centre front has a mighty
five-bay pediment supported by two-
storey Ionic pilasters rising above a
rusticated ground floor which contains
a low entrance hall. The rear elevation
is entirely rusticated and is flanked by
full height curved bays
Wardstown, near Ballyshannon,
Co. Donegal, 1740; symmetrical with
tower-like bays in the style of
Vanbrugh (now a ruin)
Russborough, Blessington, Co. Wicklow,
1741–c. 1750, by Richard Castle; a
213m (700ft) long frontage and a
central block, closely modelled on
Bellamont Forest. Colonnaded
quadrant wings to seven-bay, two-
storey pavilions are linked by a long
wall with a centrally-placed rusticated
and pedimented arch to a single-storey
barn and stables
Bessborough, Piltown, Co. Kilkenny,
1744, by Francis Bindon; nine-bay,
pedimented front with pedimented
door topped by a niche (destroyed by
fire in 1922 and later rebuilt)
Mantua House, Castlerea,
Co. Roscommon, 1747, thought to be
by Castle; a tripartite central feature
of a door flanked by Doric columns
with niche and demi-windows topped
by pediment on first floor, niche on
second floor (now a ruin)
Bellinter, Navan, Co. Meath, 1750, by
Castle; also with extensive wings
Castle Blunden, Kilkenny, Co. Kilkenny,
c. 1750; a seven-bay house with Gibbs
windows, tripartite Doric porch, and
central first floor niche

Sir Edward Lovett Pearce was to become the leading influential designer of Palladian country-house architecture in Ireland. Responsible for the detailing at Castletown, he developed a style which combined the baroque inventiveness, movement and boldness typical of Vanbrugh (to whom he was related) with the grammar and gravity of the English Palladians. Richard Castle, who worked closely with Pearce, became another formative influence. Castle brought mainstream Franco-Dutch Palladian-baroque attitudes from Hesse Kassel to the Irish building world.

The first foursquare Palladian villa constructed in Ireland was Pearce's Bellamont Forest, Co. Cavan, of c. 1730. Its plan was loosely inspired by Palladio's Villa Pisani at Montagnana, being composed of an oblong entrance hall leading into a slightly squarer saloon, with the long sides of the two rooms running parallel with each other and with the front and back façades. The stairs are arranged as at Castletown, just off the hall. There is no rustic, just a squat rusticated basement, which forms the base for the small-scale portico. The cornice of the portico runs around the house and sits between the *piano nobile* and the first-floor windows.

Pearce introduced a spacious first-floor staircase landing supported on columns and, to the side elevations, a variation on the Venetian window theme where blank niches are closely flanked and architecturally united with the windows.

Although Pearce had designed that first important Irish Palladian villa, Castle, the other major architectural force, provided the second in c. 1733 at Ballyhaise, Co. Cavan. His design was in the European baroque tradition, but internally he adapted the conventional Palladian plan with the addition of an oval saloon on the axis of the hall, and expressed in the centre of the garden front as an elliptical bay rising to the full height of the elevation.

Castle also pioneered the canted bay in Ireland, using it first at Anneville, Mullingar, Co. Westmeath, c. 1740–45. Here he arranged a five-bay, two-storey entrance front with a full-height, centrally-placed canted bay containing the front door and serving a square staircase hall.

Holkham-inspired Palladian tower houses

Much of Holkham's living accommodation was sacrificed to provide space for the magnificent double-height hall, and to compensate for this, four wings were built at the corner. Such towers became a favourite device in the Palladian repertoire.

The tower house then became the most imitated of all country-house forms, and the Holkham model, with towers placed on virtually the same plane as the long, low *piano-nobile* main façade with a feature centrally placed, inspired the most direct copies.

Lydiard Tregoze, Wiltshire, 1743–49; remodelling, thought to be by Roger Morris
Langley Park, Norfolk, 1745; alterations by Matthew Brettingham the Elder
Croome Court, Hereford and Worcester, 1751, by Lancelot Brown with Sanderson Miller
Hagley Hall, Hereford and Worcester, 1754–60, by Sanderson Miller
Kimberley Hall, Norfolk, *c.* 1755, remodelling by Thomas Prowse (original house, 1712)

Holkham Hall, Norfolk, 1731–64. A vast essay in dogmatic Palladian style, it was built in Norfolk from 1734–61 to the designs of William Kent and Lord Burlington. The Hall was constructed in brick in the decorated Palladian style, and displays a variety of preferred Palladian details, the most notable of which are the Venetian windows in the piano nobile

In England at the time there were other country properties being built in a bigger and grander style to a larger scale, purely to impress and with costs a secondary consideration. These Palladian-inspired statements of power and importance were built throughout the country with Houghton Hall, Norfolk, being the first major one. It was begun for Sir Robert Walpole in 1721, to designs by Colen Campbell. The principal storey, once again, is placed upon a rustic.

As well as changing the external appearance of the country house, this element had also revolutionized its use, adding another and more formal dimension to country house life and entertaining. The principal front at Holkham Hall, Norfolk, was begun in 1734 to designs of *c.* 1731 by William Kent and Lord Burlington. The grand external stair, which was never completed, was designed to reach up to the portico in the conventional way and thus to emphasize the *piano nobile*. In contrast, the entrance on the other side of the house is via a small door in the rustic. The floor above the rustic was extremely opulent; around the formal central hall-saloon axis there was a series of four symmetrically-designed three-room apartments, though they were not in enfilade.

Rokeby Hall in North Yorkshire was another large composition, built for himself between 1725–30 by the amateur architect Sir Thomas Robinson. One of the first true Palladian country houses, it strictly embodied the Palladian precept of proportions based on the cube. The south front has a single-storey

Opposite: *Houghton Hall, Norfolk, begun in 1722 by Colen Campbell; the south front as designed by Campbell. The towers at the corners were derived from Wilton House, Wiltshire*

porch framed by baseless Doric columns, while inside there is a double-height saloon.

It was the forerunner of Claydon House, Buckinghamshire, which was first begun by Sir Thomas Robinson c. 1750. Here he created a massive austere Palladian shell; however his patron Earl Verney, who like Walpole was also building to impress, died a bankrupt with much of the composition incomplete. The plan included a massive ballroom 21.33 x 15.25 x 12.2m (70 x 50 x 40ft) with the decoration carried out in the most sumptuous rococo plasterwork. Unfortunately this was demolished in 1791, along with the majority of the original house.

A major problem of these larger country houses was that time and changing fashions acted against them. By the time the properties were designed and construction completed tastes would have evolved, and many interiors were rearranged to take account of this. Even if determined owners were prepared to wait years to realise their dreams, others would happily amend and adapt halfway through construction in order to keep abreast of the shifting trends.

For this reason Palladian country houses of the first wave were still being begun at the mid-century, by which time the fashionable interior had reverted back towards the baroque. Similarly, English baroque houses were still being commissioned even after the revolutionary arrival of the Palladian ideal. In the first half of the eighteenth century more than a few baroque Palladian buildings were completed, and indeed from the earliest days of the Palladian movement, there were baroque Palladian architects who designed to appeal to the traditional baroque tastes of the generality of their clients. The Earl of Malton, when remodelling at Wentworth Woodhouse, South Yorkshire, began building a baroque west front c. 1725 and at the insistence of his wife simultaneously commissioned Henry Flitcroft to design a Palladian east front, which he began building in 1734.

Wentworth Woodhouse, Yorkshire, c. 1735, by Henry Flitcroft (Burlington Harry); one of the grandest Palladian compositions to be derived from Wanstead

James Gibbs, who is best known today for the eponymous Gibbs surround to windows and doors, was one of the most accomplished of these baroque-inclined Palladian architects. His work includes Ditchley Park, Oxfordshire, 1720–31; additions to Orleans House, Twickenham, of 1720, and remodelling at Wimpole Hall, Cambridgeshire, c. 1719–21. In addition, Gibbs also influenced many others, as can be seen in buildings such as Stocken Hall, Leicestershire, c. 1735 and Gilling Castle Court, North Yorkshire, where remodelling was carried out by William Wakefield *c.* 1725.

Giacomo Leoni was perhaps more adventurous in his Palladian interpretations. The first translator of Palladio's *Quattro Libri* into English, this Italian was far freer in his designs for instance than Burlington, who tended to have a rather narrow definition of the Palladian ethos. Leoni's work includes Clandon Park, Surrey, of 1730–33 and Alkrington Hall, Lancashire, of 1735; both of these have an internal layout not dissimilar to that of Wanstead, but which could never be considered truly Palladian externally.

At Clandon Leoni raised the attic prominently above the cornice, while to the east front he emphasized the centre of the *piano nobile* by using small one-storey pilasters far too superficially and decoratively to be deemed pure Palladian.

Arguably a rejuvenation or second coming of Palladianism occurred as a direct result of the influence of Holkham Hall, the exterior of which provided an ideal fount of inspiration and a perfect starting point for architects undertaking more modest works. Holkham became a model to be copied, as did Wanstead, Marble Hill, Piercefield Park and Wilton House, with perhaps the most notable feature to be replicated being Wanstead's corner towers. These were echoed in such Palladian tower houses as Langley Park, Norfolk, remodelled by Matthew Brettingham the Elder in 1745 and Hagley Hall, Hereford and Worcester, 1754, by Sanderson Miller.

By the middle of the century, stern formality of the Palladian kind was being pushed aside to make room for a new informal plan. This evolved so that both the interior and exterior were based on a single key element; the centrally placed, top-lit staircase internally, and externally the bay.

Isaac Ware designed a Palladian country house in 1754 at Wrotham Park, Hertfordshire. It was full of movement, and included a detached portico fronting the entrance hall and flanking bays containing Venetian windows and octagonal domed pavilions. This was followed by Sir Robert Taylor's Harleyford Manor, Buckinghamshire, in 1755, for which the design incorporated a variety of bays in combination.

Also by the middle of the century, owners no longer felt the necessity to live above ground level in order to enjoy panoramic views of the countryside. Landscape garden designs had been pioneered by William Kent and developed by Lancelot Brown and later Humphry Repton. As a result, as the century progressed more and more houses were being built with their main floors on the ground level.

At the same time the internal layout was rearranged to dispense with the axially-related saloon and hall, replacing them with a circuit of rooms for communal use and for formal entertaining. They were given equal importance by making them of equal size. These rooms were also arranged round and generally connected with the central top-lit staircase.

The new rococo dominance

Chute Lodge, Wiltshire, 1760, thought to be by Sir Robert Taylor; pedimented three-bay projection on entrance front, canted bay to garden and stair in a central top-lit oval compartment

Asgill House, Richmond-upon-Thames, 1760–65, by Sir Robert Taylor; river frontage of three bays, with broad canted bay flanked by low wings capped with half pediments and central top-lit staircase inside

Danson Park, Bexley, 1760–65, by Sir Robert Taylor with internal completion by Sir William Chambers, c. 1770. Three storeys over rusticated basement, with a pedimented centre breaking forward on entrance front, canted bays in centre of other elevations

Constable Burton Hall, North Yorkshire, 1762–68, by John Carr; inspired by Palladio's Villa Emo

Purbrook, Hampshire, 1770, by Sir Robert Taylor; with colonnaded atrium instead of a central staircase (demolished 1829)

Sharpham, Devon, 1770, by Sir Robert Taylor; considered to be one of his best villas, with a top-lit curving staircase

Denton Hall, North Yorkshire, 1770–81, by John Carr; a nine-bay entrance front and full-height bay on side elevation. A magnificent stair leading into a domed gallery inside

Norton Place, Lincolnshire, 1776, by John Carr. A pedimented front with entrance emphasized by Doric porch and Ionic Venetian window above, deep canted bays to side elevations. An oval top-lit stair with galleried landing internally

Manresa House, originally called Bessborough House and now a Jesuit College. This is a splendid example of William Chambers' early work. The chaste Palladian block is lightly rusticated on the bottom storey and has a giant Ionic portico approached by steps which curve up on both sides

By this time, the Palladian convention was now in decline and the rococo spirit of invention was beginning to assert itself on the outside of the house, as it had already done on the inside.

Sir William Chambers' Bessborough House (now Manresa House), Roehampton, London, 1760–68, was conceived as a villa modelled on Campbell's Stourhead; yet just two years later, in 1762 at Duddingston, Chambers created an altogether different composition. Gone was the Palladian-baroque, usurped by a chastely-detailed two-storey villa with a five-bay entrance front supporting a freestanding Corinthian portico which had columns sitting firmly on the ground. It coincided with Robert Adam's Corinthian portico at Shardeloes, Buckinghamshire, 1759–61. The service block at Duddingston is set asymmetrically to the main block, foreshadowing a picturesque grouping that would become common later in the century. Here Chambers had created a building in the vanguard of mainstream country-house development, which he followed in 1765 with Peper Harow, Surrey (since considerably altered), which reaffirmed his intentions and the direction in which villa design would proceed.

This transitional period also included work by James Paine. At Brocket Hall, Hertfordshire, he designed a large tall house between 1760–65. This was four storeys high over a basement, five bays wide and flanked by a pair of three window-wide four-storey high, canted bays. The interior was in a form of Adam

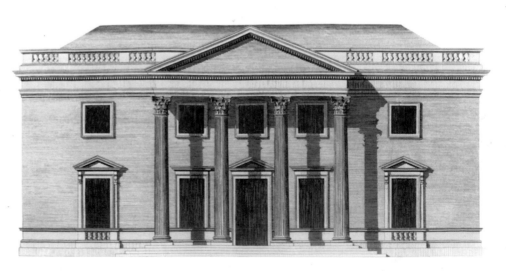

An elevation of the Earl of Abercorn's house at Duddingston, near Edinburgh, 1763–68, by Sir William Chambers. The prostyle tetrastyle Corinthian portico sits on four steps rather than on a basement storey

Palladian style, but with a neoclassical-rococo flavour. Paine went on to design a most dramatic façade for Sandbeck Park, South Yorkshire, 1763–68. The garden front has a deeply projecting Corinthian portico of irregularly-spaced columns, all sitting on a rustic arcade. The main rooms are on the first floor with the saloon, which stretches the length of the house, having a ceiling designed in 1775 in Paine's neoclassical style. This had evolved out of his earlier rococo manner, which had been evident at his Wadworth Hall, South Yorkshire, c. 1750, and was to climax at Wardour Castle, Wiltshire, 1770–76, *illustrated overleaf.*

Wardour Castle has a refined, inventive and highly original Palladian manner, with a nine-bay south front of two storeys over a rusticated ground floor. The centre pediment is of three bays on irregularly-spaced Corinthian columns. The entrance front is astylar with a central Venetian window. Again, the main rooms are on the first floor and are connected to the ground floor by a magnificent top-lit circular staircase, which is placed in a colonnaded circular compartment 18.25m (60ft) high. The rooms on the *piano nobile*, which has pedimented windows, are decorated in a delicate rococo-neoclassical style. Paine's Palladian design, with its minuscule rustic entrance door and squashed attic windows, verged on the ironic and perhaps can be regarded as an epitaph for the Palladian movement.

Stowe House, Buckinghamshire; the south front was designed by Robert Adam and executed by Borra in 1774. It consists of a porticoed centre connected by recessed lower seven-bay buildings to higher three-bay pavilions

Wardour Castle, Wiltshire, 1770–76, by James Paine is a refined, inventive and highly original Palladian building with a nine-bay south front of two storeys over a rusticated ground floor. It has a three-bay central pediment above six Corinthian columns

Batty Langley (1696–1751)

The son of a gardener, Langley was an ambitious, populist author who, by 1728, was already advertising his services as a surveyor, joiner, engineer, canal-builder and gardener. A xenophobe in the mould of Hogarth, and a fierce opponent of Palladio, Inigo Jones and the prevailing style of Lord Burlington, he relied on his powerful masonic connections for the success of his books. His gardening books of the late 1720s helped to foster the new enthusiasm for the 'natural' garden style. However, his architectural works were rarely innovative and relied heavily on drawings pirated from other books; when he did attempt something novel, like his five 'gothic' orders of 1742, the results were often ludicrous. Yet his vast output of pattern-books, from *Practical Geometry* of 1726 to *The Workman's Golden Rule* of 1750, exercised a great influence on contemporary builders and craftsmen, expressing the Palladian proportions of the day in language simple enough for most literate workmen to understand.

The Great Hall at Strawberry Hill, Twickenham, by Walpole

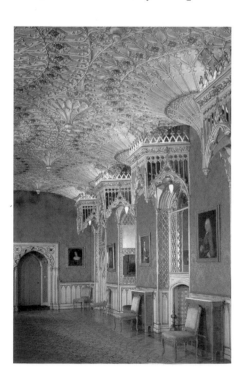

The gothic country house of the type promoted by Vanbrugh, which the Palladian style had pushed aside on its emergent popularity, now again found favour as the latter waned. This type of gothic complemented the new rococo fashion, using traditional English motifs in place of the classical Italian ones. It was a style heavily promoted by Batty Langley, who offered decorative rococo gothic designs within a framework of orders based on the classical model.

Rococo gothic was first popular primarily as a form of interior decoration, although it developed also as an alternative to classicism for the exterior embellishment of the country house. One of the earliest and certainly one of the most influential of the rococo gothic houses was Strawberry Hill, Twickenham. Horace Walpole turned it into an asymmetrical mock-medieval fantasy from 1751, with the help of many inspired designers including John Chute, Richard Bentley, Thomas Pitt, Robert Adam, James Wyatt and James Essex. It includes a staircase and hall by Bentley (1751–61), a ceiling and chimneypiece by Robert Adam (1760), and a gothic gateway together with the Beauclerk Tower by James Essex (1776).

After a short popularity for exteriors, rococo gothic soon gave way to castellated gothic. It became more refined for interiors, possibly as a result of Adam's neoclassical style. However, this apparent return to the dramatic Vanbrugh castle style was only a resurfacing of one that had never really gone away. The odd castellated house had appeared in the interim, and included such noteworthy examples as Inveraray Castle, Strathclyde, 1745–60. This was built by Roger Morris in a curious Palladian gothic manner which included turrets and battlements, but after 1760 these mock castles appeared with increasing frequency.

By the 1770s the castle movement was established. Downton Castle, Hereford and Worcester, 1772, built by Richard Payne Knight for himself, was an asymmetrical, castellated and towered stone construction, but with classical windows. These characteristics made it very much of the coming age of the picturesque movement, which influenced architecture, landscape design, and the arts in the last quarter of the eighteenth century, and distinguished it from its contemporaries such as Culzean. Whereas Culzean was of the romantic, symmetrical, backward-looking Vanbrugh type,

Other rococo gothic country houses

Arbury Hall, Warwickshire, c. 1755, the designers for which included Sanderson Miller, Henry Keen and Richard Bently. It contains arguably the best rococo interiors in the country, including the lavish fan-vaulted plasterwork of the saloon

Ecton Hall, Warwickshire, 1756, thought to be by Sanderson Miller

Castle Ward, Strangford, Co. Down, 1760–73, which was designed in two halves for a husband and wife with differing architectural tastes. Whereas the husband's elevation is textbook Palladian, the wife's garden elevation is in Strawberry Hill gothic, being of seven bays and three storeys and with a battlemented parapet. The interior is similarly divided, with a classical entrance hall and dining room and a gothic saloon and drawing room. The latter has a spectacular gothic ceiling with large elaborate pendentives

Donnington Grove, Berkshire, c. 1762, by John Chute

Moore Abbey, Monasterevin, Co. Kildare, 1767; a plain three-storey, seven-bay block with two-storey attached wings, all containing pointed windows. The interior has some modest gothic plasterwork

Below, *Inveraray Castle;* centre column above, *Culzean Castle;* and, third column, *Scone Palace*

Mock castles

Stoke Park, Stoke Gifford, Avon; castellated c. 1760 by Thomas Wright

Ugbrooke Park, Devon, 1763–68, by Robert Adam

Mellerstain, Borders, 1760s; Robert Adam additions including castellation

Midford Castle, Avon, 1775, by John Carter

Culzean Castle, Strathclyde, 1777, by Robert Adam

The new Vanbrugh-type symmetrical gothic revival castle house

Castle Upton, Templepatrick, Co. Antrim, 1783; remodelling by Robert Adam

Slane, Co. Meath, begun by James Wyatt in 1785 and completed by Francis Johnson. This is one of the earliest gothic revival castles in Ireland. The huge circular ballroom is one of the finest gothic revival rooms in the whole of Ireland

Melville Castle, Lothian, 1786–91, by James Playfair

Castle Browne, Clane, Co. Kildare, 1788, by Thomas Wogan Browne; a three-storey, symmetrical gothic-revival castle

Dalquharran Castle, Strathclyde, 1790, by Robert Adam

Seton Castle, Lothian, 1790–91, by Robert Adam; a symmetrical castle-style house with classical details mixed with medieval machicolations and cruciform windows

Stobes Castle, Borders, 1793, by Robert Adam

Gormanston Castle, Gormanston, Co. Meath, c. 1810; an early nineteenth-century symmetrical castle with classical interior

Luttrellstown Castle, Clonsilla, Co. Dublin, thought to be by Richard Morrison; an ancient castle remodelled in the early nineteenth century in symmetrical romantic style

Shelton Abbey, Arklow, Co. Wicklow, c. 1819, by Sir Richard Morrison; a vast gothic pile in Morrison's abbey style. It has a picturesque pinnacled roof line but largely symmetrical plan; some good gothic decoration inside

The Downton-inspired assymetrical castle

Lasborough Park, Gloucestershire, 1794, by James Wyatt

Charleville Forest, Tullamore, Co. Offaly, c. 1795–1800, by Francis Johnson; considered to be the first deliberately formed asymmetrical house in Ireland

Lambton Castle, Co. Durham, c. 1796, by Joseph Bonomi; asymmetrical, castellated and gothic

Norris Castle, Isle of Wight, 1799, by James Wyatt; a large round east tower with a long range of castellated buildings attached, to form an asymmetrical group

Luscombe Castle, Devon, 1799–1804, by John Nash; a picturesque asymmetrical castellated house

Pennsylvania Castle, Dorset, 1800, by James Wyatt; asymmetrical, castellated and gothic

Scone Palace, Tayside, 1803–12, by William Atkinson; the first Scottish house to have an entirely neogothic interior

Taymouth Castle, Tayside, begun in 1806 to the designs of Archibald and James Elliot; early Scottish picturesque gothic with gigantic gothic stair hall. It is grouped asymmetrically, with lower wings added in 1818

Ashridge Park, Hertfordshire, begun in 1808 by James Wyatt, later extended by Sir Jeffry Wyatville; a huge-scale asymmetrical plan, gothic style with spectacular interiors

Caerhayes Castle, Cornwall, c. 1808, by John Nash; a castellated, asymmetrical and rambling pile. It has a large round tower, square tower and octagonal tower, gothic traceried windows and battlements

Drumtochty Castle, Grampian, c. 1815, by James Gillespie Graham; a picturesque grouping of towers inspired by Warwick castle

Kinfauns Castle, Tayside, 1820, by Sir Robert Smirke; a vast stone castle of cube-like classical clarity

The early Adam houses

Syon House, Brentford, 1761–69; one of Adam's most impressive works. It includes a dining room of 1764, drawing room (extremely delicate) of 1766, the long gallery of 1766 and the entrance hall of 1761 in Adam's grand Roman manner, with domed coffered apses. The entrance gate and screen date from *c.* 1773

Mersham la Hatch, Kent, 1762–65; a simple conventional Palladian box, but inside some fine Adam rooms

Osterley Park, Hounslow, 1762–68; embellished and altered by Adam. Includes the portico of 1762 with a moulded soffit, like Adam's hall at Shardeloes. The entrance hall, 1767–68, has magnificent apsed ends; staircase of 1768, Etruscan Room *c.* 1776

Harewood House, West Yorkshire, *c.* 1765; the plan and north façade were by John Carr, 1759. Adam took over and extended the house and decorated the interiors. It was later altered by Sir Charles Barry, *c.* 1840, but Adam's fine entrance of 1765–67 survives

Nostell Priory, West Yorkshire, *c.* 1766; one of Adam's finest interiors

Kenwood, Highgate, London, 1767; built *ab initio* by Adam. The façade is of white brick and embellished with decorated pilasters and pediment. Fine interior, particularly the library; a portico was added in 1769

Newby Hall, North Yorkshire, 1767–72; original house of 1705 with two-storey wings and interiors by Adam, of which the hall, tapestry room, library and gallery are particularly fine

Saltram House, Devon, 1768–79; hall and stair in mid-century rococo manner, magnificent Adam-designed saloon and dining room

Downton was forcefully asymmetrical, with an interior fitted out in the highly-coloured neoclassical and neo-antique style that finally was to dominate.

The second half of the century witnessed the demise of the rococo gothic, with the rococo movement generally being replaced by a Greek and Roman classicism discovered from newly-published works. These publications included *Antiquities of Athens*, 1762, by James 'Athenian' Stuart and Nicholas Revett; *Ruins of Palmyra*, 1753, by Robert Ward, and *Ruins of Baalbec*, 1757. They depicted true images of the original Grecian as well as the Renaissance-Roman models, rather than the pattern books based on interpretations of these styles by later architects such as Palladio.

These new discoveries manifested themselves initially in decorative interior schemes. The Painted Room was completed by James Stuart in 1759 at Spencer House, St James, Westminster, London (1756, by John Vardy). This represents the earliest complete neoclassical room in Europe, while the first major country house to be designed in the neoclassical style was Robert Adam's Kedleston Hall, Derbyshire, 1760–65.

Adam had spent the years 1754–58 in Italy. After his return to England, he had created a tall Roman Corinthian portico at Shardeloes, Buckinghamshire, in 1759. Rising directly from the ground, this was identical in all essentials to the portico that his future rival, Sir William Chambers, was to raise at Duddingston, Lothian, *illustrated on page 38*. The following year Adam talked his way, against fierce competition, into the commission for all of the design work for the central block of Kedleston, Derbyshire.

Here he created a dazzling masterpiece which displayed all his originality and his creative talent. He evoked the spirit of Rome for the south front, building a four-column frontispiece, which was based on the Arch of Constantine, on a Palladian rustic basement. The attic of the arch rises above the parapet of the flanking elevation, which also breaks back from the arch, and the columns and entablature thrust forward within the arch. This composition marks Adam's commitment to 'movement' in architecture. The hall at Kedleston, which was placed on the same axis as the saloon in the old

Kedleston Hall, Derbyshire, 1765–70, south front by Robert Adam. The strong relief of the design illustrates his theory of movement

Palladian way, is entered through a Wanstead-like north front and was treated as a Roman atrium. The saloon is a domed rotunda.

Adam was now the century's most fashionable architect, and he was able to develop his decorative style in a series of magnificent country houses. He dominated for a decade, inspiring others who were enthusiastic for the original full-blooded Greek rather than Roman precedents.

Among these new competitors, who were prepared to experiment and to push the barriers to further limits were Nicholas Revett, Giovanni Borra, John Plaw and James Wyatt. The latter developed, with his brother Samuel, a refined neoclassical style in the Adam mode for interiors, but they complemented this with their own style of exterior which is evident at Heaton Hall, Manchester, of 1772.

There were also experiments in what can only be termed Graeco-Palladian in the early 1770s. A mix of Greek austerity and Palladian authority can be seen at Woodhouse, Shropshire, 1773, by Robert Mylne, with its quite original portico formed by a pair of Ionic columns set *in antis* with another pair in front of them to form a porch.

Another architect to practice in this style was Henry Holland, the future son-in-law of Lancelot Brown with whom he built Claremont, Esher, Surrey, 1771, and Benham Place, Berkshire, 1774.

Harewood House, West Yorkshire, 1759. John Carr devised the plan and the north façade before the scheme was taken over by Robert Adam, who extended the house and decorated the interiors c. 1765. The house was later altered by Sir Charles Barry, in the mid-nineteenth century

Heveningham Hall, Suffolk, 1778–80, by Sir Robert Taylor. It is one of the grandest Georgian houses, with interiors by James Wyatt and Biagio Rebecca
Above: *the entrance hall was by James Wyatt, c. 1782, with 'fluted-shell' fan-vaulting and ceiling ribs that were repeated in the floor design*
Below: *the seven-bay central part, with enormous detached Corinthian columns, is based on John Webb's Queen's Gallery at Somerset House of 1662, and the end pavilions on Palladian examples*

Benham was a neo-Palladian house with the main rooms on the ground floor and a central top-lit oval staircase. In 1778 Holland built Berrington Hall, Hereford and Worcester, where he faced a seven-bay front with a giant four-columned Ionic portico emphasizing the entrance which leads to ground-floor main rooms and a bold centrally-lit staircase.

The next important architect to emerge, in what was now an era of rapidly shifting experimentation in taste, was George Dance. He designed a ballroom at Granbury Park, Hampshire, *c.* 1775, that was free of any reference to Adam. This reaction to the pervasive Adam style led Thomas Leverton to create an exquisite neo-antique staircase hall at Woodhall Park, Hertfordshire, 1777, and John Carr to produce an original neo-Palladian development where the stair rises ingeniously from the rustic entrance door straight to an external landing behind the portico columns on the *piano nobile,* at Basildon Park, Berkshire, in 1776. Sir Robert Taylor designed Heveningham Hall, Suffolk, in 1778 with a seven-bay centre and a deep arcaded rustic supporting a Corinthian colonnade and a tall attic.

The neoclassical movement developed briskly until the end of the century, and while the austere Graeco-Palladian rose in popularity the polychromatic neoclassicism of Adam and the Wyatts subsided. By 1815 the dogmas that had dominated country house design throughout the eighteenth century had been effectively challenged and replaced by the stylistic pluralism of the Regency period, resulting in the adoption of totally different styles according to the functions and situations of the different buildings.

One obvious result of this architectural metamorphosis was the continual desire to revive previous styles, even recent ones. James Wyatt revived the French rococo manner for a saloon at Belvoir Castle, and Lewis Wyatt added a neo-Wren dining room to Leoni's Lyme Park, but the most dominant of all revivals of the early nineteenth century was the Greek revival.

At Longford Hall, Shropshire, in 1789 Joseph Bonomi gave the first indications of this revival with his bold two-storey four-columned Tuscan portico sitting firmly on the ground and leading to an entrance hall bedecked with a Grecian frieze. In 1803 George Dance designed Stratton Park, Hampshire, with a massive austere two-storey Greek Doric portico that had been inspired by the temples at Paestum. Inside, a magnificent staircase rose to a first-floor Greek Ionic colonnade standing on a basement of channelled rustication, all of which had been inspired by *Maisons de Ville et de Campagne*, 1803, by L-A Dubut.

During the next few years the Greek revival became established, and then developed along varied lines. Some houses followed the direction of James Playfair's Cairness House, Grampian, 1791, where the Greek revival elements of eighteenth-century French neoclassicism were taken up and emphasized. Others, such as Sir Robert Smirke, sought to evolve a modern architecture by stripping Greek of its embellishments and reducing all to primary forms.

Whatever the architect's approach, the typical Greek revival house from the late eighteenth century onwards tended to be lower in height. This was partly because a two-storey house is easier to disguise as a Greek temple. The guest bedrooms, utility areas and the domestics' quarters were also relocated into attached wings.

Though dominant, the Greek revival was not all-pervasive in early nineteeth-century house design. Among other styles to emerge were those which echoed the themes of the picturesque, asymmetry, romantic antiquity and rusticity and reflected the desire by the aristocracy for a country house design which evoked the authority of the ruling class.

This desire at least to appear to be impregnable probably fuelled the neo-Norman trend that showed itself at the very end of the century. It can be seen at James Wyatt's Norris Castle, Isle of Wight, 1799, and at Eastnor Castle, Hereford and Worcester, where Smirke designed a symmetrical neo-Norman castellated manor.

Changing styles at the turn of the century

1782 Belmont Park, Kent, by Samuel Wyatt; a fine neoclassical house with shallow bows, Coade stone plaques set in mathematical tiles, and round corner towers

1783 Attingham Hall, Shropshire, by George Steuart; an eleven-bay entrance front decorated with a pediment supported on attenuated columns, principal rooms on the ground floor in the style of Wyatt

1784 Brasted Place, Kent, by Adams; a two-storey, three-bay villa clad in stone and embellished with a mighty portico of Greek Doric derivation

1785 Shotesham Park, Norfolk, by Soane; a superimposed screen of six Ionic pilasters and an entablature on a wide façade with three-bay pediment

1785 Coton House, Warwickshire, by Samuel Wyatt; contains typical Wyattesque motifs – shallow full-height bows, tripartite windows in blank arches

1788 Bentley Priory, Stanmore, by Soane; entrance hall with a pendentive ceiling on sturdy Greek Doric columns supporting blocks of entablature

1788 Daylesford House, Gloucestershire, by S P Cockerell; neoclassical mansion with French details; top of dome derived from Muslim architecture; circular boudoir with lotus capitals and cloud-painted ceiling

1789 Beaumont Lodge, Berkshire, by Henry Emlyn who 'improved' the composition by using his 'British Order' comprising paired columns

joined by an Order of the Garter symbol with capitals composed of oak leaves, acorns and feathers

c. **1790** Castle Goring, West Sussex, by Biagio Rebecca; gothic castellated entrance front and a Graeco-Palladian garden front

1792 Tyringham, Buckinghamshire, by Sir John Soane; rectangular in plan. It has shallow bows in centre of south-east and northwest fronts; the former ringed by freestanding Ionic columns set against horizontally-chanelled French neoclassically-inspired rustication

c. **1795** Ickworth, Suffolk, by Francis Sandys to a design by Marco Asprucci for the Earl Bishop of Derry. This gigantic domed round house with lower wings displays an exuberant neo-antique enthusiasm for the house as a temple of the arts

1795 Emsworth, Malahide, Co. Dublin, by James Gandon; an exquisite villa with its ground-floor windows in blank arches, segmental-ended apsed hall and dining room and tripartite windows

1795 Southill Park, Bedfordshire, by Henry Holland; an austere Graeco-Palladian house with a chaste ashlar exterior. The pedimented centre block has Ionic colonnades and loggias on south front; inside a red and gold Empire-style (Regency) saloon

1796 Bowden House, Wiltshire, by James Wyatt; a compact two-storey villa with bold two-storey bow to garden façade. Decorated by four freestanding Ionic columns flanked by

tripartite windows within relieving arches, behind which is an oval saloon

1800 Pitzhanger Manor, Ealing, by Soane; alterations to an earlier home brought for himself. A mix of Roman elements with Soane's characteristic classical detailing

c. **1800** The Gleanings, Rochester, Kent; a Greek front, castellated to the river

1802 Cronkhill, Shropshire, by John Nash; the first picturesque Italianate villa, asymmetrical with a round tower that has a conical roof and deep projecting eaves

1803 Scampston, Humberside, by Thomas Leverton; a nine-bay south front with domed-pilastered bow and on west front a bow ringed with detached Tuscan columns

1805 Sezincote House, Gloucestershire, by S P Cockerell for his brother, an Indian nabob; an essay in the Mogul/Hindoo manner with Mogul dome and Indian cornice

c. **1805** Sandridge Park, Stoke Gabriel, Devon, by Nash; a repetition of his Italianate stuccoed Cronkhill villa, with round and square towers

1806 Dunstall Priory, Shoreham, Kent, by Roger Lugar; another early example of the asymmetrical Italianate villa

1814 Dalmeny House, Lothian, by William Wilkins; a large and influential Tudor gothic mansion

1815 Royal Pavilion, Brighton, by Nash; the exotic onion-domed Hindoo-gothic palace for the Prince Regent

Eastnor Castle, Herefordshire, 1810–15, by Sir Robert Smirke; a monumental example of his 'square' style

This revival reached its climax with Thomas Hopper's Gosford Castle, Markethall, Co. Armagh, 1819, and at Penrhyn Castle, Bangor, Gwynedd, 1825. Both of Hopper's constructions were huge, asymmetrically grouped and picturesque.

Examples of the fleeting Neo-Tudor, neo-Elizabethan revival were Nonsuch Park, Surrey, 1802, by Sir Jeffry Wyatville and William Wilkins the Younger's elaborate asymmetrical neo-Tudor mansion, Tregotham, near Truro, Cornwall, of 1816. Later still were the Elizabethan-styled Carstairs House, Strathclyde, 1822, by William Burn, and Lilleshall Hall, Shropshire, 1826, by Wyatville.

Finally came the Jacobean revival, evident in John Buonarotti Papworth's 1818 design for St Julian's Underriver, Kent; Underlay Hall, Kirkby Lonsdale, Cumbria, 1825, by George Webster; and at Babraham Hall, Cambridgeshire, 1829–32 by Philip Hardwick.

The *cottage orné* is the epitome of the picturesque, characterised by gothic detailing. These were overtly rustic constructions, asymmetrical in plan; good examples are A-la-Ronde, Exmouth, Devon, *c.* 1795, with its 18.25m (60ft) high central hall decorated with shells and birds modelled out of feathers; Derrymore House, Bessbrook, Co. Armagh, *c.* 1790–1800, of symmetrical Palladian layout, and perhaps the most typical, the Lodge of Grant's House, near Hinton Martell, Dorset, *c.* 1810, which has an umbrella-like thatched roof, gothic windows and a rustic tree-trunk colonnaded thatched porch.

From the very beginning of the eighteenth century architects had the scope to indulge their imaginations with the construction of garden buildings. They were regarded as romantic settings, a counterbalance to the formality of the classical house and a picturesque element in the composed landscape garden. These playful buildings often took on oriental forms, while others were baroque or even gothic. They existed alongside others that were

Cottage Orné, Suffolk, c. *1815, in the manner of John Nash*

Greek-revival buildings

Townley Hall, Drogheda, Co. Louth, 1794, by Francis Johnson; another austere neoclassical house, with a square plan and a single-storey Greek Doric porch

The Grange, Hampshire, 1804; remodelling by William Wilkins. The first and best rendering of a country house as a Greek Doric temple

Osberton Hall, Nottinghamshire, 1806, by Wilkins; one of the earliest Greek Doric porticoes on a British country house

Belsay Hall, Northumberland, 1806, by Sir Charles Monck; the most stunning, austere and powerful Greek revival style, square in plan with a Greek Doric portico set *in antis*

Storrs Hall, Bowness-in-Windermere, Cumbria, 1808, by J M Gandy; an entrance front with a single-storey Greek Doric colonnade supporting an entablature with prominent antefixae

Arlington Court, Devon, 1820, by Thomas Lee; two storeys with a Greek Doric entablature running all round, and an entrance marked by a pair of massive Greek Doric columns set *in antis*

Eighteenth-century garden buildings

Belvedere, *c.* 1715, Claremont, Surrey; by Sir John Vanbrugh, designed in an austere castellated style

Summerhouse, 1718, Ebberston Hall, near Scarborough, North Yorkshire; by Colen Campbell, a single-storey rusticated building in baroque manner

Alfred's Hall, 1721, Cirencester Park, Gloucestershire; by Alexander Pope, picturesque gothic ruin *cum* cottage

Temple of the Four Winds, 1725, Castle Howard, North Yorkshire; by Sir John Vanbrugh, domed with four porticos inspired by Palladio's Villa Rotunda

Gothic folly arch, *c.* 1730, Gobions, Brookmans Park, Hertfordshire; thought to be by Gibbs

Kennels, 1731, Chatelherault, Strathclyde; by William Adam, lavish and baroque

Temple of British Worthies, 1733, Stowe, Buckinghamshire; by William Kent, in rusticated classic style

Temple of Ancient Virtue, 1736, Stowe, Buckinghamshire; by William Kent, chaste, classical and domed

Bridge, 1737, Wilton, Wiltshire; by Roger Morris and Lord Pembroke, an ornamental bridge inspired by a Palladio design

Chinese pavilion, 1738, Stowe, Buckinghamshire; built of timber and long gone

Arch, *c.* 1740, Holkham Hall, Norfolk; by William Kent, a Roman triumphial arch rendered in Palladian detail

Gothic temple, 1742–45, Painshill Park, Cobham, Surrey; rococo gothic with pendant tracery and ogee openings

Gothic tower, 1745, Edge Hill, Warwickshire; by Sanderson Miller, octagonal and castellated

Worcester Lodge, 1746, Badminton House, Great Badminton, Avon; by William Kent, in decorative and inventive Palladian

Chinese pavilion, 1747, Shugborough, Staffordshire

Orangery, *c.* 1750, Frampton Court, Frampton, Gloucestershire; gothic with plan based on octagons and with ogee-arched windows

Temple of Hercules, 1754–56, Stourhead, Wiltshire; by Henry Flitcroft

Bridge, *c.* 1755, Prior Park, Bath, Avon; by John Wood the Elder, Palladian

Temple of Theseus, 1758, Hagley, Worcestershire; by James Stuart

Temple of Bellona, *c.* 1760, Kew, Kingston-upon-Thames; by Sir William Chambers

Pagoda, 1761, Kew, Richmond-upon-Thames; by Sir William Chambers

Bridge, 1764, Hagley, Worcestershire; by Thomas Hagley

Lanthorn of Demosthenes, 1764, Shugborough, Staffordshire; by James Stuart, based on the Choragic Monument of Lysicrates in Athens

Tower of the Winds, 1764, Shugborough, Staffordshire; by James Stuart, based on the octagonal towers in Athens

Corinthian Arch, 1766, Stowe, Buckinghamshire; by Thomas Pitt, Palladian-rendered Roman triumphial arch

Chinese pavilion, *c.* 1770, Wrest Park, Bedfordshire; by Sir William Chambers

Chinese temple, 1772, Amesbury Abbey, Wiltshire; by Sir William Chambers

Bridge, 1782, Audley End, Essex; by Robert Adam

Chinese dairy, 1791, Woburn Abbey, Bedfordshire; by Henry Holland

Hiorne's Tower, Arundel, West Sussex, c. 1790, by Francis Hiorne, built to a triangular plan and with gothic detailing

sophisticated and inventive, classically-based garden buildings that came to the fore in the mid-century. An excellent example is the Casino at Marino, Clontarf, Co. Dublin, 1758–76, by Sir William Chambers.

The Palladian movement produced ornamental bridges (eg Stowe), arches (eg Holkham Hall) and temples (eg Stourhead), but the second half of the eighteenth century and the early nineteenth century witnessed a serious approach to archaeological reconstruction. James Stuart produced the first fully Greek-revival garden building, the Temple of Theseus, at Hagley, Worcestershire, in 1760.

Above: *James Stuart's copy of the Athenian Tower of the Winds, 1764, at Shugborough, Staffordshire*

Below: *the Lanthorn of Demosthenes, 1764–70, also by Stuart, in the grounds of Shugborough. It was based on the Choragic Monument of Lysicrates in Athens*

Left: *the Palladian bridge, c. 1738–42, at Stowe, Buckinghamshire, viewed through the Doric arch*

Above right: *the Casino, Marino, Clontarf, Co. Dublin, 1758–76, to a design of Sir William Chambers. Built in the form of a Roman Doric temple, it is regarded as having introduced French neoclassicism into Irish architecture*
Below right: *the crescent-shaped Temple of British Worthies at Stowe, 1733, by William Kent*

Far right, above: *the Temple of Venus at Stowe, c. 1732;* and below: *the triangular Gothic Temple, Stowe, 1741–48, by James Gibbs*

Overleaf, main picture: *the Palladian Bridge, Stowe, c. 1738–42, thought to be by James Gibbs, seen in its tranquil setting across the Octagon lake*

Overleaf, inset left: *the Temple of Ancient Virtue at Stowe, 1736, by Kent; formed by a cellular rotunda with Ionic columns;* inset, right: *the Temple of Concorde and Victory at Stowe, c. 1748–62, thought to be by Kent; an early neoclassical design with portico and peristyle in the manner of a Roman temple*

By the turn of the century garden building design encompassed an amazing range of architectural style, more than any other form. Greek and Roman-inspired reconstructions sat side by side with exotic oriental and gothic designs while the emerging austere neoclassicism also made its appearance. By 1820, garden building design had become the testbed for new building technology; cast iron and glass roofs were two popular examples, and appear in our companion volume, *Victorian and Edwardian Architecture*

Chapter Five

Churches

FOLLOWING THE EVENTS of 1666, Wren had produced a plethora of church designs with various plan forms as well as ceiling and vault designs. The early eighteenth-century church designers tended to turn to these designs for inspiration, and thus kept alive the prevailing baroque long after it had fallen from grace elsewhere.

In 1711 the government introduced the 'fifty churches act' for London. Funded by a tax on coal, these new churches were to represent the Tory High Church ethos and be a symbol of State power and control scattered throughout the capital's suburbs.

The church commissioners included Wren, Vanbrugh and Archer. All three vigorously advocated that the fifty churches should all be freestanding on insular sites, and with handsome porticoes so that they would stand as monuments for posterity.

In the event only 16 churches were built, and of those four were heavily subsidized by the 1711 Church Building Commission. The architects appointed to build them were, in the main, pupils of Wren. Their buildings, together with Wren's City churches, acted as the inspiration for provincial church designers for many years.

Despite this, the single most influential church of the period was unquestionably that of St Martin-in-the-Fields, London. It was designed by James Gibbs, a Scottish Roman Catholic, between 1722 and 1726. It is essentially a baroque building, although it combines the classical propriety of its temple front and basilica plan with contemporary ecclesiastical requirements such as its tower and spire. The general design of its exterior, with its dominant portico and tall steeple, superseded anything that Hawksmoor or the other commissioners' architects achieved, for no architect had combined a basilica with a giant portico to provide the gravity, grandeur and scale that transformed this church into a Roman temple.

Internally the plan of the Roman basilica is used; there is a nave and aisles, but no transept. There is a single axis from the

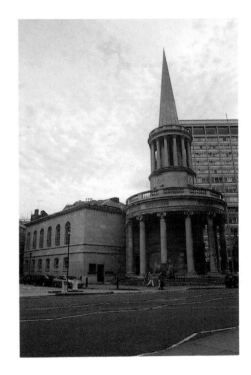

Above: *All Souls Church, Langham Place, London, 1822–25, by John Nash for the New Church Commissioners. The circular vestibule, towered and spired, forms a terminal feature to Regent Street and at the same time rounds off the turning from Langham Place into Portland Place*

Opposite: *Marylebone Parish Church, London, 1813–17, by Thomas Hardwick*

St George's Church, by John James, was built between 1720–25; the house (No. 30) next to it on the extreme right of the illustration is still standing. It is thought to be by Thomas Barlow, and is typical of several in the area

According to Ralph in A Critical Review of Public Buildings in and about London *(1734) 'the view down George Street, from the upper side of the Square, is one of the most entertaining in the whole City; the sides of the Square, the area in the middle, the breaks of buildings that form the entrance of the vista, the vista itself, but, overall the beautiful projection of the portico of St George's Church, are all circumstances that unite in beauty, and make the scene perfect'*

west front along the centre of the nave to the altar, which is in the chancel. The nave is separated from the aisles by Corinthian columns on plinths. Within the aisles are galleries which were provided to accommodate part of the congregation, placed above plinth-level halfway up the aisle columns. Gibbs, like many other architects, had been forced to add elements to his original design; in this instance these galleries which together with the pews interrupt and partly obscure the line of the giant columns between vault and floor. The Corinthian columns in the aisle are supported on pedestals, and themselves support square entablature blocks from which the vault of the nave springs, similar to those used at St Bride's, Fleet Street, London and St Andrew's, Holborn, London.

St Martin's success and the reverence in which it is held in the language of church architecture are owed to a number of factors. These are its versatility of plan, the lightness of its architectural style, its prominent site and what it had supplanted, and, significantly, that Gibbs published the complete building plans for the church in his 1728 *Book of Architecture,* precisely with the intention that it should be universally copied. In addition to the more or less complete copies

Left: *St Mary-le-Strand, London, 1714–17, by James Gibbs, from his* Book of Architecture

Right: *St John's Church, Smith Square, London, 1713–28, by Archer; cruciform with a vaulted crossing, symmetrical on both axes*

Provincial baroque churches

St Michael's, Aynho,
Northamptonshire, begun in 1723 and
thought to be by local mason Edward
Wing
St John the Baptist's, Honiley,
Warwickshire, 1723
Gayhurst, Buckinghamshire, 1728; also
by Edward Wing

Provincial baroque churches

St Michael's, Aynho,
Northamptonshire, begun in 1723 and
thought to be by local mason Edward
Wing
St John the Baptist's, Honiley,
Warwickshire, 1723
Gayhurst, Buckinghamshire, 1728; also
by Edward Wing

Early basilica-plan churches

St James's, Piccadilly, London,
1676–84, by Wren
St Paul's, Sheffield, 1720, by John Platt
(now demolished)
Holy Trinity, Leeds, 1720, by
William Etty
St Peter's, Vere Street, Westminster,
London, 1721, by James Gibbs

Copies of St Martin's

St Giles-in-the-Fields, St Giles High
Street, Holborn, London, 1731–33, by
Henry Flitcroft. A Palladian essay on
St Martin's, the front door has a Gibbs
surround and the tower is pure
St Martin's
St Andrew's, St Andrew's Square,
Glasgow, 1739–56, by Allan Dreghorn;
a fully-fledged copy of St Martin's but
the steeple is based on another of
Gibbs' designs which was also
published in his *Book of Architecture*. It
has a barrel-vaulted ceiling
Holy Cross, Daventry, Northampton,
1752, by David Hiorne; in the tradition
of St Martin's, with a Doric arcade
and tower based on Flitcroft's St Giles
St John's, St John's Square,
Wolverhampton, 1758–76, by
William Baker; with Gibbs windows
and tower but without portico
St Martin's, Cornmarket, Worcester,
1768–72, by Anthony Keck; with
Gibbs surrounds to windows, and
St Martin's-inspired vaulting and
column arrangement
Church of Ireland Cathedral,
Waterford, Co. Waterford, 1773–79,
by John Roberts. A nave of
Corinthian columns on high pedestals
supports blocks of entablature from
which springs the vaulted ceiling; a
splendid Doric portico
St Paul's, St Paul's Square, Birmingham,
1777–79, by Roger Eykyns; in Gibbs
tradition, minus portico
Christ Church, Broad Street, Bristol,
Avon, 1786–90, by William Paty; the
interior is closely based on St Martin's
St Mary's, Wanstead, London,
1787–90, by Thomas Hardwick;
Gibbs-inspired interior with tall
Corinthian columns on high pedestals
St George's, Hardwicke Place, Dublin,
1802–13, by Francis Johnson; portico,
tower and spire derived from Gibbs
but with Grecian details
North Leigh Church, Prince Regent
Street, Leith, Edinburgh, 1814–16, by
William Burn; a Grecian version of St
Martin's
St John's, Waterloo Road, London,
1823–24, by Francis Bedford; Greek
Doric portico with tower set above, in
the manner of James Gibbs

that followed, there were also many provincial churches that incorporated single elements of either the windows, the nave elevations, or the tower of St Martin's. The most impressive duplication of the tower is at St Nicholas's, Worcester, 1730–35, by Humphrey Hollins.

Gibbs, however, was not the only inspirational church designer and there were alternatives to his solution of springing vaults from blocks of entablature carried on columns supported on pedestals. Either the ceiling could be allowed to rise in a barrel vault from a continuous entablature running the length of the nave, the aisles having flat ceilings divided into compartments by entablatures as used by Wren; or the aisle vaults could be treated as a series of barrel vaults lit by high-level windows, as used by Hawksmore.

The basilica plan additionally afforded the possibility of placing the nave columns on pedestals which were themselves supported on piers. This formation visually integrated the gallery into the design of the interior, and Wren had used it in St James's, Piccadilly, 1676–84. Although the basilica type of plan tended to

Left: *St Giles-in-the-Fields, St Giles High Street, Holborn, London, 1731–33, by Henry Flitcroft*

Far left: *Christ Church, Broad Street, Bristol, 1786–90, by William Paty*

Below: *Grosvenor Chapel, South Audley Street, London, c. 1730, by Benjamin Timball; handsomely finished in yelllow brick and white stone*

dominate, other plans were followed: the baroque type with a cross-axis expressed externally on the aisle elevations; the cruciform plan church with transepts expressed externally and, finally, a hotch-potch of provincial church designs distinguished by archaic features or decorated with details straight out of pattern books based, not

necessarily directly or accurately, on designs by Palladio or Gibbs.

There were also small, modest, cell-like vernacular churches, often arranged with a Venetian window at the east end and a gallery at the west end. In the wake of John Wesley's popularity the parish churches of the Nonconformist chapels evolved handsome and generally unadorned symmetrical and often centralized preaching halls.

It is perhaps puzzling that the Palladian church is noticable by its absence, having dominated every other area of building up to the mid-century. There were spasmodic attempts to create a Palladian church, such as at Holy Trinity, Leeds, 1722. This was based on a Roman basilica plan like St Martin-in-the-Fields, with monumental Corinthian columns supporting a straight entablature running the length of the nave. The nave windows are embellished externally by alternating triangular and segmental pediments, a method which is early Palladian in style, typical of Burlington.

St Lawrence's Church, Mereworth, Kent, designed in 1722 by Colen Campbell, was one serious attempt at a Palladian church, built to a basilica plan for the Earl of Westmorland between 1744–46. Its tower is derived from St Martin's and its Tuscan portal and columns, which support a deep eaved cornice, are from Inigo Jones' prototype Palladian church of St Paul's, Covent Garden, London, 1632.

Before the Palladian style had any significant effect upon church building it was eclipsed by the gothic taste, which began to emerge as early as the 1740s. Palladian style in churches ended before it had ever become popular, with the publications of the 1750s and 1760s which highlighted the limitations of Palladio's interpretation of ancient classical architecture. Church design was slow to feel the influence of this neoclassical shift which initially affected only a few elements such as the towers.

Eventually there were internal alterations, with a greater emphasis being placed on central planning, such as symmetrical Greek Cross plans and central domes. Typical of these new developments, and an early example of the Greek/Roman temple church, was James Stuart's All Saints' Church. This was designed with the Earl of Harcourt for the grounds, landscaped by Capability Brown, of the Earl's Nuneham Park, Nuneham Courtney, Oxfordshire in 1764. This had a centralised plan and dome and a hexastyle Greek Ionic portico based on the fifth-century Ionic of the Temple of Ilissus.

Centrally planned churches were more popular in Scotland than south of the border. The most popular was the octagonal plan, which gained favour from about 1770 and remained popular though not dominant for a long period.

Notable among the English churches to have a centralised plan was St Mary's, Paddington, London, 1788, by John Plaw. This had the same Greek-cross plan as that used for St James's, Great Packington, Warwickshire, in 1790 by Joseph Bonomi. The

---

Palladian churches

Knockbreda Church (now Newtownbreda), Co. Antrim, 1737, by Richard Castle. Cruciform in plan with semi-circular transept; west tower has a spire, pedimented west door has Gibbs surround

St Catherine's, Thomas Street, Dublin, 1769, by John Smyth; standard aisled and galleried basilica plan has barrel vault, magnificent north elevation of five bays with three-bay pediment supported on giant Doric engaged columns, pedimented centre door

St Nicholas, Hardenhuish, Wiltshire, 1779, by John Wood the Younger; Venetian windows in north and south nave walls, tower with octagonal top and stone dome

---

Far left, bottom left: *St Martin-in-the-Fields;* centre, *alternative tower designs published by James Gibbs in 1728 and,* right, *Gibbs' Italian baroque St Mary-le-Strand in 1714–17*

Central-plan churches

Kilarrow Kirk, Bowmore, Islay, Strathclyde, 1769, for Daniel Campbell

Kelso, Borders, 1773, by John Laidlaw, John Nisbet and Robert Purves; one of the earliest octagonal churches with a fine columned and galleried interior

Glassite Chapel, King Street, Dundee, 1777; octagonal with round-headed windows

Dreghorn, Strathclyde, 1780; octagonal

St George's Episcopalian Chapel, Edinburgh, 1794, by John Adam; gothic revival

St Michael's, Madeley, Shropshire, 1794–96, by Thomas Telford; octagonal neoclassical

St John's, Lockwinnoch, Strathclyde, 1806; gothic octagonal plan

St Paul's, Perth, 1807, by John Paterson; gothic

St Mary's, Micheldever, Hampshire, 1808–10, by George Dance the Younger; the addition of an octagonal brick nave to a medieval church

Glen Orchy, Strathclyde, 1811, by James Elliot; gothic octagonal plan

St George's, Charlotte Square, Edinburgh, 1811–14, by Robert Reid; a Greek-cross plan set below a colonnaded dome and unrelated to it. A portico of Greek Ionic columns set *in antis*

latter is a most splendid church, with a symmetrical body and four red-brick corner turrets, embellished with massive Diocletian windows. Internally there are four tunnel vaults radiating from a square nave, where the cross-vaulting springs from four Greek Doric columns derived from those at the Temple of Neptune at Paestum.

St Mary's, Banbury, Oxfordshire, 1792, by S P Cockerell is another remarkable centralized church. It design was based on a circle within a square, with a square nave in which eight freestanding composite columns are linked by arches and support a round dome-like roof.

However, throughout the century it was the gothic revival church that prevailed, progressing from the early picturesque gothic, the decorative rococo and the Adamesque gothic of the middle and late century to the antiquarian gothic at the end. A common theme throughout was the classical, usually Doric, interior within a gothic shell. This unlikely marriage was displayed particularly dramatically by classically detailed churches furnished with a tall, tapering, pointed spire. During the first half of the century modern gothic additions were made to existing gothic buildings, a practice which increased during the second half.

Those churches of the early-generation gothic of the eighteenth century are, for the most part, unremarkable architectural pieces. The gothic of the mid-eighteenth century was essentially a decorative style, so the later eighteenth-century gothic churches differ from their classical counterparts only in their embellishment, being of a similar structure.

St John's, Shobdon, Hereford and Worcester, 1753, is a notable example of the rococo gothic. Although some of the details are straight out of Batty Langley's pattern books others, like the ogee tracery in the windows, are copied from Strawberry Hill.

At Croome d'Abitot, Hereford and Worcester, St Mary Magdalene's Church of 1761 is the work of Robert Adam, probably with advice from Lancelot Brown as the church stands in a park of his design. The exterior is a serious attempt at the gothic ideal, whereas internally it is the elegant light decorative style typical of Adam's contemporary classical work. It differs from the freedom of the rococo gothic, which can be seen in the church of St John the Baptist, King's Norton, Leicestershire, c. 1760–75, by John Wing the Younger. Here large Perpendicular windows were used, which were the preferred genuine gothic style of the later eighteenth-century antiquarian gothic designers.

The church building act of 1818 granted its commissioners one million pounds to build new churches, and as in the earlier Act of 1711, political concerns were as prominent as spiritual concerns. Some 600 new churches were built within the next 35 years as a result of the Act; the consequence was that the money available was insufficient to ensure a uniformly high standard of architecture. The commissioners' constraints and lack of finance resulted in a plethora of cheap, uniform and liturgically unadventurous oblong brick boxes built on a basilica plan. Their one saving grace was that they were often well sited, and would eventually have a good effect on their immediate townscape.

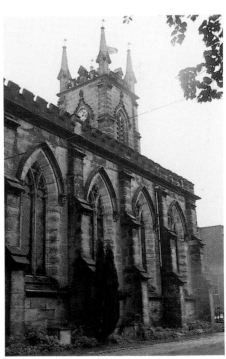

Above, left: *St Luke's Church, Sydney Street, Chelsea, 1820–24, by James Savage. One of the most daring gothic structures of the time, it is vaulted from end to end in stone and supported by flying buttresses spanning the aisle roofs. This vault was structural in function, rather than decorative like those of wood and plaster*

Above, right: *Holy Trinity Church, Church Road, Tunbridge Wells, 1827–29, by Decimus Burton; thin gothic parish church, now a lively arts centre*

Chapter Six

Market and Industrial Buildings

Banks

Given the current appearance of affluence promoted by today's financial houses, it is surprising that at the beginning of the eighteenth century the purpose-built bank was invariably a building of domestic appearance. Another surprise is that by the 1820s there were well in excess of 750 private banks in England, and that it was well into the Victorian age before the bank began to emerge as a recognisable building type.

One of the notable early banking establishments was the Bank of England in the City of London by Soane, 1788–1833. Almost grim in appearance, it was surrounded by a high rusticated

Far left: *Abingdon County Hall*

Left: *Lloyds Bank, The Square, Petersfield, Hampshire; a good provincial Palladian composition of mid-century*

wall with few windows, pierced by pedimented doors and decorated with neoclassical details including a Corinthian-columned corner of *c.* 1805 which was inspired by the Temple of Vesta at Tivoli. The Bank had originally been designed by Sir Robert Taylor between 1765 and 1744, and Soane added internally a series of spacious top-lit apartments of Roman grandeur. These rooms, which included the Five Pound Note Office, and the Accounts Office, were purposely designed to represent the institution's power, being much more spacious than their function actually demanded. They mark an important phase in the development of Soane's architecture, and were the most romantic if not the most representative of eighteenth-century commercial interiors. Tragically, all but the screen wall of the building was demolished between 1921–1937.

British provincial arcades

Crown Arcade, Virginia Street, Glasgow, *c.* 1820
Upper and Lower Arcades, Bristol, 1824–25, by James Foster
The Corridor, High Street, Bath, Avon, 1825, by H E Goodridge
Argyle Arcade, Argyle Street, Glasgow, 1827–28, by James Baird

The Corridor, off the High Street, Bath; a bold neoclassical façade with Doric columns at ground level flanking the shops

Shops and arcades

The design of shops made very little progress during the eighteenth century, although in detail they reflected the changing fashions from Palladian through rococo to neoclassical and their traditional bow-windows remained in evidence, though gradually flattened out. The typical mid-century shop was double-bayed, with a door squeezed in between.

The London building act of 1774 ruled that bay windows should not project more than ten inches into the street, but it was not until the turn of the century, with the emergence of large panes of plate glass, that the shop front was finally flattened. This enabled the entrance door to be more prominent, often being flanked by columns of pilasters to divide the door from the windows.

By 1825 shops were beginning to be designed as uniform groups in arcades, courts and occasionally in streets. An early example of the uniform shopping street was D'Olier Street, Dublin, *c.* 1799, laid out by the Wide Streets Commission. The elevations and shop-fronts were uniform, arcaded with Ionic pilasters used to define each unit. Internally they had U-shaped galleries on a mezzanine floor, with cast-iron balconies.

Arcades were more common, having already appeared in England as roofed streets of shops as early as 1566 (Gresham's Royal Exchange in the City of London), and later in 1676 (Exeter Change, Strand, London). They were made popular in the late eighteenth century by the Parisians and established in England in the early nineteenth century. Examples are the Royal Opera Arcade, Pall Mall, of 1816–18 by Nash and Repton and the Burlington Arcade, 1818–19, by Samuel Ware, for which he designed a pitched-glass roof on transverse arches. Glass and iron vaulted roofs were not used until a little later, with the construction of the Gallerie d'Orléans in Paris of 1828.

External and internal views of the Burlington Arcade, Piccadilly, London; said by its designer Samuel Ware to have been based on the Exeter Change

Exchanges and markets

The seventeenth-century Exchange was founded on a cloister-like plan with covered arcades surrounding an open court, typical of which was the Corn Exchange, City of London, *c.* 1755.

However from that mid-century point other building types were to be utilised for the large-scale exchanges. The Exchange at Corn Street, Bristol, by John Wood the Elder, was of town mansion type being an eleven-bay, three-storey ashlar Palladian composition with a three-bay pediment and engaged Corinthian columns on a rusticated ground floor. It was completed in 1745, nine years before his Exchange at Liverpool (now the Town Hall) which was of very

Right: *the Exchange, Corn Street, Bristol, 1740–45, by John Wood the Elder; an eleven-bay, three-storey ashlar Palladian composition with three-bay pediment and engaged Corinthian columns on a rusticated ground floor*

Far right: *Market House, now the Butter Market, North Street, Chichester, 1807, in the Greek Doric manner; the top storey was added in 1900 and the whole restored in 1955*

similar design. It was damaged by fire in 1795 and rebuilt by Foster in 1802, who added a dome. The portico was added in 1811.

A circular plan was submitted for the design of the Royal Exchange, Dublin, by Thomas Cooley in a competition of 1768. This proposed a domed neoclassical temple, and possibly was influenced by the 1763 Paris Corn Exchange. The Dublin Royal Exchange was built between 1769 and 1779 and hailed as a neoclassical temple of commerce but it was not very practical, and the building later became the City Hall. It was entered via a giant Corinthian portico; the open space on the ground floor was defined by a ring of columns coupled with piers and supporting the dome.

The Royal Exchange (now Stirling's Library), Glasgow, 1827–29, by David Hamilton also made use of a huge Corinthian portico. It has a Graeco-Roman interior with a Corinthian arcade, supporting a shallow barrel-vaulted coffered ceiling.

The Exchange's smaller brother was the market hall, used for more diverse functions but sharing the common denominating element of the open arcade. Its influential predecessor was that at seventeenth-century Abingdon (now the County Hall), 1678–80, by Christopher Kempster, with its open arcaded substructure.

Both the Butter Cross, Ludlow, Shropshire, 1743, by William Baker, and Martock market, Somerset, *c.* 1750, are freestanding markets as at Abingdon, but this type of market was also sometimes constructed as part of a terrace as at the main street in Midleton, Co. Cork, known as Market House.

The Industrial Revolution brought a revolution in the market hall, with a drastic change in scale, construction and design. The Piece Hall, Halifax, West Yorkshire, 1775, thought to be by Thomas Bradley and designed as a cloth market, is typical of those in the rapidly-expanding manufacturing and industrial centres in the north of England. It is massive, with tiers of colonnades, now containing small shops and offices, surrounding a truly enormous square of parade-ground proportions which is entered via a pedimented gate.

London's Covent Garden market, *c.* 1828–30, by Charles Fowler, heralded a new generation of markets. Of advanced design, they reflected contemporary international thinking. Here granite Tuscan arcades sheltered rows of shops, while the glass-roofed central arcade reflected current French and North American concepts in market design. The original construction of Covent Garden market was in brick, stone and timber, shunning the new technology of cast iron.

Covent Garden Market, the Piazza, Covent Garden, London; a magnificent classical design incorporating Tuscan colonnades and a central Greek-detailed covered arcade

Merchant and city halls

Coopers' Hall, King Street, Bristol, 1743–44, by William Halfpenny (destroyed); had a provincial Palladian street façade

Trinity House, Kingston-upon-Hull, Humberside, 1753–59; a pedimented nine-bay entrance front. The courtroom inside of 1773 by Joseph Page has a strange mixture of lavish rococo and neoclassical plasterwork

Waterman's Hall, St Mary-at-Hill, City of London, 1778–80, by William Blackburn; an over-embellished neoclassical façade

Merchants' Hall, Hunter Square, Edinburgh, 1788, by John Baxter the Younger

Trades House, Glassford Street, Glasgow, 1791–94, by Robert Adam; complex elevation displaying Adam's belief in 'movement' (alterations were made in 1808, 1824 and 1887, from when the interior dates)

Trinity House, Tower Hill, City of London, 1792–94, by Samuel Wyatt; five bays with tripartite windows

Merchant halls

The merchant halls, and those of the City livery companies, built in the latter half of the eighteenth century were styled as town mansions or country houses, while their immediate successors presaged the grandeur to be lavished on them by the Victorians.

Prestige was seen to have been achieved merely by employing the top architect of the day, and encouraging him to over-embellish the exterior and richly to decorate the interior. Other halls such as the Stationers' Hall, Ludgate Hill, City of London, 1800, by Robert Mylne, had a dignity lent by a Graeco-Palladian elevation and could be more closely associated with institutional buildings such as town halls.

Mills and warehouses

The system of cottage industry did survive to some extent throughout the eighteenth century, most often on the basis of living quarters provided on the ground floor with the well-lit rooms in the upper storey(s) providing a manufacturing base.

The pattern of construction for the eighteenth-century mills and warehouses had been created as early as 1718, with Thomas and John Lombe's silk mill in Derby. This pioneered a scale of manufacturing that would enable the mass-production system to flourish. Although it was 33.5m (110ft) long and five storeys high. it was shallow in depth and the maximum effort had been made to provide good light, by the inclusion of many windows. Power for the mill was provided by a 7m (23ft) diameter waterwheel.

It was this sheer scale of approach of the Lombe mill that was revolutionary, although the structure within the shell would undergo considerable change in future, especially as building technology developed and architects continually sought to improve safety and find fireproof methods of construction.

The call for fire safety reached its zenith when the Albion Mill, London, 1783–86, by Samuel Wyatt, was destroyed by fire in 1791. It had been a conventional structure with a loadbearing brick shell and a timber-framed interior.

There had been half-hearted attempts at fireproofing mills, but the first 'fireproof' mill did not appear until 1792, when William Strutt built a mill in Derby for his father. He used iron colonnades instead of wooden posts, with the floors supported on shallow brick arches although the beams which were supported by the

Right: Thomas and John Lombe's water-powered silk mill, 1718–21, sited on the River Derwent

Below: Samuel Wyatt's Albion Mill, 1783–86, with entrance via a central shipping hole from the River Thames

iron colonnades and those supporting the brick arches were still timber. This approach was not altered until 1796, when iron beams were introduced for the Charles Bage-designed Marshall, Benyon and Bage flour mill (now Allied Breweries), Ditherington, Shrewsbury, Shropshire.

Thus it was still the practice to make general use of timber long after 1792, although cast iron was used to a limited extent to improve construction techniques, especially for the building of warehouses in London's dockland. Here it was used predominantly for colonnettes of various forms, sizes and section, because cast iron, in addition to its fireproof qualities, had other attractive characteristics. Members could be made thinner and still be of equal strength to wood; this not only saved space, but spans could be made wider, which also meant that fewer components were necessary and assembly times were quicker, and there was a uniformity of production. Even then the iron-frame building was not fully developed, for the outer brick walls were still loadbearing. The first fully skeletal structure was not to appear for many years to come, but the idea of a complete inner iron frame was quickly accepted in Britain. An excellent example of this type of construction can be seen in the Cloth Mill, King's Stanley, Stroud Valley, Gloucestershire, of 1812. Built entirely without wood, it is comprised of an iron frame within a brick and stone exterior.

These mills and warehouses were always huge austere structures, conveying the impression of impregnability. The architectural opportunities offered by buildings on a heroic Roman scale were not missed by the mill designers. One of these was Richard Arkwright, who designed Masson Mill, Cromford, Derbyshire, in 1783 with a façade of eight Venetian windows stacked in pairs and separated by three Diocletian windows, all topped by a lantern.

Right: *the façade of the Masson Mill, which was sited on the River Derwent*

Far right: *Pulteney Bridge, Bath, 1771, by Robert Adam; lined with shops and inspired by Florence's Ponte Vecchio, it was named after William Pulteney, first Earl of Bath*

Bridges

Eighteenth-century bridge elevations tended to mirror the current architectural fashion, although there were also extreme examples that reflected an architect's absorbtion in archaeology or with revolutionary engineering technology and new materials. Thus we are endowed with such diversities as the Pulteney Bridge, Bath, 1764–74, by Robert Adam but since much altered. It was an interpretation of a design by Palladio for the Rialto Bridge, Venice, but with shops and pedimented end pavilions replacing Palladio's colonnade-covered walkway. At the other extreme is the Iron Bridge, Ironbridge, Shropshire, 1777–79, designed by Thomas F Pritchard and modified by Abraham Darby.

The Iron Bridge pioneered the technology of large-scale cast-iron construction, having a single arch span of 30.6m (100.5ft) achieved with slender, elegant cast-iron structural members. However, even with the success of the Iron Bridge it was not until the early part of the nineteenth century that iron bridge technology was fully exploited by exponents such as Thomas Telford, who mastered the design for large-span bridges with the suspension principle. His first suspension bridge, which was also the world's first, was the Menai Suspension Bridge, Gwynedd, of 1819–26.

Above: *the prefabricated Iron Bridge was put into place over several months in 1779 without disturbing the barge traffic on the River Severn. It has an elegant single span of 30.6m (100.5ft) and weighs just over 384 metric tonnes (423 US tons). The individual main ribs weigh 5.1 metric tonnes (5.6 US tons)*

Chapter Seven

Government and Institutional Buildings

I
T WAS NOT UNTIL 1723 that national government finally began to build anew instead of continually housing its departments in ancient premises which it then adapted for its needs. The first of these was the Admiralty in Whitehall, 1723–26, by Thomas Ripley. Unfortunately it was not an impressive start; the Admiralty was archaic in design, with a tall Ionic portico squeezed awkwardly into a small court, its pilaster strips and segmental windows completing the elements, but in disastrous proportion.

The Paymaster General's Office, designed by John Lane, followed in 1732–33. It lies to the south of the Admiralty in Whitehall, and is domestic in character with a five-bay brick front and a three-bay pediment and Gibbs surrounds to the ground floor.

Meanwhile in Ireland, Sir Edward Lovett Pearce had designed Parliament House (now the Bank of Ireland), College

Far left: *King Edward's School, Broad Street, Bath, 1752–54, by Thomas Jelly; a two-storey building with a three-bay pediment*

Left: *Robert Adam's screen of 1760 at the Admiralty, Whitehall, London, with Tuscan columns and Roman Doric entablature, concealing Thomas Ripley's Admiralty building of 1723–26*

Above: *Horse Guards, designed by Kent, was completed after his death by John Vardy. It remains little altered, a monument to George II's passion for military order and display. It was designed to be the headquarters of the General Staff and continued as such until 1872. The building remains the most considerable public building to come from the Burlington group*

Below, right: *Somerset House, by Sir William Chambers. Built under an Act of Parliament of 1775, it involved the clearance of a number of buildings, many of which had been erected by James I and Charles I. The plan for the new building consisted of a great central courtyard, shown here, flanked by narrower courtyards, but only the main one was to be built in the first instance. It was to be approached from the Strand through a block of narrow frontage compared with the width of the building as a whole, and this narrower block was built to accommodate the headquarters of learned societies*

Green, Dublin, 1729. It is a highly successful Palladian public building that emanates power, with its classically correct detailing.

The next building to appear in Whitehall was the Treasury, 1733, by William Kent. This impressive Palladian building in the early Burlington style looks onto Horse Guards Parade and was designed with a fully rusticated façade divided by pilasters, placed upon a rustic base and topped by a pediment.

The Treasury was quickly followed by one of the major government-financed administrative buildings of the eighteenth century, the Horse Guards, Whitehall, London, designed c. 1745–48 by William Kent and built after his death by John Vardy c. 1750–60. The Horse Guards is another decorated Palladian building, with various self-contained elements on different planes linked to make a symmetrical composition. The Whitehall elevation is in the form of a courtyard with a screen wall and gate. Some of the attic

windows are blank, while a number of Venetian windows on the *piano nobile* are partially dummy and light only small rooms.

Somerset House, Strand, London, was begun in 1776 by Sir William Chambers. This was not just the next major government building; for the first time various government offices – the Audit Office, Salt and Land Tax Offices, the Stamp Office, the Duchies of Cornwall and of Lancaster, the Navy, the Royal Academy and the Society of Antiquaries – were gathered under one purpose-built roof. This first attempt to create a large-scale public building has a remarkably academic appearance. Both the planning and the detail are masterly; the Strand elevation is excellent, with an astonishingly French ashlar elevation to the internal courtyard. The river elevation on the other hand is a wonderful combination of Roman gravity, a Palladian composition with French neoclassical detailing. The remaining two sides, which complete one of London's most magnificent squares, are filled by more modest terraces. Most of the buildings in the square, though not in the flanking terraces, are connected by a long corridor with rooms front and back and a centrally placed top-lit or dog-leg stair.

This type of arrangement also prevailed at the prestigious Four Courts, Dublin, 1786, by James Gandon, where terrace houses serve as office accommodation.

Because of the Act of Union of 1707 between England and Scotland, Edinburgh was almost devoid of major government buildings. The most ambitious was the Royal Exchange, High Street, 1753, by John Adam, and the Register House which overlooks North Bridge in the New Town, 1774, by Robert Adam.

Designed to house the city's records, Register House is an essay in neoclassically-detailed Palladian design. It is thirteen bays wide and two storeys high, with a domed library. The ground-floor windows are set between engaged columns beneath a pediment. At each end the bays break forward to form pavilions which contain Venetian windows and support classical clock towers.

Local government buildings

Abingdon County Hall, Oxfordshire, 1678–80, by Christopher Kempster, (*see page 67*, market halls) formalized the plan and disposition of space while reflecting its medieval origins. A first-floor council room was placed over an open ground-floor arcade, which was used as a market or merchants' exchange. This Abingdon template of double function of local government and commercial building was reflected in Monmouth Town Hall, 1724, the Town Hall and Market House at Dursley, Gloucestershire, 1738, at Rye Town Hall, East Sussex, 1743 and at Whitby Town Hall, North Yorkshire, 1788, which together illustrate the widespread and long-lasting influence of the Abingdon building.

Slightly more ambitious projects were undertaken in the second half of the eighteenth century. In the larger towns which were able to support a separate market and exchange, the town hall and guild hall were conceived as independent structures. The town hall then either followed the convention established by the combination of exchange, market and council chamber, or was almost entirely domestic in character.

One of the more successful and original designs is that of the Guildhall at Salisbury, 1788, by Sir Robert Taylor. He created a building which looked like neither an exchange nor a market nor even a town house, but much more like an impressive office.

Palladian style had a far greater effect, and for a far longer time, on local government buildings than it ever had on church buildings. At the Council House, North Street, Chichester, West Sussex, 1731–33, its leading practitioner Roger Morris made a central entablature and attic flanked by recessed lower half-pediments and an open arcade, beneath part of the ground floor, to the street.

The style was to prevail throughout the middle and well into the second half of the century, far outlasting its fashion in other spheres. Indeed, as late as 1789 John Johnson designed the Shire Hall, Chelmsford, Essex, which was important in that it was only then that the conventional Palladian composition of three-bay pediment and rusticated basement was adorned with neoclassical details. During the time when the Palladian style otherwise prevailed for local government buildings there were naturally a few exceptions. These curiosities include the Guildhall, Guildhall Yard, City of London, 1789, by George Dance the Younger which had a façade of a strange mixture of classical, gothic

The Council House and Assembly Room, North Street, Chichester, 1731, by Roger Morris; the former was built by public subscription at a cost of £1,189. The Assembly Room was added to the east of the house by James Watt in 1783 and it is approached from the landing of the Council House through an anteroom

Local government buildings

Town Hall, Morpeth, Northumberland, 1714, by Vanbrugh (rebuilt *c.* 1875 as replica); centre three bays pedimented, end bays support pedimented towers

Town Hall, Market Place, Blandford Forum, Dorset, 1734, by John and William Bastard; a notable Palladian design, which was unusual for the Bastard brothers

Town Hall, Market Hill, Huntingdon, Cambridgeshire, 1745; contains a court as well as an assembly room on the second floor

Shire Hall, Northgate Street, Warwick, Warwickshire, 1754, by Sanderson Miller; Palladian with a pair of octagonal domed court rooms, three-bay pediment supported on engaged Corinthian columns. The gaol, an advanced neoclassical design, adjoins

Guildhall, High Wycombe, Buckinghamshire, 1757, by Henry Keene; three wide bays with a pedimented centre and an open ground-floor colonnade

Mayoralty House, Drogheda, Co. Louth, *c.* 1760–65, by Hugh Darley; Palladian with centre pediment over first-floor Venetian window, arcaded ground floor

Guildhall, Market Square, Poole, Dorset, 1761; arcaded ground floor and a first-floor chamber reached by a pair of external semicircular stairs

Town Hall, High Street, Maidstone, Kent, 1762–63; north and south fronts of five bays. Ground floor of ashlar with blank arcading, pediments to first floor windows. Internally, the council

chamber has fine rococo plasterwork

Town Hall, Woodstock, Oxfordshire, 1766, by Sir William Chambers; refined mid-Palladian style. Three-bay pediment, arcaded ground floor

Town Hall, Sheep Street, Stratford-upon-Avon, 1767, by Timothy Lightoler and / or Robert Newman; a standard late-Palladian design with open ground floor

Shire Hall, Hertford, Hertfordshire, 1767–69, by Robert and James Adam; a large yellow-brick block with arcades (since closed in) along part of the ground floor; top-lit rotunda to upper floor

Town Hall and Assembly Rooms, Market Place, Newark-on-Trent, Nottinghamshire, 1773–76, by John Carr; originally occupied by a butter market. An ashlar Palladian composition of seven bays; rusticated ground floor with arched window. The centre has a three-bay loggia with Tuscan columns and a pediment

Guildhall, Market Place, Salisbury, Wiltshire, 1788, by Sir Robert Taylor and William Pilkington (altered 1829, 1889 and 1896); originally a tall single-storey building, with elevational movement typical of Taylor's villa designs. Venetian windows are set within tall, rusticated, relieving arches. The entrance was via a Doric screen, running between projecting bays, and a concave flight of steps

Old Aberdeen Town House, High Street, Aberdeen, 1788, by George Jaffray; in a simple Palladian manner

Town Hall, Petworth, West Sussex, 1793; dour stone façade with three-bay pediment, blind arcading to first floor

Shire Hall, High Street West, Dorchester, Dorset, 1795–97, by Thomas Hardwick; austerely constructed in Portland stone, centre three bays on ground floor formed on rusticated entrance arcade

Town Hall, Market Place, Ripon, North Yorkshire, 1798, by James Wyatt; five bays and two storeys forming part of a terrace. This standard Graeco-Palladian temple composition has a three-bay pediment supported on engaged Greek Ionic columns on a rusticated ground floor

Town Hall and Assembly Rooms, Devizes, Wiltshire, 1806–08, by Thomas Baldwin; front elevation Palladian, rear neoclassical with centrally placed three-bay full-height curved bow dressed with Greek Ionic columns

Guildhall, corner of High Street and Quay Street, Newport, Isle of Wight, 1814–16, by John Nash; a three-bay pedimented main front formed by Ionic portico over an open arcade continues along the side elevation to High Street, which also has a first-floor Ionic loggia

Town Hall, Magdalene Street, Glastonbury, Somerset, 1813, by J B Beard; still in the Palladian style, yet not begun until 1818

Town Hall, Leith, Edinburgh, 1827–28, by Richard and Robert Dickinson

The Guildhall, High Street, Bath, 1776, by Thomas Baldwin; externally in the Bath Palladian tradition but with some contemporary Adamesque detailing. The building was extended in the nineteenth century, and has an exceptional cast-iron stair balustrade

and 'Hindoo' motifs. The Old Town Hall, Lancaster, 1781–83, by Major Jarrat has a four-bay Doric porch and a Greek revival tower which produces a church-like appearance.

Another town hall to imitate ecclesiastical buildings can be seen at Berwick-upon-Tweed, *c.* 1750–55, built by Joseph Dodds to designs by Samuel and John Worrall. This not only manages to accommodate the town gaol on its upper floor, but in addition has a steeple influenced by St Martin-in-the-Fields.

Berwick was not unique in including a gaol, because so did the New Town Hall, Nottingham, 1789, by S and W Stratton. The town halls of Richmond, North Yorkshire, 1756; Deal in Kent, 1803; Macclesfield, Cheshire, 1823, by Goodwin; and Salford, Greater Manchester, 1825, instead contain assembly rooms. Shire halls contained courts.

Thomas Harrison reconstructed Chester Castle between 1788 and 1822 to form a county court, barracks, exchequer and gaol. He created one of the earliest Greek-revival complexes in Britain, and from that time the style was to flourish and establish itself as the symbol of local government authority. In 1810 the Moot Hall, Newcastle-upon-Tyne, was given a giant Doric portico by John Stokoe, while Glasgow Public Offices, Court House and gaol were designed by William Stark with a massive Greek Doric hexastyle portico, 1807–11. After these Sir Robert Smirk designed a number of equally temple-like shire halls at Gloucester, 1814; Hereford, 1815; Perth, 1815, and Bristol, 1824. Other designers created town halls and assembly rooms in larger towns and cities throughout the country, including Thomas Cooper who built the massive Brighton Town Hall, East Sussex, 1830–32.

Mansion houses

This brief entry establishes the mansion house as a separate entity. They were usually more ambitious in scale than town halls, though usually lacking any degree of adventurous architectural style.

However, two worthy of individual comment are those in

The Old Town Hall, Manchester, 1822–24, by Francis Goodwin (demolished 1912). The Greek disposition of the columnar screen is in antis *and extends in front of the terminal blocks*

Left: *Chester Castle, 1788–1822, by Thomas Harrison; a distinguished neoclassical complex. Its highlights are the Greek Doric entrance gateway of blank unfluted columns, behind which lies the elegant semi-circular Shire Hall with its coffered semi-dome*

the City of London, 1737, by George Dance the Elder which has a nine-bay ashlar front with a giant six-column Corinthian portico standing on a rustic base; and at York, 1726 33, by William Etty, which was inspired by Palladio's Palazzo Iseppo Porto, Vicenza, via Webb's 1662 Queen's Gallery, Old Somerset House, London.

Below: *the Town Hall, Market Place, Brighton, 1830–32, by Thomas Cooper; a massive Grecian pile, although somewhat ungainly*

Court houses

The elevations of court houses also reflected the changing trends of architectural fashions through the period. Like the town halls, they culminated in a group of Greek-revival structures reflecting the architects' taste for the authority of the Grecian portico.

From the early eighteenth century there were external similarities between court houses, town halls and exchanges, until the former developed a highly individual plan. There was a tradition in England for court rooms to be open-ended, reflecting the practice of justice being seen to be done, and for them to be placed off from a public hall. The publication of Vitruvius' *Britannicus* vol V in 1771 contained plans of the recently-completed Shire Hall, High Pavement, Nottingham, 1770, designed by James Gandon and built by Joseph Pickford, with its pair of courts separated by a screen of columns from a large public hall. A similar layout was followed for Waterford Court House, 1784 and also by Gandon; Kilkenny Court House, 1794, and Derry Court House, 1813, by John Bowden.

Mansion House, London, 1753, by George Dance the Elder. Shown here as completed, the Mansion House was the first appearance of the monumental Palladian style within the City of London. It has a tall pilastered façade with an ungenerously shallow portico, giving the impression of uneasily restricted bulk. Also visible are the two ark-like attics at the front and the rear it possessed when originally built, which were removed in 1784 and 1843. These had done nothing to enhance the overall design, which was basically a monumental shrine to money rather than good taste

Gandon's greatest triumph was his Four Courts in Dublin, begun in 1786. The most powerful eighteenth-century neoclassical public building in the British Isles, it has a central block fronted by an imposing giant Corinthian hexastyle portico, topped by a colonnaded drum supporting a rather shallow saucerish dome. Inside the four courts radiate from a huge central hall and are separated from it by a double screen of columns. The screen was curtained in 1802 and destroyed by fire in 1922. Now, after rebuilding, it is filled with masonry, but effectively the first curtaining signalled the demise of the open-ended court room.

The Court House, Glasgow Green, 1807–14, to the designs of William Stark; it was rebuilt in 1910, in the Grecian manner, retaining the giant Doric portico which was one of the earliest Greek Revival porticoes

Professional institutions

No real development of buildings for either the legal or medical professions occurred until towards the end of the eighteenth century. Traditionally, the buildings that housed the former were apartments within more or less conventionally-designed terrace houses, with their dining halls and chapels occupying ancient buildings and arranged in a collegiate manner.

The Six Clerks' and Enrolment Office, Lincoln's Inn Fields, London, 1774–80, by Sir Robert Taylor was an early example of a purpose-built office. Modest in scale, and partly terraced, it is perhaps only exceptional because of its double-height first-floor arched windows which give the first indications of an office building.

The King's Inns, Henrietta Street, Dublin, begun in 1800 to designs by Gandon, can claim to be the leader when it comes to purpose-designed legal chambers. Exquisitely detailed in the neoclassical Greek-revival manner, it provides chambers, a library and a magnificent Benchers' dining hall within elevations that rise behind a handsome screen wall.

Around the turn of the century surgeons' colleges were designed for both Dublin and London. The Royal College of Surgeons, St Stephen's Green, Dublin, 1806, by Edward Park and William Murray is an imposing building with a respectable façade embellished by pediment, a sturdy colonnade of attached Doric columns and a rusticated ground floor. Its London counterpart, also of 1806, was fronted by a powerful unfluted Greek Ionic portico. This was our capital city's first such, and it was copied in 1822 by Sir Robert Smirke for his Royal College of Physicians in Trafalgar Square, London. Of the same time, the Royal Institution (now Royal Scottish Academy), The Mount, Edinburgh, by W H Playfair was a truly powerful Greek Doric temple, reaching the zenith of the style of Greek expression for a professional institution.

Military buildings

Sir John Vanbrugh was appointed Comptroller of the Board of Works in 1702, and thus was a deputy of Wren whose position was that of Surveyor of the Royal Works. Vanbrugh's close Whig connections enabled him to impose his muscular 'castle' style on military works, in which there was a boom after 1715 following victories in combat, but with the continuing threat to England's security Vanbrugh's work became hugely influential.

The Royal Foundry was relocated to larger premises at Woolwich, where the Board of Works was responsible for designing both the Royal Brass Foundry, 1716, and the Gun-Boring Foundry and Smithy in the following year.

At the same time, work was begun on new barracks at Berwick-upon-Tweed, and Chatham received its great Dock Yard Gate. This was followed immediately by the Board of Ordnance Model Room, at Woolwich, 1718, and the Officers' Terrace at Chatham was begun in 1721. Although none of these can be attributed directly to Vanbrugh himself, it was his guiding hand and direct influence that held sway and we see in all of them his bold 'castle' style with its minimum of decoration.

His influence was still to be seen long after his death in 1726. Fort George, Highland Region, was begun after the 1745 rebellion to Board of Ordnance specifications of 1746, by William Adam working under Colonel Skinner. Fort Clemence, Rochester, Kent, was not begun until 1812; it was brick built with bold round corner towers, but still bore the signs of Vanbrugh's touch.

Prison buildings

Perhaps no other building type was destined to change so dramatically during the period as that of the prison. Plans for prisons were primitive for the first half of the eighteenth century, with little thought given to any aspect of the building other than its façade. Plans for prisons pre-1778 followed a long-established system, epitomised by Newgate Gaol in the City of London by George Dance the Younger, demolished in 1902. Here, the blocks arranged round a central exercise yard were in the form of wards. Individual cells, of which there were precious few, were reserved for special prisoners; that is, those who could afford to pay for them.

An Act of Parliament forced a reform of prison design in 1778. It was thought that many of the evils of prisons were caused by their design. A blueprint was drawn up for a new revolutionary prison design after studies of St Michael's Prison, Rome, and the Maison de Force, Ackerghem near Ghent, Belgium.

The plan provided for the siting of prisons away from town centres and alongside rivers. Cell blocks were to be raised on arches, leaving a court beneath for exercise. Prisoners were to be segregated by sex, age and crime. There were to be good heating and ventilation and a minimum cell size. Useful employment and moral and religious instruction would be provided.

Unfortunately these ideas were not acted upon for almost another 40 years. Meanwhile, long-term prisoners, who could no longer be shipped to America, were detained in hulks moored off the coast or transported to Australia, a practice that began in 1787.

Following a further Act in 1782, William Blackburn was commissioned to build a series of county gaols, but these were small-scale versions of what was really needed. After the turn of the century there was a general improvement in gaol design, with cell blocks radiating from a taller octagonal centre block. One such early example is at Abingdon; another is Robert Reid's four-armed radial prison in Edinburgh Road, Perth, Tayside, built in 1810. The next stage was the first penitentiary at Millbank, London, which was begun in 1812 by Thomas Hardwick but has since been demolished; here, the arms of the radial design were linked to form a pentagon.

The radial design was developed to a logical conclusion on paper, with the centralized panopticon prison. In this design, cells were arranged symmetrically around a central point of observation. Cast iron was to be used in the construction, thus creating a fireproof structure. However, good as the design was, it was never implemented until well into the nineteenth century, and then not in the UK but across the Atlantic in the United States.

Abingdon Old Gaol, Oxfordshire, 1805–11, by Sir Jeffry Wyatville; it is now a leisure centre

Infirmaries

Generally these were domestic in appearance throughout the period, and seldom more than a regular terraced house. More often they took on the appearance of an unembellished brick-built country house, stranded in the centre of town.

The main block was usually disposed parallel to the street. Others were quadrangular, an arrangement that was developed by the Navy which enjoyed government finance. Most infirmaries of the period were financed by endowment and gifts from individuals or by subscription.

After the first decade of the nineteenth-century infirmaries, in common with other public buildings, began to assume a Greek, sometimes gothic, revival appearance.

Above: *the Foundling Hospital, London, 1742–52, by Theodore Jacobsen (demolished 1928); elaborately composed, it was the product of private wealth*

Below: *the Radcliffe Infirmary, Woodstock Road, Oxford, 1766–70, by Stiff Leadbetter, as it is today. It was completed by John Sanderson*

Austere infirmaries

London Hospital, Whitechapel Road, London, 1752–77, by Boulton Mainwaring and Joel Johnson

Gloucester Royal Infirmary, off Southgate Street, Gloucester, Gloucestershire, 1758–61, by Stiff Leadbetter and Luke Singleton

Worcester Royal Infirmary, Castle Street, Worcester, 1767–70, by Anthony Keck

Salisbury General Infirmary, Fisherton Street, Salisbury, Wiltshire, 1767–71, by John Wood the Younger

Leicester Royal Infirmary, Infirmary Road, Leicester, 1771, by Benjamin Wyatt

Royal Infirmary, Infirmary Road, Sheffield, South Yorkshire, 1793, by John Rawsthorne

Grander infirmaries

St Bartholomew's Hospital, Smithfield, London, 1730, by James Giggs; three detached, stone-faced, pedimented blocks with spare Palladian detailing

General Infirmary (now Royal Mineral Water Hospital), Bath, Avon, 1738, by John Wood the Elder; an eleven-bay Palladian composition with three-bay pediment, ashlar-faced and Ionic-porticoed

Rotunda Lying-in Hospital, Parnell Street, Dublin, c. 1751, by Richard Castle; in Palladian country-house style with rusticated ground floor, central pediment on Doric engaged columns, first-floor Venetian windows. A tall square central tower carries the arcaded drum, supporting cupola and obelisk

Radcliffe Infirmary, Woodstock Road, Oxford, 1759–70, by Stiff Leadbetter and John Sanderson

Bishop's College Hospital (formerly Infirmary), Wordsworth Street, Lincoln, Lincolnshire, 1776, by John Carr; pedimented three-bay centre, wings with Venetian windows

General Infirmary, Billing Road, Northampton, 1791–93, by Samuel Saxon; ashlar-faced and nineteen bays long with a three-bay pediment

Naval hospitals

Haslar Royal Naval Hospital, Hampshire, 1745, by Theodore Jacobsen with John Turner; paired ranges form three sides of a huge square, the centre range pedimented with arcades at ground level

Royal Naval Hospital (now St Nicholas's Hospital), Great Yarmouth, Norfolk, 1809–11, by William Pilkington and Edward Holl; four blocks each of 29 bays, approached through a triumphal arch

ROYAL MINERAL WATER HOSPITAL

Early nineteenth-century infirmaries

Royal Sea Bathing Hospital,
  Canterbury Road, Margate, Kent,
  1820; Grecian with monumental four-
  columned Doric portico behind, which
  is an earlier building of 1792–96
George Stiel's Hospital (now
  St Joseph's School), Tranent, Lothian,
  1822, by William Burn; Greek Ionic
Royal Salop Infirmary, St Mary's

Place, Shrewsbury, Shropshire,
  1826, by Edward Haycock and Sir
  Robert Smirke; a large Greek Doric
  edifice
Murray Royal Asylum for the
  Insane, Kinnoull, near Perth,
  Tayside, 1827, by William Burn;
  Roman Doric portico, central
  octagon

St George's Hospital, Hyde Park Corner,
  London, 1828, by William Wilkins in
  Grecian-detailed stucco skin; now the
  Lanesborough Hotel
Cumberland Infirmary, Carlisle,
  Cumbria, 1830–32, by Robert
  Tattershall; Greek revival with giant
  Doric portico set against a part-
  rusticated wall

Almshouses

Closely related to infirmaries in form, function and origin, the almshouses of the eighteenth century were charitable institutions for the sick and elderly or were schoolrooms for poor children.

The charity schools, known as Bluecoat Schools because of the uniforms worn, were usually in the same building complex as the almshouses. They were generally built and supported by capital sums and endowments from livery companies, the local gentry and nobility and by leading members of trades and professions.

The most obvious architectural manifestation of this charity was that the structures were generally overtly archaic in design, possibly as a symbolic reflection of the grateful humility of the inmates. Their form, established in the previous century, was of

Above: *the General Infirmary, now the Royal Mineral Water Hospital, Bath, 1738, by John Wood the Elder; a large 11-bay Palladian composition with a central pediment covering three bays*

Almshouses

Bluecoat School, Liverpool, Merseyside, 1716–17; a large red-brick building with pediment in centre block and complex fenestration

Spalden Almshouses, Ashbourne, Derbyshire, 1723; two-storey building next to the church, arranged around three sides of a courtyard and with very conservative detail such as low two-light mullioned windows

Cart Almshouses, High Street South, Dunstable, Bedfordshire, c. 1723; in red brick

Almshouses, Sevenoaks, Kent, 1724–32, to designs of Lord Burlington; a pair of two-storey almshouses with a taller, pedimented and rusticated arch leading to rear courtyard combining almshouses with charity school

Bluecoat School and Almshouses, Frome, Somerset, 1726; wings with mullioned two-light windows on each side

Marlborough Almshouses, Hatfield Road, St Albans, Hertfordshire, c. 1730; planned around a quadrangle, in two storeys with seventeen bays, pedimented centre

Southwell School and Almshouses, Downpatrick, Co.Down, 1733, probably to design of Sir Edward Lovett Pearce; central one-bay pedimented block supports stone tower, flanked by lower ranges of cottages terminating in school rooms

Almshouses, East Street, Wareham, Dorset, 1741; designed as a terrace, bold brick rustication makes them look earlier

Hopton Almshouses, Hopton Street, Southwark, London, 1752; designed as a linked block

Hosyers' Almshouses, Ludlow, Shropshire, 1758, by Thomas Pritchard; shallow quadrangle with central pediment

Blaise Hamlet, Avon, 1810–11, by John Nash; picturesque grouped almshouses in the style of *cottages ornés*

angle quoins, bold wooden cornices, richly-coloured bricks and steep pitched roofs. Their plan was usually quadrangular, although they were sometimes designed on straight terraces or occasionally as linked blocks. These compositions frequently included a pedimented centre containing a chapel flanked by one or two-storey blocks, a single room deep and containing modest rooms in almshouses or classrooms in schools.

There were also exceptional almshouses, for instance the Royal Naval Hospital at Greenwich, which in the mid-eighteenth century provided accommodation for 1,550 aged seamen.

Schools and universities

The grander educational establishments kept school architecture abreast of fashion. Lord Burlington designed the Palladian Dormitory at Westminster School in 1722. Strikingly appropriate for its use, it had a noble pedimented *piano nobile* set between an open, arcaded ground floor and a square-windowed second floor.

Another Palladian essay of the period was Wilson's Hospital, Multyfarnham, Co. Westmeath, c. 1760, by John Pentland. At this school for Protestant boys, the tradition and atmosphere of the almshouse charity school are combined with the Palladian villa-with-wings composition. The building has a pedimented central block, surmounted by a cupola and containing an arcaded court which is linked via curved wings to end pavilions.

By the early nineteenth century, the great teaching chambers that epitomised the eighteenth century were being replaced by smaller classrooms which could be presided over by an individual master. An example is Mill Hill School (originally the Protestant Dissenters' Grammar School), Ridgeway, Mill Hill, London, 1825–27, by Sir William Tite. This is in the Grecian manner, with a giant Ionic portico centrally placed on the long low block.

As well as adopting a rearranged internal plan, some schools also received a fashionable Greek-revival frontage. Perhaps the most striking is the Royal High School, Regent Road, Calton Hill, Edinburgh, 1825–29, by Thomas Hamilton. This school was open to all boys who attained a sufficiently high educational standard.

Among the more venerable educational establishments, Rugby School received some Tudor gothic additions in 1809–13 by Henry Hakewill; and Harrow was extended by Charles Robert Cockerell in 1818, again in the Tudor gothic style. This style was also used for St David's College, Lampeter, Dyfed, 1822, also by Cockerell, and Elizabeth College, St Peter Port, Guernsey, 1826, by John Wilson. The pointed gothic-revival style was used for Mildenhall School, Wiltshire, 1823, by Robert Abraham, and Sebright School, Wolverley, Hereford and Worcester, 1829, which is thought to be by William Knight.

England's two universities provided the architectural excitement of the period, with Oxford particularly proving a breeding ground for innovation and development.

The springboard for Oxford was the Clarendon Building, designed by Nicholas Hawksmoor for Oxford University Press and constructed between 1711–15. Ashlar, with a giant portico to the street and layered wall surface, it transported the architectural language of Blenheim right into the heart of the city.

The hall and chapel front of Queen's College then followed in similar style, in 1714. The screen to the street was not added until 1733, and was by Hawksmoor. By the time George Clarke, Fellow of All Souls, and Provost Lancaster of Queen's designed the library block at Worcester College in 1720 and the New Building at Magdalen in 1733, Oxford had taken on a really baroque appearance.

Above: *the imposing frontispiece of the Royal High School, Regent Road, Edinburgh, 1825–29, by Thomas Hamilton. Designed and sited with spectacular imagination, it is one of the finest Greek Revival buildings in Britain*

Right: *the Provost's Lodge, Trinity College, Dublin, begun in 1759 and based directly on Lord Burlington's house for General Wade*

University buildings
Cambridge

Emmanuel College Westmorland Building, 1719–22, by John Lumley; in provincial baroque
Queen's College Mathematical Bridge, 1749, by William Etherbridge and James Essex; timber-built bridge over the River Cam at back of college
Trinity Bridge, 1763–65, by James Essex
Emmanuel College street front, 1769, by James Essex
Sidney Sussex College chapel and library, 1776–87, by James Essex
St John's College New Court, 1825–31, by Rickman & Hutchinson; gothic incorporating a 'Bridge of Sighs'

Dublin

Trinity College is the largest eighteenth-century college complex in the British Isles and includes:
Library, 1712–32, by Thomas Burgh; 27 bays
Printing House, 1734; thought to be by either Richard Castle or Sir Edward Lovett Pearce
Dining Hall situated behind the Quad, c. 1741, by Richard Castle and Hugh Darley (altered 1760 and damaged by fire 1984)
West front to College Green, 1752, thought to be by Theodore Jacobsen; pedimented centre and rusticated base. The massive stone quadrangle behind the façade terminates in a pair of porticoed buildings, 1775, by Sir Richard Chambers
Provost's House, begun in 1759
Chapel, 1787–1800, by Chambers; contained within one of the terminating buildings

Oxford

University College Radcliffe Quadrangle, 1716–19, by George Clarke
Balliol College alterations to former hall and library, 1792–94, by James Wyatt; gothic in style
Oriel College St Mary's Quad west side, c. 1825, by Daniel Robertson; also gothic
Balliol College Garden Quad, 1826, by George Basevi

Peckwater Quad had been conceived in 1706 by Henry Aldrich, Dean of Christ Church, as three matching palace fronts, embellished with giant Ionic pilasters rising from a rusticated ground floor. It was the first composition of its kind, and years ahead of the Palladian palace schemes of Colen Campbell and John Wood the Elder. The Library was added to the fourth side of the Quad in 1717, and was based on Michelangelo's side palaces at the Capitol, Rome.

Just as Oxford had been at the forefront of Palladian and baroque style, so it was with the gothic revival when All Souls decided to expand with a new North Quad in 1716–35, by Hawksmoor. It is a picturesque composition in a fanciful rococo style, intended to be in sympathy with the existing medieval gothic buildings.

In 1737 the last major eighteenth-century baroque building in England was begun by James Gibbs. The Radcliffe Camera, a circular temple to the arts, combines baroque elements with conventional Palladian motifs.

Still in Oxford, the Clarenden Press in Walton Street of 1826–27 by Daniel Robertson (north wings completed by Edward Blore 1829–30) echoes the full-blooded archaeological spirit of the early nineteenth century. It is Roman-inspired rather than Greek, with a handsome Corinthian triumphal arch embellishing the entrance elevation.

The Fellows' Building, Peterhouse, Cambridge, 1738–42, was designed by the amateur architect Sir James Burrough in a provincial Palladian style. He later re-fronted the Principal Court, 1754–56, and the chapel at Clare College, 1763, in a similar style, but the refreshing elements of Cambridge were supplied by James Gibbs.

Burrough's scheme for the Senate House was improved by Gibbs out of all recognition, 1722–30, establishing Gibbs as an original designer with a style falling between the Palladian and baroque. The sash windows of the ground storey are headed by alternately triangular and segmental pediments, the upper windows being round-headed. In 1723 Gibbs designed the Fellows' Building at King's College, which is very baroque in detail with its keystoned windows and a giant two-storey pedimented porch beneath a Diocletian window.

The first expression of the Greek revival in Cambridge was at Downing College, 1804, by William Wilkins. This influential building of two storeys has a full-height hexastyle Greek Ionic portico. Wilkins went on to reject the Greek style and extended other colleges in Cambridge in a neo-Perpendicular and neo-Tudor manner, giving Trinity College the Tudor gothic New Court, 1821–25, Corpus Christi the neo-Perpendicular New Court, Chapel and other buildings, 1823–27, and neo-Perpendicular additions to King's College.

Far left, above: *Peckwater Quad, Christ Church, Oxford;* below, *Peckwater Library*

Above: *the entrance to New Buildings, North Quad, All Souls College, Oxford, by Hawksmoor*

Below: *Senate House, Cambridge, 1722–30, by James Gibbs; two storeys are included in a single order of Corinthian pilasters, coupled at the ends. The centrepiece of four half-columns is surmounted by a sculptured pediment, flanked by balustrades*

Chapter Eight

Museums, Theatres, Clubs, Inns and Hotels

HE MUSEUM was a phenomenon that had appeared by the end of the eighteenth century, when it expressed a then-fashionable neoclassical ideal of the theatre of the arts. Greek temple-inspired museum buildings were designed throughout Europe just after the turn of the century. In England the Dulwich College Picture Gallery, 1811–14, by Sir John Soane, became the pioneering work of gallery design that reached its zenith with the massive Greek-detailed quadrangle round a large open court of the British Museum, 1823, by Sir Robert Smirke.

Very few theatres have escaped unscathed from the ravages of fire or even mere changes in fashion. Though some do survive, they are not indicative of theatre development during the period. The few survivors are listed *overleaf*.

The few survivors are listed *overleaf*.

Museums and galleries

Picture Gallery, Corsham Court, Wiltshire, 1761–64, by Lancelot Brown

Sculpture Gallery, Newby Hall, North Yorkshire, c. 1767, by Robert Adam

Exhibition Room, Somerset House, London, 1776, by Sir William Chambers

Sculpture Gallery and Museum, Castle Howard, North Yorkshire, 1800–01, by Charles Heathcote Tatham

Pantheon Room, Ince Blundell Hall, Merseyside, 1802, thought to be by John Hope

Picture Gallery, Attingham Hall, Shropshire, 1807, by John Nash; a revolutionary cast-iron roof with top lighting

Yorkshire Museum, York, 1827–30, by William Wilkins the Younger

Rotunda Museum, Scarborough, North Yorkshire, 1828–29, by Richard Hay Sharp

---

Far left: *the Doric door case of the Southgate Hotel, Southgate Street, Winchester, c. 1715*

Left: *the British Museum, Great Russell Street, London, begun in 1823. It was important in the development of the museum building type*

Theatres

Theatre Royal, King Street, Bristol, Avon, 1764–66, by James Paty
Market Hall and Theatre, Market Cross, Bury St Edmunds, Suffolk, 1774–80, by Robert Adam; Palladian composition with neoclassical detail (it became the Town Hall after 1819)
Theatre Royal, situated behind Market Place, Richmond, North Yorkshire, 1788; an undistinguished exterior, but the only surviving small-scale eighteenth-century theatre in Britain (now much restored)
Theatre Royal, Westgate Street, Bury St Edmunds, Suffolk, 1819, by William Wilkins the Younger; Greek-detailed interior with gallery and boxes supported on cast-iron columns

The English theatre in the eighteenth and early nineteenth centuries was not subsidised by public funds; it was a free market with each company being a private business. Therefore the theatre manager was more concerned by the number of paying customers he could have rather than by the niceties of fashionable architecture.

In all English theatres of the eighteenth century the pit and higher galleries were packed with benches running from side to side, with no aisle, which filled up on a first-come, first-served basis. They were generally therefore modest affairs, frequently erected on cheaper land off the main street and backing onto the rear of a terrace rather than being detached.

The few exceptions included two London theatres, that of Drury Lane of 1792 by Henry Holland that was destroyed by fire in 1808, and that of Covent Garden of 1809 by Sir Robert Smirke, destroyed by fire in 1855.

Above, right: *Covent Garden Theatre by Pugin and Rowlandson from* The Microcosm of London, *1808*

Above, left: *Strawson's Corn Exchange, Tunbridge Wells, built as a theatre in 1802*

Holland's theatre had been neither completed nor paid for before it burnt down. It was replaced by the Theatre Royal, Drury Lane, 1810–12, by Benjamin Dean Wyatt. He arranged the foyer around a magnificent rotunda, but the long side elevation was not given its magnificent Ionic colonnade until 1831.

The Haymarket Theatre, London, 1820–21, by Nash, was part of the Regent Street improvement and had a Corinthian portico on an axis with the distant St James's Square.

The development of the club really took place after 1830, although in the eighteenth century various politically-orientated clubs were housed in purpose-built structures which had been based on institutional buildings. The pioneers of the building form for clubs were Decimus Burton and John Nash. Their Athenaeum

Above: *the Theatre Royal, Bristol, 1764–66, by James Paty*

and United Services Clubs (USC) faced each other across Waterloo Place, St James's. The Athenaeum was begun a year earlier than the USC in 1827, but both are arranged around magnificent staircase halls, with the dining room on the first floor and reading rooms above. Charles Barry designed the influential Travellers' Club, Pall Mall in the Italianate style in 1829.

Clubs

Boodles', 28 St James's Street, London, 1775, by John Crunden; the ground-floor bow was added in 1821 by John Buenarotti Papworth

Brooks's Club, 60 St James's Street, London, 1776–78, by Henry Holland; austere façade with giant pilasters

White's Club, 37–38 St James's Street, London, 1787–88, by James Wyatt; re-fronted 1852

Lyceum Club, Bold Street, Liverpool, Merseyside, 1800–02, by Thomas Harrison; austere early example of Greek revival with a giant Greek Ionic pedimented portico set *in antis*

Athenaeum, King Street, Stirling, Central Region, 1814–16, by William Stirling; a curved frontage with spire

Left: *the garden elevation, Travellers' Club, London, 1832, by Sir Charles Barry*

Above: *the Southgate Hotel, Southgate Street, Winchester, c. 1715; the centre first-floor window has brick pilasters*

Far right, above: *the Old Ship Hotel, West Street, Brighton, which contains an assembly room of 1767 by Robert Golden*

Far right, below: *the Royal Sussex and Victoria Hotel, Tunbridge Wells, c. 1820*

Eighteenth-century inns and hotels have their origins in the monasteries of the Middle Ages. While some inns, particularly those in High Streets, may be grandiose there are others which are quite basic. There are also those inns of country towns with plain elevations, often with a single-storey colonnaded porch projecting out across the pavement.

By the late eighteenth century the inn was beginning to undergo its metamorphosis into the hotel, a cross between the inn and the country house, complete with restaurant, entertaining rooms, and even a ballroom. It was designed to flatter the conceits and attract the custom of the richer travelling public in late Georgian Britain, who had previously lodged at inns.

The hotel began to emerge in the 1770s, when inns began to add extra rooms for entertainment. The Old Ship Hotel, Brighton, East Sussex, acquired an ornate Adamesque assembly room in 1767 by Robert Golden. The hotel proper began to appear in the 1790s. Such early examples as the Swan Hotel, Litchfield, Staffordshire, and the Warwick Arms Hotel, High Street, Warwick, Warwickshire, *c.* 1790, heralded a building boom for the type.

As the century progressed, so the scale of the hotels grew, benefitting from the growing popularity of seaside resorts and spas, the easier travel afforded by the stage coaches, and business generated by the canals. Although the steam locomotive had been invented, the London & Manchester Railway did not open until 1830 and its impact will be discussed in our companion volume, *Victorian and Edwardian Architecture.*

Architects and Buildings of the Period

The years of birth and death of each architect are given in parentheses where these are known

Abraham, Robert (1774–1850)
Arundel Castle, Arundel, West Sussex; additions including library, 1801
The School, Mildenhall, Wiltshire, 1823–24
Alton Towers, Staffordshire; garden buildings including conservatory, Prospect Tower and pagoda in lake, c. 1824

Adam, John
House, Arniston, Lothian; west wing,1753
Royal Exchange, High Street, Edinburgh, 1753–61 (now City Chambers)
Town House, Inveraray, Strathclyde, 1755–57
with Robert Adam:
Ravelin Gate, Fort George near Nairn, Highlands, c. 1753
Dumfries House, near Ayr, Strathclyde, 1754–59

Adam, Robert (1728–92)
The second son of William Adam, whose other three sons also became architects; Robert became the inspirational leader of the Adams brothers. Educated at Edinburgh High School and Edinburgh University, he travelled through France and Italy in 1754. He worked in Rome with his brother James for three years, and set up practice with him on returning to London in 1758. One of his early patrons was fellow-Scot and the King's First Minister, Lord Bute. He was architect to King George III 1762 68, and was elected MP for Kinross-shire.
The influence of Robert Adam's work has been as strong on British architecture, especially on domestic interiors, as that of any other classical architect. Adam added a rich variety of ancient Roman decorative features to the English Palladian vocabulary and created a manner, still in use, known as the 'Adam style'
Hatchlands, near Guildford, Surrey; interior, c. 1759–60
Bowood House, near Calne, Wiltshire, date unknown (mostly demolished, only south 'Diocletian wing' remains)
Kedleston, near Derby, Derbyshire; gothic temple, 1759–60
Shardeloes, near Beaconsfield, Buckinghamshire; portico, 1759–61
Admiralty, Whitehall, London; concealing screen, 1759–61
Kedleston, near Derby, Derbyshire; completion, from 1760
Mellerstain, near Kelso, Borders; completion and interior, 1760
Croome Court, Croome d'Abitot, Hereford and Worcester; completion of interior, 1760
Market Hall, High Street, High Wycombe, Buckinghamshire, 1761
Kedleston, near Derby, Derbyshire; north lodge and bath house, 1761

Bowood House grounds, Wiltshire; mausoleum, 1761–64
Compton Verney, near Stratford-upon-Avon, Warwickshire; remodelling of south and east fronts, 1761–67
Syon House, Brentford, Hounslow, London; internal remodelling, 1761–69
Mersham le Hatch, near Ashford, Kent, 1762–65
Lansdowne Club (originally Lansdowne House), Berkeley Square, London, 1762–68 (façade reconstructed)
Osterley Park, Osterley, Hounslow, London; alterations, 1762–68
Osterley Park, Osterley, Hounslow, London, lodge, c. 1763
Moor Park, near Rickmansworth, Hertfordshire; Tea Pavilion (17 Moor Lane) and gateway, 1763–65
Ugbrooke Park, near Newton Abbot, Devon, 1763–68
Pulteney Bridge, Bath, Avon, 1764–74 (now altered)
Harewood House, near Leeds, West Yorkshire; extensions and interior decorations c. 1765 (later greatly altered by Sir Charles Barry)
Nostell Priory, near Wakefield, West Yorkshire; interior, c. 1766
Luton Hoo, Bedfordshire, 1766 (remodelled by Smirke, c. 1815; later alterations in 1843 and 1903)
West Wycombe Park, West Wycombe, Buckinghamshire; stable in the grounds, 1767–68
Kenwood House, Highgate, Camden, London, 1767–69
Kedleston, near Derby, Derbyshire; stables, 1767–69
Newby Hall, near Ripon, North Yorkshire; two-storey wings and interiors, c. 1767–72
Saltram House, near Plympton, Devon; alterations, 1768–69
Whitehaven Castle, Whitehaven, Cumbria, 1768–69 (now a hospital)
St Andrew's Chapel, Gunton Park, near North Walsham, Norfolk, 1769
Kedleston, near Derby, Derbyshire; bridge, 1769–70
10 Hertford Street, London, 1769–71
Kedleston, near Derby, Derbyshire; boathouse, c. 1770
1 Queen Street, Edinburgh, 1770–71
33 Duke of York Street, St James's, Westminster, London, 1770–72
Chandos House, Chandos Street, Marylebone, London, 1771
St Bartholomew's Church, Binley, Coventry, Warwickshire, 1771 (thought to be by)
20 Duke of York Street, Westminster, London; façade, 1771–74 (extended 1936)
Wedderburn Castle, Duns, Borders, 1771–75
Apsley House, Hyde Park Corner, London, 1771–78
Audley End, Essex; Temple of Victory, 1772
8 John Adam Street (now Royal Society of Arts), Charing Cross, London, 1772–74
11 Duke of York Street, Westminster, London; refronting, 1774–76

Woolton Hall, Woolton, Merseyside; enlarging and remodelling, 1774–80
Register House, overlooking North Bridge, Edinburgh, 1774–92
Market Hall, Market Cross, Bury St Edmunds, Suffolk, 1774–80
Theatre, Market Cross, Bury St Edmunds, Suffolk, 1774–80 (became town hall chamber from 1819)
Marlborough House, Old Steine, Brighton, East Sussex, c. 1775 (thought to be by)

Marlborough House has a pair of pedimented end pavilions containing large Venetian windows; sadly, it is now in need of much repair

Garrick's Villa, Hampton Court Road, Hampton, Richmond-upon-Thames, London; modernisation, c. 1775
5–15 and 16–22 Mansfield Street, Marylebone, London, c. 1775–80
20 Portman Square, Marylebone, London, 1776
Frederick's Place, City of London, 1776 (much altered)
Red Lion Hotel, Market Place, Pontefract, West Yorkshire; remodelling, c. 1776
Headfort, Kells, Co. Meath, Ireland; interior, c. 1776
Brizlee Tower, Hulme Park, Alnwick, Northumberland, 1777–83
Culzean Castle, Strathclyde; large additions, 1777–92
Palladian Bridge and teahouse, Audley End, Essex, 1782–83
Dalquharran Castle, Strathclyde, 1782–85 (wings added 1881; now a ruin)
Castle Upton, Templepatrick, Co. Antrim, Ireland; remodelling, from 1783 (altered 1837)
Brasted Park, near Sevenoaks, Kent; villa, 1784
Sunnyside House, Liberton, Lothian, 1785 (now a golf club)
Yester House, near Haddington, Lothian; internal embellishments, 1789
Newliston House, near Queensferry, Lothian, 1789–90
University, Chambers Street, Edinburgh, c. 1789

Left: *the Royal Pavilion, Brighton, 1815–21 by John Nash*

Wilson Street, Glasgow, Strathclyde, *c.* 1790
(much altered; it forms a square with Garth,
Hutcheson and Glassford streets)
Seton Castle, near Tranent, Lothian, 1790–91

*Seton Castle, Lothian, 1790–91;
a symmetrical castle-style house,
with classical details mixed with
medieval machicolations and
cruciform windows*

Airthrey Castle, central Scotland, 1790–91
Fitzroy Square, St Pancras, Camden, London;
east and south sides, 1790–94
Gosford House, near Tranent, Lothian,
1790–1800 (largely gutted 1940)
Balavil House (formerly Belleville House), near
Kingussie, Highlands, 1790–96
Charlotte Square, Edinburgh, 1791
Trades House, Glassford Street, Glasgow,
Strathclyde, 1791–94
Stobs Castle, near Hawick, Borders, 1793
St Mary Magdalene's Church, Croome d'Abitot,
Hereford and Worcester; interior, date not
known
with James Adam:
Shire Hall, Hertford, Hertfordshire, 1767–69
Lion Bridge, Alnwick, Northumberland, 1773

Adam, William (1689–1748)
The father of the four architect Adam brothers,
John, Robert, James and William; he was one
of the first purely classical architects of Scotland
Floors Castle, Kelso, Borders, 1720s (remodelled
1837)
Mavisbank, near Dalkeith, Lothian, 1723 (ruin)
Hopetoun House, near South Queensferry,
Lothian; east front, 1723–56
Lawers House, near Aberfeldy, Tayside,
1724–26 (remodelled 1810)
Mellerstain, near Kelso, Borders, 1725
Dalmahoy House, near Queensferry, Lothian,
1725–28
House, Arniston, Lothian, 1726
The Drum, Edinburgh, 1726–30
Yester House, near Haddington, Lothian;
embellishments, *c.* 1729
Robert Gordon Hospital, 1730–32
Chatelherault, near Hamilton, Strathclyde; dog
kennel, 1731
Church, Hamilton, Strathclyde, 1732
Haddo House, near Huntly, Grampian, 1732–35
Duff House, Banff, Grampian, 1735–39
Town House / Assembly Rooms, Haddington,
Lothian, 1742 (rebuilt)
Pollok House, Rutherglen, Strathclyde, 1752

Aikin, Edmund (1780–1820)
A contributor to *Rees's Encyclopedia*
Wellington Rooms, Mount Pleasant, Liverpool,
Merseyside, 1815–16

Aldrich, Henry
Christ Church College, Oxford, Oxfordshire;
Peckwater Quadrangle, 1706-13

*The exquisite Peckwater
Quadrangle, Oxford, 1706–13;
this was the first Palladian
palace-fronted composition of the
eighteenth century*

Alexander, Daniel Asher (1768–1846)
Educated at St Paul's School, London, and a
winner of the Silver Medal of the Royal
Academy, he was appointed surveyor to the
London Dock Company 1796–1831 and to
Trinity House, for which he designed the
lighthouses at Harwich and Lundy Island
Mote Park, off Mote Road, Maidstone, Kent,
1793–1801
London Docks, Wapping, London, 1796–1820
(little survives)
Dartmoor Prison, Devon, 1805–09
Blocks, each side of and linked to, Queen's House,
Romney Road, Greenwich, London, 1807–16
Gaol, Lower Boxley Road, Maidstone, Kent,
1811–19

Allen, James
St Thomas's Church, Bristol, Avon, 1793

Anderson, William *see* **Henderson, William**

Archer, Thomas (*c.* 1668–1743)
Born at Umberslade, Warwickshire, and
educated at Trinity College, Oxford, from
1686; he was groom-porter to Queen Anne in
1705, and then to George I and George II
Cathedral of St Philip, Birmingham, West
Midlands, 1709–15
Queen Mary's Hospital (originally Roehampton
House), Roehampton Lane, Roehampton,
Wandsworth, London, 1710–12
St Paul's Church, Deptford High Street,
Deptford, London, 1713–20

St John's Church, Smith Square, London,
1714–18
Chettle House, near Blandford, Dorset,
c. 1715–25 (thought to be by)
43 King Street, Covent Garden, London,
1716–17 (thought to be by)
St Mary's Church, Hale, near Salisbury,
Hampshire; remodelling, 1717

Arkwright, Richard
North Street, Cromford, Derbyshire; workers'
housing, 1771–76
Masson Mill, Cromford, Derbyshire, 1783 (later
enlarged)

Arrow, James
Gateway, Royal Navy Victualling Yard, Pepys
Estate, Deptford, London, 1788

Atkinson, Peter the Elder (1725–1805)
Practised architecture in York; he was an
assistant to John Carr, to whose practice he
succeeded
Hackness Hall, near Scarborough, North
Yorkshire, 1797
Female prison (now a museum), York, North
Yorkshire; addition of end bays, 1802
Ouse Bridge, York, North Yorkshire, 1810–20
Foss Bridge, York, North Yorkshire, 1811–12

Atkinson, Peter the Younger (1776–?)
Layerthorp Bridge, York, North Yorkshire, 1829

Atkinson, Thomas
Town Hall, Market Place, Richmond, North
Yorkshire, 1756 (thought to be by)
Girls' High School, Norwood, Beverley,
Humberside, 1765 (thought to be by)
Bar Convent, Blossom Street, York, Yorkshire,
begun in 1765
All Saints' Church, Brandsby, North Yorkshire,
1767
Brough Hall, near Richmond, North Yorkshire;
extensions and alterations, 1772–75
20 St Andrewgate, York, Yorkshire; own house,
c. 1780
Workhouse, Maygate, York, North Yorkshire,
1792

Atkinson, William (*c.* 1773–1839)
Scone Palace, near Perth, Tayside, 1803–12
Mulgrave Castle, North Yorkshire, *c.* 1804–11
Broughton Hall, North Yorkshire, 1809–11
Bowhill, near Selkirk, Borders, 1812–17
Garnons, Hereford and Worcester,
1815– *c.* 1830 (additions and alterations 1855
and 1958)
Abbotsford, Borders; for Sir Walter Scott,
1816–23
Gorhambury, near St Albans, Hertfordshire;
alterations, 1816–26 (there were also further
alterations in 1847)
Tulliallan Castle, Fife, 1817–20
Taymouth Castle, near Aberfeldy, Tayside;
enlargement, 1818–28
Hylands, near Chelmsford, Essex, 1819–25

Left: *St Paul's Church,
Deptford, 1712–30; the first of
two churches Archer designed as a
Commissioner for the fifty new
churches. St Paul's sits massively,
its great semi-circular portico
rising to a circular Borromini-like
tower and a very English spire.
Rusticated pilasters all round
make the flanks rather ponderous*

Dudley House, 100 Park Lane, Mayfair, London, 1824

Himley Hall, Staffordshire; remodelling, 1824–27

Atwood, Thomas Warr
The Paragon, Bath, Avon, 1768

The Paragon, Bath, begun in 1768; a long curving terrace

Old Gaol, Grove Street, Bath, Avon, 1772 (now flats)

Backhouse, James
West Lodge, West Crescent, Darlington, Co. Durham; front, c. 1805

Bacon, Charles (c. 1784–1818)
Woodford House, Woodford, Northamptonshire, 1813–26
Oaklands, near Oakhampton, Devon, c. 1816 (begun by)
St Mary the Virgin's Church, High Road, Woodford, Redbridge, London; body, 1817

Badger, Joseph (1738–1817)
Renishaw Hall, Derbyshire, enlargement, 1793–1808

Baird, H
Avon Aqueduct, Union Canal, central Scotland, 1818–22

Baird, John
Argyle Arcade, 98–102 Argyle Street, Glasgow, Strathclyde, 1827–28

Baker, William (1705–71)
Born in London, he is thought to have succeeded to the north Midlands practice of William Smith; his style is derived from that of Gibbs
Butter Cross, Ludlow, Shropshire, 1743–44
Town Hall, Montgomery, Powys, 1748
Patshull Hall, Patshull, Staffordshire; completion, 1754
St John's Church, St John's Square, Wolverhampton, West Midlands, 1758–76
Church, Kenmore, Tayside, 1760 (thought to be by)
with William Robinson
St Michael's Church, Stone, Staffordshire, 1753–58 (altered internally 1887)

Baldwin, Thomas (1750–1820)
City architect at Bath, c. 1775–1800
Guildhall, High Street, Bath, Avon, 1776 (extended in the nineteenth century)
Somersetshire Buildings, Milsom Street, Bath, Avon, 1781–83
Cross Bath, Bath, Avon, 1787

Great Pulteney Street, Bath, Avon, 1789
Argyle Street, Bath, Avon, 1789
Laura Place, Bath, Avon, 1789
Bath Street Colonnade, Bath, Avon, 1791
Great Pump Room, Abbey Churchyard, Bath, Avon, 1791–92 (completed by John Palmer)
Town Hall, Devizes, Wiltshire, 1806–08
Rainscombe House, near Oare, Wiltshire, c. 1816

Barnes, George
23, 25 and 27–29 Brook Street, London, c. 1720–22

Barry, Sir Charles (1795–1860)
Articled as a surveyor in Lambeth 1810–16, he was a regular exhibitor at the Royal Academy and was awarded the Queen's Gold Medal for Architecture
St Peter's Church, Victoria Gardens, Brighton, East Sussex, 1824–28
Royal Institute of Fine Arts (now City Art Gallery), Mosley Street, Manchester, 1824–35
Buile Hill (now Science Museum), Eccles Old Road, Salford, Greater Manchester, 1825–27 (later additions)
St Paul's Church, corner of Balls Pond Road and Essex Road, Islington, London, 1826
St John the Evangelist's Church, Holloway Road, Islington, London, begun in 1826
Holy Trinity Church, Cloudesley Square, Barnsbury, Islington, London 1826
St Andrew's Church, Waterloo Road, Brighton, East Sussex, 1827–28
Travellers' Club, Pall Mall, Westminster, London, 1829–32

Basevi, George (1794–1845)
Trained as a pupil of Sir John Soane
Gatcombe Park, Gloucestershire; addition of wings, c. 1820
St Thomas's Church, Wellington Road South, Stockport, Greater Manchester, 1822–25
Belgrave Square, Westminster, London, 1825–40

Belgrave Square, London, 1825–40. The development had freestanding corner mansions by various architects

Balliol College, Oxford, Oxfordshire; Garden Quadrangle west side, 1826
Painswick House, Painswick, near Stroud, Gloucestershire; wings, c. 1827–32
Egerton Crescent, Pelham Crescent and Pelham Place, South Kensington, London, c. 1830

Bastard, John (1687–1770) and **William** (1689–1766)
Carpenters of Blandford, Dorset, they succeeded to the business of their father, Thomas (d. 1720).

It is thought that they built Chettle House, Dorset, c.1715–25, which is attributed to Thomas Archer, and from him derived the Borromini capital with inturning volutes that is regarded as characteristic of many of their buildings
Town Hall, Market Place, Blandford Forum, Dorset, 1734
Red Lion Inn and Greyhound Inn, Market Place, Blandford Forum, Dorset, c. 1734
Houses, Market Place, Blandford Forum, Dorset, c. 1734
Couper House, Church Lane, Blandford Forum, Dorset, c. 1734
1 West Street, Blandford Forum, Dorset, date not known
Church of St Peter and St Paul, Blandford Forum, Dorset, 1735–39
Sir Peter Thompson's House (Poole College), Market Street, Poole, Dorset, 1746–49

Baxter, John the Younger
Morton Hall House, Edinburgh, 1769 (thought to be by)
Gordonstoun House, near Lossiemouth, Grampian; alterations, 1772–76
Town House, Peterhead, Grampian, 1788
Merchant's Hall, 3–4 Hunter Square, Edinburgh, 1788 (altered 1894)
Bellie Church, Fochabers Newtown, Grampian, 1795–97

Beard, J B
Town Hall, Magdalene Street, Glastonbury, Somerset, 1813

Beazley, Charles (c. 1769–1829)
A pupil of Sir Robert Taylor
St Mary of Charity's Church, Faversham, Kent; tower and steeple, 1799
Ospringe House, Kent, c. 1799
Hollingbourne House, near Maidstone, Kent, 1799–1800

Beazley, Samuel (1786–1851)
Architect and playwright who, in addition to designing theatres, wrote over 100 dramatic pieces
Royal Assembly Rooms, Beth Street, Leamington Spa, Warwickshire, 1820–21
Theatre Royal, Drury Lane, Covent Garden, London; external colonnades and porch, 1831

Bedford, Francis Octavius (1784–1858)
St George's Church, Wells Way, Walworth, London, 1822–24
Holy Trinity, Trinity Church Square, Southwark, London, 1823–24 (interior reconstructed)
St John's Church, Waterloo Road, Lambeth, London, 1823–24
St Luke's Church, Norwood High Street, Lambeth, London, 1823–25 (interior remodelled 1878)

Bell, Samuel
St Andrew's Church, Dundee, Tayside, 1772
Nethergate House, 158 Nethergate, Dundee, Tayside, 1790 (thought to be by)
Milns Buildings, 136–40 Nethergate, Dundee, Tayside, c. 1790 (thought to be by)
Morgan Tower, 135–39 Nethergate, Dundee, Tayside, 1794
Theatre Royal, 7–21 Castle Street, Dundee, Tayside, 1807–09 (façade remains)

Benson, William (1682–1754)
Sheriff of Wiltshire 1710 and MP for Shaftsbury 1715; he was appointed Surveyor-General of Works in place of Sir Christopher Wren and Auditor of the Imprest
Wilbury House, Wiltshire, c. 1708 (altered and added to in 1740 and 1775)

Bevens, J
Retreat (Friends' Mental Hospital), Heslington Lane, York, North Yorkshire, 1794–96

Bindon, Francis (*d.* 1765)
Clermont, Co. Wicklow, Ireland, 1730 (house thought to be by)
Bessborough, Piltown, Co. Kilkenny, Ireland, *c.* 1744 (burnt in 1922 and rebuilt)
Drewstown, Athboy, Co. Meath, Ireland, *c.* 1745 (thought to be by)
Woodstock, Inistioge, Co. Kilkenny, Ireland, *c.* 1745 (ruin)
New Hall, Ennis, Co. Clare, Ireland, *c.* 1766 (thought to be by)

Blackburn, William (1750–90)
Surveyor and architect, he studied at the Royal Academy; he obtained the highest premium in competition for penitentiary houses in 1782, and subsequently executed designs for prisons and other structures throughout the country
Watermans' Hall, St Mary-at-Hill, City of London, 1778–80
County Gaol, Ipswich, Suffolk, 1786–90
House of Correction (now a museum), Northleach, Gloucestershire, 1787–91
House of Correction (now Record Office), Littledean, Gloucestershire, 1787–91
County Gaol, Monmouth, Gwent, 1788–90
Gaol, Gloucester, Gloucestershire, 1788–91 (enlarged 1845)
County Gaol, off North Square, Dorchester, Dorset; 1789–95 (portal survives)

Blore, Edward (1787–1879)
Corehouse, Strathclyde, 1824–27
Clarendon Press, Walton Street, Oxford, Oxfordshire; completion of north wings, 1829–30
Market House, Woburn, Bedfordshire, 1830
Bishop's Palace (former), St Asaph, Clwyd; west wing, 1830–31
with William Burn
Freeland House, Tayside, 1825–26 (later additions)

Bond, John Linnell (1764–1837)
Gold medallist at the Royal Academy, 1786
Stamford Hotel, St Mary's Street, Stamford, Lincolnshire, 1810–19

Bonnar, Thomas (*d. c.* 1832)
Bellevue Crescent, Edinburgh, 1818
India Street, Edinburgh, 1819
Atholl Crescent, Western New Town, Edinburgh, 1825
with R Burn
Nelson Monument, Calton Hill, Edinburgh, 1807–16

Bonner, John
Phoenix Lodge, Queen Street East, Sunderland, Tyne and Wear, 1785

Bonomi, Ignatius (*c.* 1787–1870)
St James's Church, Great Packington, Warwickshire, 1790
Crown Court (formerly Assize Court) and Gaol, Durham, Co. Durham; completion, 1811
Lambton Castle, near Chester-le-Street, Co. Durham; enlargements, *c.* 1820–28
Burn Hall, Co. Durham, 1821–34
St Cuthbert's Roman Catholic Church, Court Lane, Durham, Co. Durham, 1827 (later alterations)
St Peter's Church, Redcar Lane, Redcar, Cleveland, 1828–29

Bonomi, Joseph (1739–1808)
Born in Rome, he came to England in 1767 and established a practice in London in 1784. He exhibited drawings of his work, which was chiefly in the Grecian renaissance style, at the Royal Acadamy from 1783–1806
Packington Hall, West Midlands; interiors, from 1784
Longford Hall, near Newport, Shropshire, 1789–94
Blickling Park, Norfolk, 1794
Lambton Castle, near Chester-le-Street, Co. Durham, *c.* 1796

Hatchlands, near Guildford, Surrey; alterations, 1797
Piercefield, Chepstow, Gwent; completion, 1797 (now a ruin)

Borra, Giovanni Battista
Rotondo, in the grounds of Stowe, near Buckingham, Buckinghamshire; alterations, *c.* 1763
Boycott Pavilions, in the grounds of Stowe, near Buckingham, Buckinghamshire; alterations, *c.* 1770
Stowe, near Buckingham, Buckinghamshire; alterations and additions, 1770–72
Stowe, near Buckingham, Buckinghamshire; south front, 1774 (original design by Robert Adam)

The central portico of Stowe House, Buckinghamshire; the south front designed by Robert Adam, and executed by Borra, 1774

Boscawen, George
Marfield village estate, near Wrexham, Clwyd, 1806–16

Bowden, John
Court House, Cavan, Co. Cavan, Ireland, *c.* 1800
Court House, Bishop Street, Derry, Co. Londonderry, Ireland, 1813–17
Old Foyle College, Strand Road, Derry, Co. Londonderry, Ireland, 1814
St George's Anglican Church, High Street, Belfast, Co. Antrim, Ireland, 1816
St Stephen's Church, Upper Mount Street, Dublin, Ireland, 1824–25

Bowen, John
Market Hall, Bridgwater, Somerset, 1826

Bowie, Alexander (*d. c.* 1829)
Allan Park, Stirling, central Scotland, *c.* 1810–27 (partly by)
Craigs House, Stirling, central Scotland, *c.* 1820

Brettingham, Matthew the Elder (1699–1769)
A pupil of William Kent, he formed a large practice in Norwich, partly as a result of his long and successful association with the building of Holkham House for the Earl of Leicester
Gunton Park, near North Walsham, Norfolk; entrance front, 1742 (gutted)
Langley Park, near Norwich, Norfolk; major alterations, 1745
5 St James's Square, St James's, Westminster, London, 1748–51
94 Piccadilly, London, 1756
Kedleston, near Derby, Derbyshire; rebuilding, begun in 1759

with Robert Brettingham
Holkham House, 15–17 Cow Hill, Norwich, Norfolk *c.* 1750

Brettingham, Matthew the Younger (1725–1803)
Published the plans of Holkham House in 1773, claiming the credit for them for his father 'who laid every brick from the foundation to the roof'
Charlton Park, near Malmesbury, Wiltshire; alterations, 1772

Brettingham, Robert (1750–1806)
Nephew of Matthew Brettingham the Elder, he studied in Italy before becoming resident architect of the Board of Works, 1771–1805
Gaol, off George Row, Northampton, Northamptonshire, 1791–94 (mostly demolished 1930)

Bridges, James
The Royal Fort, Woodland Road, Bristol, Avon, 1761

Above: *The Royal Fort, Bristol, by James Bridges; and* below, *St Nicholas's Church, which is now the tourist information office*

St Nicholas's Church, High Street, Bristol, Avon, 1762–68 (only tower and shell survive)

with Thomas Paty
Arno's Court, Arno Vale, Bristol, Avon, *c.* 1760

Bromfield, Joseph (*c.* 1743–1824)
Glansevern Hall, Berriew, Powys, *c.* 1805

Brooks, William (1786–1867)
St Thomas's Church, High Street, Dudley, West
Midlands, 1816–17

Brooks, William McIntosh (*d.* 1849)
Peterhouse College, Cambridge,
Cambridgeshire; Gisborne Court, 1825–26

Brown, James
George Street, Edinburgh; west side and part
east side, *c.* 1765
Nos 1–6 Buccleuch Place, Edinburgh, *c.* 1790

Brown, Lancelot ('Capability') (1716–83)
He combined a considerable architectural
practice with landscaping. A list of 19 country
houses of which he was architect was compiled
by his son-in-law, Henry Holland, with whom
he went into partnership in 1772. Those
belonging to his rococo phase and still existing
are Croome Court and the reconstruction of
Corsham Court with which Sanderson Miller
was also later associated. His conventional
houses have a neoclassic simplicity and were
noted for their convenient planning
Croome Court, Croome d'Abitot, Hereford and
Worcester, 1751
St Mary Magdalene's Church, Croome d'Abitot,
Hereford and Worcester, 1761–63 (exterior
thought to be by)
Corsham Court, Corsham, Wiltshire;
enlargements, 1761–64 (later altered)
Benham Park, Speen, Berkshire, 1772–75
(altered 1870)

Benham Park by Capability Brown for the sixth Earl of Craven. Brown also laid out the gardens. The house, which is built in stone, is three storeys high and nine bays wide with a portico of four unfluted Ionic columns and no pediment

Palladian Bridge, in the grounds of Scampston
Hall, near Pickering, Humberside, *c.* 1775
Milton Abbey, Milton Abbas, Dorset;
completion, *c.* 1776
Nuneham Park, Nuneham Courtenay,
Oxfordshire; alterations, 1781

Richmond Gate, Richmond Park, Richmond-
upon-Thames, London, 1798

Brown, Robert
Coates Crescent, Western New Town,
Edinburgh, 1813
Melville Street, Western New Town, Edinburgh,
1814

Brown, Sir Samuel (1776–1852)
An engineer who became a naval officer in 1795,
commander in 1811 and captain in 1842. He
was knighted in 1834 and was responsible for
having devised an improved method of chain
links for ships' cables and suspension bridges
Union Chain Bridge, Berwick-upon-Tweed,
Northumberland, 1820
Suspension Bridge, Hutton, Borders, 1820

Brown, Thomas (*c.* 1781–1850)
Exchange Building, Constitution Street, Leith,
Edinburgh, 1809
Trinity House, Leith, Edinburgh, 1816–17
St Mary's Church, Bellevue Crescent,
Edinburgh, 1823–26

Browne, Thomas Wogan
Castle Browne (or Clongowes Wood), Clane,
Co. Kildare, Ireland, 1788

Browning, Bryan (1773–1856)
Sessions House, Bourne, Lincolnshire, 1821
House of Correction, Folkingham, Lincolnshire,
1824–25

Brunel, Isambard Kingdom (1806–59)
A civil engineer and only son of Sir Marc
Isambard Brunel; he was educated privately
and in Paris, after which he became clerk to his
father in 1823. He was appointed resident
engineer of the Thames Tunnel in 1826 and
engineer to the Great Western Railway in 1833.
He was responsible for application of the screw
propeller to steam ships in 1845, and designed
the *Great Eastern* steamship in 1852–58
Clifton Suspension Bridge, Clifton, Avon,
1829–64

Brunel, Sir Marc Isambard (1769–1849)
A civil engineer born in Normandy, France, he
was educated at Rouen for the Church but
served for six years in the French navy before
emigrating to America in 1793, where he
practised as a surveyor, architect and civil
engineer and was responsible for planning the
defences of New York. He came to England in
1799, to patent his machinery for making ships'
blocks and was imprisoned for debt in 1821.
Between 1825 and 1843 he was engineer for
the Thames Tunnel, for which work he was
knighted in 1841
Sawmill, Chatham Docks, Chatham, Kent, 1814

Buckler, John (1770–1851)
A topographical artist who practised architecture
in London until 1826. He issued aquatint
engravings of colleges and cathedrals 1797–
1815, and his watercolours were exhibited at
the Royal Academy, 1796–1849
Halkyn Castle, Clwyd, 1824–27 (enlarged 1886)
Holy Trinity Church, Theale, Berkshire; tower,
1827
Tate almshouses, Cricket Green, Merton,
London, 1829

Burgh, Thomas
Oldtown, Naas, Co. Kildare, Ireland; own
house, *c.* 1709
Library, Trinity College, Dublin, Ireland,
1712–32
Dr Steeven's Hospital, Dublin, Ireland, 1721–23
Celbridge School (former), Celbridge,
Co. Kildare, Ireland, *c.* 1728 (thought to be by)

Burlington, Lord (Richard Boyle) (1694–1753)
The third Earl of Burlington and the fourth Earl
of Cork; he was a leading Whig aristocrat from

the north of England and patron of the arts. He
visited Italy in 1719, to study the work of
Palladio, returning to build one of the earliest
and most influential English Palladian
buildings, Burlington House in Piccadilly,
London, 1716–19, for which he commissioned
Colen Campbell. He was by far the most
important single influence in the Palladian
movement which supplanted the English
baroque style and by the second quarter of the
eighteenth century had established the late
Italian Renaissance ideals as the only acceptable
architecture in England
Tottenham Park, near Marlborough, Wiltshire,
begun in 1721
Westminster School, Westminster Abbey,
London; dormitory, 1722–30
Chiswick House, Burlington Lane, Chiswick,
London *c.* 1723–29. The most important of the
Earl's buildings, it was built to accomodate his
library and as a place to entertain friends. The
rich interiors were by Kent. The villa is
approached by a quadruple stone stairway
where a six-column portico dominates the
entrance front, forming an airy relief from the
solid walls on both sides. Above it rises the
octagonal dome which is the villa's most original
feature. The form is truly Italian, with its low
basement storey and high *piano nobile* above

Chiswick House by Burlington

Sevenoaks School and Almshouse, Sevenoaks,
Kent, 1724–32
Assembly Rooms, Blake Street, York, North
Yorkshire, 1731
Northwick Park, near Bristol, Avon;
remodelling, 1732

Burn, William (1789–1870)
Practised in Edinburgh *c.* 1814, before moving to
London in 1844
North Leith Church, Prince Regent Street, Leith,
Edinburgh, 1814–16

Gallanach House, Strathclyde, 1814–17
(enlarged 1903)
St John, Princes Street, Edinburgh, 1816–18
Custom House, Greenock, Strathclyde, 1817–18
Saltoun Hall, near Tranent, Lothian, 1818–26
Dundas Castle, near Queensferry, Lothian, 1818
Alderstone Hall, near Belford, Northumberland,
1819
Blairquhan, Straiton, Strathclyde, 1820–24
St Joseph's School (formerly George Stiell's
Hospital), Tranent, Lothian, 1821–22
Carstairs House, near Wishaw, Strathclyde,
1822–24
Edinburgh Academy, Henderson Row,
Edinburgh, 1823–26
Ratho Park, Ratho, Lothian, 1824
Camperdown House, near Dundee, Tayside,
1824
Reform Street, Dundee, Tayside, 1824
John Watson's Hospital School (now Gallery of
Modern Art), Bedford Road, Edinburgh,
1825–28
Fettercain, Laurencekirk, Grampion, 1826
Kinnoull parish church, Perth, Tayside, 1826
Dalhousie Castle, Lothian; remodelling and
extensions, 1826–28
Murray Royal Asylum for the Insane, Kinnoull,
Perth, Tayside, 1827
Whittinghame House (now hospital), near East
Linton, Lothian; alterations, 1827
Lauriston Castle, Edinburgh; enlargement, 1827
Pitcairns, Dunning, Tayside, 1827
Faskally, Tayside, 1829
Tyninghame House, near Dunbar, Lothian,
1829–30
Raehills, near Moffat, Dumfries and Galloway;
enlargements, 1829–34
Spott House, Lothian; remodelling, 1830
Pitcaple Castle, Grampian; additions, c. 1830
Drumlanrig Castle, Dumfries and Galloway;
wings, c. 1830–34; (thought to be by)

Burrough, Sir James (1691–1764)
An amateur architect educated at Bury
St Edmunds and Caius College, Cambridge, he
attained his degree in 1711; was a Fellow
1712–19; Master 1754–64; Vice-Chancellor in
1759 and Esquire Bedell in 1727. He was
knighted in 1759 and was consulted or
employed on most of the Cambridge buildings
of his day
Senate House, Cambridge, Cambridgeshire;
initial design, 1722–30; the design was finished
by James Gibbs
The Manor House, 5 Honey Hill, Bury
St Edmunds, Suffolk, 1735 (now County
Education Offices)
Peterhouse College Cambridge,
Cambridgeshire; New Building, 1736–42
Clare College Chapel, Cambridge,
Cambridgeshire, 1763

Burton, Decimus (1800–1881)
The twelfth son of James Burton, he trained
with his father and at the Royal Academy
Schools from 1817
The Holme, in Regent's Park, Marylebone,
London, c. 1818
Cornwall Terrace, Regent's Park, Marylebone,
London, 1821
Grove House (now Nuffield Lodge), in Regent's
Park, Marylebone, London, 1822–24
Clarence Terrace, Regent's Park, Marylebone,
London, 1823
Holwood House, Bromley, London, 1823–26
Hyde Park Screen and Arch, Hyde Park Corner,
London, 1824–25
Holmwood (formerly Mitchells), Langton
Green, Kent, 1827
Constitution Arch, Hyde Park Corner, London,
1827–28
Holy Trinity Church, Church Road, Tunbridge,
Kent, 1827–29
Athenaeum Club, Pall Mall, Westminster,
London, 1827–30
Calverley Park Crescent, Tunbridge Wells, Kent,
c. 1830

Calverley Park Crescent,
Tunbridge Wells, Kent, c. 1830;
a single curve of 17 houses with
continuous ground-floor verandas

Adelaide Crescent, Brighton, East Sussex,
1830–34

Burton, James (1761–1837)
Originally known as Haliburton, he was the
favourite building contractor of John Nash
18–27 Bloomsbury Square, Bloomsbury,
London, 1800

21 Bloomsbury Square, London,
part of a terrace including
numbers 18–27, built at the turn
of the century by James Burton

1–11 and 12–29 Montague Street, Bloomsbury,
London, 1800
Bedford Place, Bloomsbury, London, 1800–01
38–43 Russell Square, Bloomsbury, London,
c. 1800–10
Cartwright Gardens, Bloomsbury, London,
begun c. 1807
Burton Street, Bloomsbury, London, c. 1810

Busby, Charles Augustus (1788–1834)
Commercial Rooms, Corn Street, Bristol, Avon,
1810–11

The Commercial Rooms, Corn
Street, Bristol, 1810

Kemp Town, Brighton, East Sussex, from 1823
Sussex Square, Brighton, East Sussex, c. 1823
Brunswick Terrace, Hove, East Sussex,
c. 1824–30
Brunswick Square, Hove, East Sussex,
c. 1824–30
Lewes Crescent, Brighton, East Sussex, c. 1825

Lewes Crescent, Brighton, c. 1825

Butter, Charles and **William**
Gayfield House, East London Road, Edinburgh,
1765

Byfield, George (c. 1756–1813)
Craycombe House, Fladbury, Hereford and
Worcester, 1791
Old Gaol, Bury St Edmunds, Suffolk, 1803
(known as The Fort; only the façade remains)

County Gaol and Sessions House, Longport, Canterbury, Kent, 1806–10
Papworth Hall (now Papworth Hospital), near Cambridge, Cambridgeshire, 1809
Perridge House, Devon, c. 1827

Cabanel, Rudolph (1762–1839)
Born at Aix-la-Chapelle, France, he came to England early in life and invented the Cabanel roof
The Old Vic (originally Royal Coburg Theatre), Waterloo Road, Lambeth, London, 1816 (only side wall remains)

Cairncross, Hugh
Broughton Place, Edinburgh, 1807

Campbell, Colen (1676–1729)
A lowland Scot, educated in Edinburgh, he originally trained as a lawyer. His first villa was completed in 1712, at Shawfield near Glasgow. His great works date from the mid-1720s, by which time he had moved to London, and include the classical Palladian villa at Stourhead which he built for the banker, Henry Hoare. Houghton Hall was built for Robert Walpole, and Mereworth Castle for John Fane, Earl of Westmorland. He was appointed to the post of Surveyor of Greenwich Hospital on Vanbrugh's death in 1726
Burlington House (Royal Academy), Piccadilly, London, 1717–19

Above: *Burlington House as refronted by Colen Campbell in 1719* and below, *today, as the Royal Academy with an upper storey and entrance loggia added*

Summer House, Ebberston Hall, near Scarborough, North Yorkshire, 1718
31–32 Old Burlington Street, Piccadilly, London, 1718–23
Baldersby (formerly Newby) Park, near Ripon, North Yorkshire, 1718–26
Stourhead, near Gillingham, Wiltshire, begun c. 1720
Houghton Hall, near King's Lynn, Norfolk, 1721–35
Mereworth Castle, near Tonbridge, Kent, begun 1722
76 Brook Street, Mayfair, London; own house, c. 1726 (top storey added later)

Carline, John (1761–1835)
Welsh Bridge, Shrewsbury, Shropshire, 1793–95
St Alkmund's Church, St Alkmund's Place, Shrewsbury, Shropshire, 1794–95

Carr, John (1723–1807)
Known as Carr of York
Peasholme House, St Saviour's Place, York, North Yorkshire, 1752
Micklegate House, 88–90 Micklegate, York, North Yorkshire, 1753
Heath Hall, Heath, West Yorkshire, 1754–80
St James's Church, Ravenfield, South Yorkshire, 1756
Lytham Hall, Lytham St Ann's, Lancashire, 1757–64
Harewood House, near Leeds, West Yorkshire; plan and north façade, 1759

Design for the northern elevation of Harewood House, Yorkshire

Abbot Hall (now art gallery), Kendal, Cumbria, 1759
Model village near Harewood House, West Yorkshire, c. 1760
Castlegate House, 26 Castlegate, York, North Yorkshire, 1762
Constable Burton Hall, near Richmond, North Yorkshire, 1762–68
St Cuthbert's Church, Kirkleatham, Cleveland, 1763 (thought to be by)
Cannon Hall, near Barnsley, South Yorkshire; alterations, 1764–8 (now Museum of Barnsley)
Somerset House, George Street, Halifax, West Yorkshire, 1766
Denton Hall, near Ilkley, North Yorkshire, 1770–81
Thirsk Hall, Thirsk, North Yorkshire; enlargement with wings added, 1771–73
Bootham Park Hospital (former County Lunatic Asylum), York, North Yorkshire, 1772–77 (altered 1814)
Greta Bridge, near Barnard Castle, Co. Durham, 1773
Town Hall, Market Place, Newark-on-Trent, Nottinghamshire, 1773–76
Assize and Crown Court, York, North Yorkshire, 1773–77
Basildon Park, near Reading, Berkshire, 1776
Norton Place, near Market Rasen, Lincolnshire, 1776
Bishop's College Hospital (formerly Infirmary), Wordsworth Street, Lincoln, Lincolnshire, 1776
Grandstand, Doncaster Racecourse, Doncaster, South Yorkshire, 1776 (enlarged 1810–20)
Keppel's Column, Wentworth Woodhouse, near Rawmarsh, South Yorkshire, 1778

Female prison (now a museum), York, North Yorkshire, 1780–83
Castle Farm, Sledmere House, near Great Driffield, Humberside, c. 1780 (thought to be by)
Assembly Room, Crescent, Buxton, Derbyshire, 1780–90
Holy Rood Church, Ossington, Nottinghamshire, 1782
Wentworth Woodhouse, near Rawmarsh, South Yorkshire; wings to east front, 1782–84
Court House and House of Correction (now HM Prison), Zetland Street, Northallerton, North Yorkshire 1784–88
Devonshire Royal Hospital, Buxton, Derbyshire; stables, 1785–90
Rockingham Mausoleum, Wentworth Woodhouse, near Rawmarsh, South Yorkshire, 1788
St James's Church, Clerkenwell Green, Clerkenwell, London, 1788–92
Bridge, Richmond, North Yorkshire, 1789
Unitarian chapel, Wilmslow Road, Fallowfield, Greater Manchester, 1790 (thought to be by)
St Peter and St Leonard's Church, Horbury, West Yorkshire, 1791
Ormsby Hall, near Horncastle, Lincolnshire; entrance porch and additions, 1803
with William Lumby
Gaol (now Lincolnshire Record Office), Lincoln Castle, Lincoln, Lincolnshire, 1787

Carter, Francis (c. 1773–1809)
Marden Hill, near Tewin, Hertfordshire 1790–94 (remodelled 1818–19)

Carter, John (1748–1817)
A draughtsman, architect and surveyor's clerk, he was appointed draughtsman to the *Builders' Magazine* 1774–86 and to the Society of Antiquaries 1780. He published many books between 1780–1814 of his views on buildings in England
Midford Castle, near Bath, Avon, c. 1775 (thought to be by)
St Mary the Virgin and All Saints' Church, Debden, Essex; chapel, 1792
Debden church, Essex; addition of chapel and monument, 1792–93

Cartwright, Francis
Creech Grange, near Wareham, Dorset; south front, 1738–41
Kingsnympton Park, near South Molton, Devon, 1740
Came House, near Dorchester, Dorset, c. 1754

Carver, Richard (c. 1792–1862)
Holy Trinity Church, Blackford, Somerset, 1823
Christ Church, Theale, Somerset, 1828

Castle, Richard (d. 1751)
Born in Germany to German parents, he was also known as Cassel or Cassels. By 1720, he had moved to Ireland
80 St Stephen's Green, Dublin, Ireland, c. 1730
Hazlewood, Sligo, Co. Sligo, Ireland, 1731
Westport House, Westport, Co. Mayo, Ireland, c. 1731 (added to)
Ballyhaise House, Ballyhaise, Co. Cavan, Ireland, c. 1733 (wings added c. 1800)
Dollardstown, Slane, Co. Meath, Ireland; remodelling, c. 1735 (now gutted)
Ledwithstown, Ballymahon, Co. Longford, Ireland, c. 1735–40 (thought to be by)
Newbridge House, Donabate, Co. Dublin, Ireland, 1737 (thought to be by)
Tyrone House, Marlborough Street, Dublin, Ireland, c. 1740 (external alterations 1835)
Anneville, Mullingar, Co. Westmeath, Ireland, c. 1740
Belvedere, Lough Ennell, Co. Westmeath, Ireland, c. 1740
Carton, Maynooth, Co. Kildare, Ireland; remodelling, c. 1740–51 (altered c. 1815)
Russborough, Blessington, Co. Wicklow, Ireland, 1741–c. 1750

Trinity College, Dublin, Ireland; Dining Hall,
c. 1741 (damaged by fire 1984)
Bishop's Palace (former), beside Church of
Ireland Cathedral, Waterford, Co. Waterford,
Ireland, c. 1741
Tudenham (formerly Rochfort), Mullingar,
Co. Westmeath, Ireland, c. 1742 (ruin; thought
to be by)
Court and Market House, Market Square,
Dunlavin, Co. Wicklow, Ireland, 1743 (thought
to be by)
85 St Stephen's Green, Dublin, Ireland, c. 1745
Leinster House, Molesworth Field, Merrion
Square, Dublin, Ireland, 1745–47
Mantua House, Castlerea, Co. Roscommon,
Ireland, 1747 (ruin; thought to be by)
Bellinter, Navan, Co. Meath, Ireland, c. 1750
Rotunda Lying-in Hospital, Parnell Street,
Dublin, Ireland, c. 1751

Chambers, Sir William (1723–96)
Raised in Sweden by Scottish parents, he was
trained in France and Italy, and settled in
London in 1755,where he became the favourite
of King George III. Aspiring to the highest
official architectural offices, he was regarded as
one of the leading architects of the eighteenth
century. He published *Treatise of Civil Architecture*
in 1759. Just as Sir Robert Taylor and James
Paine dominated English architecture in the
years immediately after the middle of the
eighteenth century, the 1770s and 1780s were
the great period of William Chambers and
Robert Adam. Chambers made his name by his
work in the Chinese taste and then became a
byword for late academic Palladian style, while
the latter gave his name to a classical style of
his own
Harewood House, near Leeds, West Yorkshire;
stables, 1755–56
Royal Botanic Gardens, Kew, Richmond-upon-
Thames, London; Orangery, 1757
Goodwood House, near Chichester, West
Sussex; stables, 1757–63
Wilton House, Wilton, Wiltshire; triumphal
arch and casino in the grounds,1757–74
Royal Botanic Gardens, Kew, Richmond-upon-
Thames, London; Temple of Aeolus, Temple of
Arethusa, Temple of Bellona and ruined arch,
1758–63
Casino, Marino, Clontarf, Co. Dublin, Ireland,
1758–76
Manresa House (formerly Parksted), Danebury
Avenue, Roehampton, London, 1760–68
Goodwood House, near Chichester, West
Sussex; south wing, c. 1760 (thought to be by)
Castletown, Celbridge, Co. Kildare, Ireland;
redecoration, c. 1760
Royal Botanic Gardens, Kew, Richmond-upon-
Thames, London; pagoda, 1761
Styche Hall, near Market Drayton, Shropshire,
1762
Coleby Hall, near Lincoln, Lincolnshire; Temple
of Romulus and Remus, 1762
Duddingston, Edinburgh, 1762–67
Charlemont House, Parnell Square, Dublin,
Ireland, c. 1763–75
Peper Harrow, near Godalming, Surrey, 1765–68
(much altered)
Town Hall, Woodstock, Oxfordshire, 1766
Blenheim Palace, Oxfordshire, Temple of Flora
and Diana, 1766–75
Woburn Abbey, Woburn, Bedfordshire; south
wing including library, 1767–72
Observatory, Old Deer Park, Richmond,
London, 1768
21 Arlington Street, Piccadilly, London;
alterations, 1769
Ampthill Park, Bedfordshire; enlargement and
redecoration, 1769–71
Warwick House, Stable Yard Road, Westminster,
London, 1770–71 (altered externally)
Milton House, near Northampton,
Northamptonshire; dining room, tea room,
library and gallery, 1770–77
Castle Howard, near Malton, North Yorkshire;
Exclamation Gate, c. 1770

No 26 St Andrew's Square, Edinburgh, c. 1770
(thought to be by)
Danson Park, Welling, Bexley, London; interior,
c. 1770
Dundas House, St Andrew's Square, Edinburgh,
1771 (altered 1828 and 1858)
Albany (originally Melbourne House), off
Piccadilly, Piccadilly, London, 1771–76
(converted and enlarged 1802)
Milton Abbey, Milton Abbas, Dorset; rebuilding,
1771–76
Chinese Temple, Amesbury, Wiltshire, 1772
Wick House, Richmond Hill, Richmond-upon-
Thames, London, 1772 (front elevation since
altered)
Somerset House, Strand, London, begun 1776
Chapel, Trinity College, Dublin, Ireland, 1787–
1800

Changier, L L
Earl's Terrace, Kensington, London, c. 1800–10
Edwardes Square, Kensington, London,
1811–19

Chantrell, Robert Dennis (1793–1872)
Rudding Park, North Yorkshire; completion,
c. 1825

Chaplin, Robert
Royal Hotel, Ashby-de-la-Zouch, Leicestershire,
1826

Childs, Francis
Crescent Grove, Clapham, London, c. 1825

Chute, John
Donnington Grove, near Newbury, Berkshire,
c. 1762

Clark, Sir John,
Son of Sir James Clark
St Mungo's Church, Penicuik, Lothian, 1771
Roundhay Hall, Leeds, West Yorkshire, 1826
with John Baxter the Elder
Penicuik House, Penicuik, Lothian, 1761–69
(ruin)

Clarke, George
Queen's College, Oxford, Oxfordshire; Hall and
Chapel, 1714
University College, Oxford, Oxfordshire;
Radcliffe Quadrangle, 1716–19
Christ Church College, Oxford, Oxfordshire;
Peckwater Library, 1717–38

Worcester College, Oxford, Oxfordshire;
Library and entrance block, 1720
Magdalen College, Oxford, Oxfordshire; New
Building, 1733

Clarke, James
Dower House (formerly King's Arms Inn),
London Road, Newbury, Berkshire 1750

Clements, Nathaniel
Viceregal Lodge (now Arus an Uachtarain),
Phoenix Park, Dublin, Ireland, 1751 (extended
several times)
Newberry Hall, Carbury, Co. Kildare, Ireland,
c. 1765 (thought to be by)
Belview, near Kells, Co. Meath, Ireland, c. 1765
(thought to be by)
Colganstown, Newcastle, Co. Dublin, Ireland,
c. 1765 (thought to be by)
Beau Parc, near Navan, Co. Meath, Ireland,
c. 1775 (thought to be by)
Lodge Park, Straffan, Co. Kildare, Ireland,
c. 1775 (thought to be by)

Clerk, Sir James
Hailes House, Edinburgh, c. 1770

Clifton, C
Tr Mawr, Llanfrynach, Powys; remodelling,
c. 1820 (additions c. 1860–80)

Cobden, Thomas
Roman Catholic Cathedral, Carlow,
Co. Carlow, Ireland, c. 1828

Cockerell, Charles Robert (1788–1863)
Son of Samuel Pepys Cockerell, he was trained
by his father and studied architectural remains
in Greece, Asia Minor, Sicily and Italy between
1810–17. He discovered, along with two
Germans, the frieze of the Temple of Apollo at
Phigalein in 1812. He practised architecture in
London from 1817, exhibited at the Royal
Academy 1818–58, and was appointed
Professor of Architecture there 1840–57
Lady Boswell's School, London Road,
Sevenoaks, Kent, 1818
Harrow School, Harrow, London; major
additions, including Speech Room wing,
1818–20
St Mary's Church, Banbury, Oxfordshire; tower
and portico, 1818–22
Oakley Park, near Ludlow, Shropshire;
remodelling, 1819–36
Gibson School, Oldcastle, Co. Meath, Ireland,
1821–22
Library and Philosophical Institute, Park Street,
Bristol, Avon, 1821–23

Left: *Peckwater Library, Christ
Church, Oxford; originally
sketched by Henry Aldrich, and
based on Michelangelo's side
palaces on the Capitol, Rome.
The Library forms the fourth side
of Peckwater Quad, of which the
other three sides are embellished
with pilasters and columns
beneath central pediments*

Top right: *the tall, curved
Grecian portico of the Literary
and Philosophical Institute, which
remains as a façade*

Derry Ormond Tower, Dyfed, 1821–24 (thought to be by)
Loughcrew, Oldcastle, Co. Meath, Ireland, 1821–29 (gutted 1965)
Bowood House, Wiltshire; chapel, library and breakfast room, 1822–24
St David's University College, Lampeter, Dyfed, 1822–27
Lodge, Wynnstay Park, Powys, 1827
Langton House, Langton, Long Blandford, Dorset, 1827–33 (demolished)
Holy Trinity Church, Hotwell Road, Bristol, Avon, 1829–30
with SP Cockerell
32 Duke of York Street, Westminster, London, 1819–21
with WH Playfair
National Monument, Calton Hill, Edinburgh, 1824–29

Cockerell, Samuel Pepys (1753–1827)
A pupil of Sir Robert Taylor, he exhibited at the Royal Academy 1785–1803
Admiralty House, Whitehall, London, 1786–88
Daylesford House, Gloucestershire, 1788–93
St Mary's Church, Banbury, Oxfordshire, 1792–97
St Anne's Church, Wardour Street, Soho, London; tower, 1801–03
Nutwell Court, Lympstone, Devon, 1802
Tower, Llanarthney, Dyfed, c. 1805 (thought to be by)
Sezincote House, near Chipping Norton, Gloucestershire, c. 1805
Nelson Square, Southwark, London, c. 1807–10 (thought to be by)
Sezincote House, near Chipping Norton, Gloucestershire; farm in the grounds, c. 1808
Public Baths (now Laston House), St Julian's Street, Tenby, Dyfed, 1811
Fulham Palace, Fulham, London; east block, 1814
Western Courtyard, New Street, City of London; extensions, c. 1820 (elevations only survive)

Cole, Charles
with John Graham
Ely Place, Holborn, London, 1773–76

Cole, William (1800–92)
Bolesworth Castle, Cheshire, 1829

Colles, William
Tholsel, Kilkenny, Co. Kilkenny, Ireland, 1761 (thought to be by)
Millmount, Maddockstown, Co. Kilkenny, Ireland; own house, c. 1765

Coltsman, John
St Anne's, Shandon, Protestant Church, Cork, Co. Cork, Ireland, 1722 (thought to be by)
Corn Market, Cork, Co. Cork, Ireland, c. 1750 (thought to be by)

Committee of taste *see* **Sanderson Miller**

Cook, Thomas (d. 1803)
Gaol, Gaol Road, Stafford, Staffordshire, 1793–94 (enlarged 1832)

Cooley, Thomas (1740–1784)
He originally practised as a carpenter
Royal Exchange (now City Hall), Dublin, Ireland, begun 1769
Armagh Palace, Armagh, Co. Armagh, Ireland, 1770 (extended 1786)
Library, Armagh, Co. Armagh, Ireland, 1771 (extended c. 1820)
Caledon, near Armagh, Co. Tyrone, Ireland, 1779 (altered 1808)
Mount Kennedy, Co. Wicklow, Ireland, 1782–84
Rokeby Hall, Dunleer, Co. Louth, Ireland; work carried out by Francis Johnson to Cooley's designs, 1785–94

Cooper, Thomas
Bedford Hotel, Brighton, East Sussex, 1829
Town Hall, Market Place, Brighton, East Sussex, 1830–32 *below*

Cotton, Henry
Bedford Row, Worthing, West Sussex, 1802–05
Ambrose Place, Worthing, West Sussex, 1815
Liverpool Terrace, Worthing, West Sussex, c. 1830

Couse, Kenton (1721–90)
He was employed by the Board of Works
10–12 Downing Street, Whitehall, London; façades, 1766
Holy Trinity Church, Clapham Common North Side, Clapham, London, 1776
with James Paine
Richmond Bridge, Richmond-upon-Thames, London, 1774–77 (widened 1937)

Craig, James (d. 1795)
Practised in Edinburgh and published designs for laying out Edinburgh New Town in 1767
Observatory, Calton Hill, Edinburgh, 1776

Craig, John
42 Miller Street, Glasgow, Strathclyde, c. 1775

Crichton, Richard (c. 1771–1817)
Gask House, Tayside, 1801
Colinton House, Edinburgh, 1801 (extensions 1870)
Court House and Gaol, Stirling, central Scotland, 1806–11
Lawers House, Tayside; remodelling, c. 1810
Kincardine-in-Menteith church, central Scotland, 1814
Balbirnie House, Fife 1815–19

Crunden, John
Boodle's Club, 28 St James's Street, Westminster, London, 1775
Belfield House, Buxton Road, Weymouth, Dorset 1785

Cubitt, Thomas (1788–1855)
A builder who, in his early life, made a voyage to India as a ship's carpenter. He was a master carpenter in London 1809 and supporter of the Thames Embankment scheme. He guaranteed a large sum of money to the Great Exhibition of 1851
Crescent Grove, Wandsworth, London, 1822
Gordon Square, Bloomsbury, London; east side, 1824–30 *below*

Endsleigh Place, Bloomsbury, London, c. 1824
Linton Park, Kent; remodelling, c. 1825
Eaton Place, Eaton Square, Belgrave Place and Chester Square, London, 1825–53

Cundy, Thomas the Elder (1765–1825)
Bessingby Hall, Humberside, 1807
Hawarden Castle, Clwyd; extensions and remodelling, 1809–10
Tottenham Park, near Marlborough, Wiltshire; remodelling, 1823–26 (altered later)
St Matthew's Church, Normanton, Leicester; tower, 1826–29

Custance, William
Grove Lodge, Cambridge, Cambridgeshire, 1795

Dance, George the Elder (1700–68)
Architect and surveyor to the Corporation of London; his churches are noted for their rather provincial classicism with proportions that were often ungainly and detailing of patchy quality
St Leonard's Church, Shoreditch High Street, Hackney, London, 1736–40
Mansion House, Mansion House Street, City of London, 1739–42
St Botolph's Church, Aldgate, City of London, 1741–44
St Matthew's Church, St Matthew's Road, Bethnal Green, London, 1743–46
St Mary of Charity's Church, Faversham, Kent, 1754–55 (altered)
with James Gould
St Botolph's Church, Bishopsgate, City of London, 1727–29 (inside altered 1821)

Dance, George the Younger (1741–1825)
The fifth son of George Dance the Elder, he was City Surveyor 1768–1815 and professor of architecture at the Royal Academy 1798–1805. He visited Rome when aged 17, with his painter brother, Nathaniel, where they lived near to Robert and James Adam. He returned to London in December 1764 and became assistant to his father. In 1777 he was employed by the City of London for the development of Finsbury Square, since demolished after damage in the Second World War. The west side, *below*, was an original treatment of London terraced housing and was praised by Soane in preference

to the hole-in-the-wall speculative work ongoing
in Bloomsbury
All Hallows Church, London Wall, City of
London, 1765–67
Pitzhanger Manor, Walpole Park, off Mattock
Lane, Ealing, London; extension, 1768
Guildhall, Guildhall Yard, City of London;
front, 1788–89
Cranbury Park, near Eastleigh, Hampshire;
c. 1780 (additions 1830s)
42–6 Chiswell Street, City of London, c. 1790
(thought to be by)
Stratton Park, East Stratton, Hampshire, 1803
(only portico survives)
Mount Stewart, Newtownards, Co. Down,
Ireland, 1803 (enlarged 1825)
Theatre Royal, Beauford Square, Bath, Avon,
1804 *below*

Coleorton Hall, near Ashby-de-la-Zouch,
Leicestershire, 1804–08 (additions 1862)
East Stratton, Hampshire; model village, 1806
Royal College of Surgeons, Lincoln's Inn Fields,
Holborn, London; south side façade and
portico, 1806–13 (interior gutted and
remodelled after World War II)
St Mary's Church, Micheldever, Hampshire;
nave, 1808–10
Laxton Hall, near Corby, Northamptonshire;
interiors, 1812

Daniell, Thomas
Sezincote House, near Chipping Norton,
Gloucestershire; garden buildings in grounds,
c. 1808

Darley, Frederick
King's Inns, Henrietta Street, Dublin, Ireland;
Library, 1827

Darley, Hugh
Trinity College, Dublin, Ireland; completion of
Dining Hall, 1760 (damaged by fire in 1984)
Mayoralty House, Drogheda, Co. Louth,
Ireland, c. 1760
Flour mill, on the River Boyne, Slane,
Co. Meath, Ireland, 1763–76 (thought to be by)

Davis, Whitmore
Charleville, Enniskerry, Co. Wicklow, Ireland,
1797

Deane, Thomas
Commercial Buildings, South Mall, Cork,
Co. Cork, Ireland, 1811

Dent, Isaac
Watts' Charity, High Street, Rochester, Kent,
1771

Dickson, Richard and Robert
Town Hall, Leith, Lothian, 1827–28

Dixon, Joseph
St Mary's Church, Battersea Church Road,
Battersea, London, 1775–77

Dobson, John (1787–1865)
Cheeseburn Grange, Northumberland, 1813
and 1819
Prestwick Lodge, near Ponteland,
Northumberland, 1815

Doxford Hall, Northumberland, 1818 (since
altered)
Swansfield House, Alnwick, Northumberland,
1823
Angerton Hall, Northumberland, 1823
Longhirst Hall, near Morpeth, Northumberland,
1824–28 *below*

Nunnykirk Hall, Morpeth, Northumberland, 1825
Mitford Hall, Northumberland, c. 1828
St Thomas's Church, Barras Bridge, Newcastle-
upon-Tyne, Tyne and Wear, 1828–29
Castle House, Harbottle, Northumberland, 1829
Lilburn Tower, Northumberland, 1829–37
(interior mutilated)

Donaldson, James
Holy Trinity Church, Cottage Place, South
Kensington, London, 1826–29

Donthorn, William John (1799–1859)
Westacre High House, Westacre, Norfolk;
remodelling, 1829
Upton Hall, Nottinghamshire, c. 1830
Highcliffe Castle, Hampshire; remodelling,
1830–34 (now a ruin)

Doull, Alexander
Eliot Place, Blackheath, London, 1792–1805

Dreghorn, Allan
St Andrew's Church, St Andrew's Square,
Glasgow, Strathclyde, 1739–56

Dubois, Nicholas (d. 1735)
Of French birth, he served in the British army
and was appointed master mason to the Board
of Works in 1719. As translator of Leoni's
Architecture of Andrea Palladio 1715 edition, he was
an originator of the Palladian style. Apart from
Stanmer House, he designed the hanging
staircase at Chevening, Kent
Stanmer House, near Brighton, East Sussex,
1722–27

Ducart, Davis
Custom House, Limerick, Co. Limerick,
Ireland, 1765–69
Mercy Hospital (formerly Mayoralty House),
Prospect Row, Cork, Co. Cork, Ireland, 1765–73
Lota, Glanmire, Co. Cork, Ireland, c. 1765
Kilshannig, Rathcormack, Co. Cork, Ireland,
c. 1765
Castletown Cox, Piltown, Co. Kilkenny, Ireland,
1767–71
Florence Court, Enniskillen, Co. Fermanagh,
Ireland; wings, c. 1770 (thought to be by)

Duff, Thomas
Roman Catholic Cathedral, Newry, Co. Down,
Ireland, begun in 1825

Ebdon, Christopher
Assembly Room, Theatre, Truro, Cornwall 1772
(now offices)

Eboral, W
Warwick Arms Hotel, High Street, Warwick,
c. 1790

Edmonds, Christopher
St Paul's Church, Rectory Grove, Clapham,
London, 1815

Edwards, Francis (1784–1857)
St John the Baptist's Church, New North Road,
Homerton, London, 1825–29
Holmbush, near Cuckfield, West Sussex, 1829

Edwards, Thomas
Prince's House, Prince's Street, Truro, Cornwall,
1737
Mansion House, Prince's Street, Truro,
Cornwall, c. 1755

Edwards, William (1719–89)
A bridge-builder from south Wales who, in 1751,
invented the use of perforated haunches to
remove the pressures to which the single arch
of his bridge over the Taff had succumbed
Bridge (over River Taff), Pontypridd, mid-
Glamorgan, 1755–56

Edwin, Richard
Stratford Place, Marylebone, London, 1774

Eglington, Samuel
County Hall, Bayley Lane, Coventry,
Warwickshire, c. 1760–84 (thought to be by)

Elliot, Archibald the Younger (1760–1823)
Glenorchy church, Strathclyde, 1808–11
Mausoleum, Callendar House, central Scotland,
1816
Waterloo Place, Edinburgh, 1819
The Haining, Borders, c. 1820
Gaol, Jedburgh, Borders 1823
Royal Bank of Scotland, Royal Exchange
Square, Glasgow, Strathclyde, 1827
with James Elliot
Stobo Castle, near Peebles, Borders, 1805–11
Taymouth Castle, near Aberfeldy, Tayside,
1806–10

Elliot, James (1770–1810)
Church, Glen Orchy, Strathclyde, 1810–11

Elliot, William
Crailing House, Borders, 1803

Elmes, James (1782–1862)
Vice-President of the Royal Architectural Society
1809–48, he published *Letters on Architecture*,
1823, and *Memoirs of the Life and Works of Sir
Christopher Wren*, 1823
St John's Church, St John's Street, Chichester,
West Sussex, 1812 *below*

Emlyn, Henry (*c.* 1729–1815)
Published *A Proposition for a New Order in Architecture* in 1781 and introduced his division of the upper portion of the shaft into two columns as discussed in the book into the tetrastyle portico at Beaumont Lodge
Beaumont Lodge, Berkshire; improvements, 1789

Ensor, George
Furness, Naas, Co. Kildare, Ireland, *c.* 1735 (thought to be by)
Merrion Square, Dublin, Ireland; laid out possibly under control of, begun 1762
Rotunda Assembly Rooms, Parnell Street, Dublin, Ireland, 1764 (extended *c.* 1785)
Ardress House, near Armagh, Co. Armagh, Ireland; remodelling, *c.* 1770
Infirmary, Armagh, Co. Armagh, Ireland, 1774

Ensor, John
Parnell Square, Dublin, Ireland; north side, *c.* 1755

Espin, Thomas
The Priory, Eastgate, Louth, Lincolnshire; own house, 1818

Essex, James (1722–84)
Trinity Bridge, Cambridge, Cambridgeshire 1763–65
Clare College, Cambridge, Cambridgeshire; Chapel completion, 1764–69
Kenmare House, 74 Trumpington Street, Cambridge, Cambridgeshire, 1768
Emmanuel College, Cambridge, Cambridgeshire; street front, 1769
Sidney Sussex College, Cambridge, Cambridgeshire; Chapel and Library, 1776–87
with William Etherbridge
Mathematical Bridge, Queen's College, Cambridge, Cambridgeshire, 1749

Etty, William
Mansion House, St Helen's Square, York, North Yorkshire, 1726–33

Evans, Charles
Badminton House, Avon; St Michael's Church in the grounds, 1785

Evans, William (*c.* 1764–1842)
Gaunt's House, near Hinton Martell, Dorset, 1809 (additions 1880s)

Eveleigh, John
Camden Crescent, Bath, Avon, 1788
Somerset Place, Bath, Avon, *c.* 1790
Grosvenor Place, London Road, Bath, Avon, 1791
Windsor Terrace, Clifton, Bristol, Avon, 1793 (thought to be by)

Eykyns, Roger
St Paul's Church, St Paul's Square, Birmingham, West Midlands, 1777–79

Farrell, William
Court House, East Bridge Street, Enniskillen, Co. Fermanagh, Ireland; remodelling, 1821
Court House, Carrick-on-Shannon, Co. Leitrim, Ireland, *c.* 1825
with Charles Lilly
Portaferry House, Portarlington, Co. Laois, Ireland, 1790–1814

Fear, James
5, Albemarle Row, Bristol, Avon, 1762

Field, John
Ickworth, near Bury St Edmunds, Suffolk; completion, *c.* 1830

Fieldhouse, John
School house, Waterloo Road, Cranbrook, Kent, 1727–29

Flitcroft, Henry (1698–1769)
The last of the original Palladians, he was the son of Jeffry Flitcroft, the royal gardener at Hampton Court. He graduated in carpentry, 1719, and worked with Kent for the Earl of Burlington. He edited *The Designs of Inigo Jones,* published in 1727, and served on the Board of Works where he achieved the position of Comptroller of Works in England in 1758. He was architect to Frederick, Prince of Wales for the rebuilding of Carlton House, 1733
Boreham House, near Chelmsford, Essex, 1728 (altered)
Craven Street, Charing Cross, London; laid out, 1728–30
Bower House, Havering-atte-Bower, London, 1729 (wings added *c.* 1800)
St Giles-in-the-Fields, St Giles High Street, Holborn, London, 1731–33
36 Sackville Street, Piccadilly, London, 1732
Wentworth Woodhouse, near Rawmarsh, South Yorkshire; east front, begun 1734
7 Duke of York Street, Westminster, London, 1736
St Mary's Church, Stoke Edith, Hereford and Worcester, 1740 (thought to be by)
5 and 6 Bloomsbury Square, Bloomsbury, London, *c.* 1740–50 (thought to be by)
Lady Rockingham's Farm, Wentworth Woodhouse, near Rawmarsh, South Yorkshire; barn, 1742–24
Wimpole Hall, near Cambridge, Cambridgeshire; refacing of south entrance front, 1742–45
Stourhead, near Gillingham, Wiltshire; Temple of Flora in grounds, 1745–55
Woburn Abbey, Woburn, Bedfordshire; west front, 1747–61
Wimpole Hall, near Cambridge, Cambridgeshire, St Andrew's Church in the grounds, 1748–49 (altered 1887)
Fort Belvedere, Great Park, Windsor, Hampshire, *c.* 1750 (enlarged 1827–30)
Milton House, near Northampton, Northamptonshire; rebuilding and remodelling, 1750–55
Stourhead, near Gillingham, Wiltshire; Temple of Hercules or Pantheon in grounds, 1754–56
Stourhead, near Gillingham, Wiltshire; Temple of the Sun or of Apollo in the grounds, 1767

Forbes, John
Dorset House, Pittville Town, Cheltenham, Gloucestershire, *c.* 1825
Pittville Pump Room, Cheltenham, Gloucestershire, 1825–30
Segrave Place, Pittville Central Drive, Cheltenham, Gloucestershire, *c.* 1825–30 (thought to be by)
St Paul's Church, St Paul's Road, Cheltenham, Gloucestershire, 1827–31

Foss, John (1745–1827)
Clifton Castle, near Masham, North Yorkshire, 1802–10

Foster, James
Holy Trinity, Kingswood, near Bristol, Avon, 1819–21
Upper and Lower Arcades, Horsefair, Bristol, Avon, 1824–25

Foster, John (*c.* 1759–1827)
St Luke's Church, St Luke's Place, Liverpool, Merseyside, 1802 (gutted)
Exchange (now Town Hall), Liverpool, Merseyside; rebuilding, from 1802

Foster, John (*c.* 1787–1846)
Studied under James Wyatt; he discovered the sculptures from the pediment of the Temple of Athene at Aegina
St Andrew's Church, Rodney Street, Liverpool, Merseyside, 1823–24
St James's Cemetery, Liverpool, Merseyside, 1827–29

Foulston, John (1772–1842)
Town Hall, Ker Street, Devonport, Devon, 1821–23
Library (now Oddfellows' Hall), Ker Street, Devonport, Devon, *c.* 1821
Albemarle Villas and St Michael's Terrace, Plymouth, Devon, 1825–36

Fowler, Charles (1792–1867)
Syon House, Brentford, London, conservatory in the grounds, 1827–30
Covent Garden Market, Covent Garden, London; the Piazza, *c.* 1828–30

Frampton, James
St Nicholas's Church, Moreton, Dorset, 1776

Fraser, Major
St Andrew's Church, George Street, Edinburgh, 1785

Gabb, Thomas
St Thomas of Canterbury's Church, Terminus Road, Cowes, Isle of Wight, 1796

Galilei, Alessandro
St Werburgh's Church, next to Dublin Castle, Dublin, Ireland, *c.* 1715 (front thought to be by)
Castletown, Celbridge, Co. Kildare, Ireland, begun *c.* 1719

Gandon, James (1743–1823)
Articled to Sir William Chambers; he published the continuation of Campbell's *Vitruvius Britannicus* with J Woolfe in 1767–71. He was the winner of the first Gold Medal for Architecture at the Royal Academy in 1768 and was an original member of the Royal Irish Academy
Shire Hall, High Pavement, Nottingham, Nottinghamshire, 1770–72 (altered and extended)
Customs House, Dublin, Ireland, begun in 1781
below

Parliament House (now Bank of Ireland), College Green, Dublin, Ireland; extensions, 1782
Church, Coolbanagher, Co. Laois, Ireland, 1785 (altered)
Rotunda Assembly Rooms, Parnell Street, Dublin, Ireland; additions, *c.* 1785
Four Courts, Dublin, Ireland, 1786–1802
St Peter's Church, Port Laoise, Co. Laois, Ireland, *c.* 1790 (thought to be by)
Emo Park, Portarlington, Co. Laois, Ireland, begun 1791
Emsworth, Malahide, Co. Dublin, Ireland, *c.* 1795
Carrigglas Manor, near Longford, Co. Longford, Ireland; farmyard-stable complex, *c.* 1795
King's Inns, Henrietta Street, Dublin, Ireland, begun 1800

Gandy (later **Deering**), **John Peter** (1787–1850)
He travelled in Greece 1811–13, was MP for Aylesbury and High Sheriff of Buckinghamshire in 1840. He published the *Rural Architect* in 1805
St Mark's Church, North Audley Street, London, 1825–28
Stamford and Rutland Hospital, Deeping Road, Stamford, Lincolnshire, 1826
Pimlico Literary Institute, Ebury Street, London, 1830

Gandy, Joseph Michael (1771–1843)
A pupil of Wyatt, he received the Pope's medal for architecture in 1795. He exhibited at the Royal Academy 1789–1838, executed many drawings for Sir John Soane and contributed illustrations to Britton's *Architectural Antiquities*

Lancaster Castle, Lancashire; reconstruction, 1802–23
Storr's Hall, near Windermere, Cumbria, 1808–11
Doric House, Sion Hill, Bath, Avon, *c.* 1810
Garbally Court, Ballinasloe, Co. Galway, 1819 (thought to be by)
Swerford House, Hook Norton, Oxfordshire; remodelling, 1824
St Anne's House, 363 Kennington Lane, Kennington, London, *c.* 1825 (thought to be by)

Garbett, Edward William
Holy Trinity Church, Theale, Berkshire, 1820–22

Garbett, William (*c.* 1770–1834)
St John's Hospital south side, High Street, Winchester, Hampshire, 1817 (altered 1831) *below*

Gardner, Thomas
St Mary's Church, Mill Road, Cromford, Derbyshire, 1792 (altered later)

Garling, Henry (1789–1870)
Corn Exchange (former), High Street, Guildford, Surrey, 1818 (altered 1935)

Garlive, John
St John the Baptist's Church, Knutsford, Cheshire, 1741–44

Garrett, Daniel
Wallington Hall, near Morpeth, Northumberland; south and north fronts, *c.* 1735–53; the south side, *below*

Library (attached to side of cathedral), Newcastle-upon-Tyne, Tyne and Wear, 1736 (thought to be by)
The Hall, Gibside, Tyne and Wear; Gothic Banqueting House, 1744
Rothley Castle, near Morpeth, Northumberland, date unknown

Garrett, James
Powderham Castle, near Dawlish, Devon; completion, *c.* 1754 (later altered)

Gayfere, Thomas the Elder
Sherwood and Lydia House, Dartmouth Grove, Blackheath, London, 1776 (thought to be by)

Gibbs, James (1682–1754)
Born near Aberdeen of Catholic parents, he trained for the priesthood before turning his attention to architecture. He was a pupil of Carlo Fontana in Rome, and returned to Britain in 1709. His London church of St Martin-in-the-Fields had an enormous influence on the ecclesiastical architecture of the period, especially on the new churches of the American colonies. His two pattern books, *The Book of Architecture* published in 1728, and the *Rules for Drawing the Several Parts of Architecture*, proved to be fundamental to the builders of modest Georgian homes. He did not belong either to the high English baroque or to the Palladian schools of architecture although he practised while they were fashionable. Gibbs followed Dickins as one of the two surveyors to the Commission for the fifty new churches when the latter resigned in 1713.
St Mary-le-Strand Church, Strand, London, 1714–17 *below*

Sudbrook Park, Sudbrook Lane, Richmond-upon-Thames, London, *c.* 1717–20
Wimpole Hall, near Cambridge, Cambridgeshire; library wing, 1719–21
The Octagon, Orleans Road, Twickenham, London, 1720
Ditchley Park, near Woodstock, Oxfordshire, 1720–31
St Peter's Church, Vere Street, Marylebone, London, 1721–24
St Martin-in-the-Fields Church, Trafalgar Square, London, 1722–26
Senate House, Cambridge, Cambridgshire; improvements, 1722–30
All Saints' Cathedral Church, Derby, Derbyshire, 1723–25 (excluding sixteenth-century tower)
King's College, Cambridge, Cambridgeshire; Fellows' Buildings, 1723–29
Stowe, near Buckingham, Buckinghamshire; Boycott Pavilions in the grounds, *c.* 1726 (altered)
St Bartholomew's Hospital, West Smithfield, City of London; main quadrangle, 1730–59
16 Arlington Street, Piccadilly, London, 1736 (altered)
Radcliffe Library, Oxford, Oxfordshire, 1737–49 *top right*

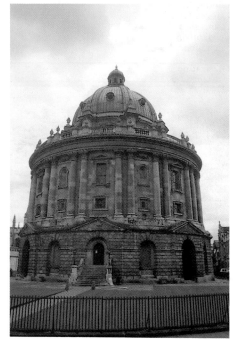

Stowe, near Buckingham, Buckinghamshire; Palladian bridge in the grounds, *c.* 1738–42 (attributed to)
St Cuthbert's Church, Kirkleatham, Cleveland; mausoleum, 1740
Stowe, near Buckingham, Buckinghamshire; Gothic Temple in the grounds, *c.* 1741 *below*

Turner's Hospital, Kirkleatham, Cleveland; rebuilding, 1741–47
St Mary's Church, Patshull, Staffordshire, 1742 (partly reconstructed 1874)
Town Hall (formerly Bank Hall), Sankey Street, Warrington, Cheshire, 1750
Patshull Hall, Patshull, Staffordshire; rebuilding, 1750–54 (altered 1855)
Ragley Hall, near Stratford-upon-Avon, Warwickshire; great hall, *c.* 1750
St Nicholas's Church West, Aberdeen; rebuild of nave, 1752–55
Stable, Compton Verney, near Stratford-upon-Avon, Warwickshire, date unknown

Gibson, George the Younger
Stone house, 281 Lewisham Way, Lewisham, London, 1771–73
Local History Library (formerly Woodlands), Mycenae Road, Greenwich, London, 1774

Gibson, Jesse
Claybury Hall, Woodford Bridge, Woodford, London, 1790

Gilbert, Thomas
St George's Church, Portland, Dorset, 1754–66

Giles, Robert
St Cuthbert's Roman Catholic Church, Albion Road, North Shields, Tyne and Wear, 1821

Gillow, Richard
Custom House, St George's Quay, Lancaster, Lancashire, 1764
Leighton Hall, near Carnforth, Lancashire; alterations, *c.* 1810

Glascodine, Samuel
Exchange Market, High Street, Bristol, Avon, 1744–45 *below*

Golden, Robert
Old Ship Hotel, West Street, Brighton, East Sussex; assembly room, 1767 *below*

Goodridge, Henry Edmund (1797–1864)
Beckford Tower, Lansdown, Bath, Avon, *c.* 1825
The Corridor, off High Street, Bath, Avon, 1825 *below*

Montebello, Bathwick Hill, Bath, Avon, 1828
Prior Park, Bath, Avon; external staircase, wings and interiors, 1829–34 and 1836

Goodwin, Francis (1784–1835)
St Matthew's Church, Walsall, West Midlands; remodelling, 1820–21 (later altered)
Holy Trinity, Camp Hill, Bardesley, West Midlands, 1820–23
Christ Church, High Street, West Bromwich, West Midlands, 1821–28
Town Hall and Assembly Rooms, Macclesfield, Cheshire, 1823–24
Gaol, Vernon street, Derby, Derbyshire, 1823–27 (altered 1880)
St Leonard, Bilston, West Midlands, 1826 (later alterations)
St George's Church, Chester Road, Hulme, Manchester, 1826–28

St Mary's Church, Oxford Street, Bilston, West Midlands, 1829–30

Graham, James Gillespie (1776–1855)
On his marriage he assumed the name of Graham or Graeme. He was responsible for introducing a purer gothic into Scotland and aided Pugin with the design of Victoria Hall, Edinburgh, 1842–44
Culdees Castle, Tayside, *c.* 1810 (burnt 1887, restored 1910)
Bowland House, Stow, Borders, *c.* 1811 (thought to be by; additions in 1890 and 1926)
Ross Priory, Strathclyde; remodelling, 1812
St Mary's Cathedral, Broughton Street, Edinburgh, 1813–14 (later alterations)
Edmondstone Castle, Strathclyde, 1815
Church, Clackmannan, central Scotland, 1815
Barr House (formerly Glenbarr Abbey), Kintyre, Strathclyde, *c.* 1815 (thought to be by)
Drumtochty Castle, near Laurencekirk, Grampian *c.* 1815
Torrisdale Castle, Kintyre, Strathclyde, *c.* 1815 (thought to be by)
Kilkerran House, Dailly, Strathclyde; addition of wings, *c.* 1815
St Andrew's Cathedral, Great Clyde Street, Glasgow, Strathclyde, 1816
Cambusnethan Priory, Wishaw, Strathclyde, 1816–19
Duns Castle, Borders, 1818–22
Moray Place, Edinburgh, 1822–30
Dunninald House, Craig, Tayside, 1823–24

Green, John
Buckland Filleigh House, Devon, 1810
Library and Philosophical Institute, Westgate Road, Newcastle-upon-Tyne, Tyne and Wear, 1822

Greenway, Francis Howard (1777–1837)
with Joseph Kay
Assembly Room, The Mall, Clifton, Avon, 1806–11

Greg, Samuel
Quarry Bank Silk Mill, Styal, Cheshire, 1784

Groves, John Thomas (*d.*1811)
He lived in Italy between 1780–90, and on returning to England exhibited Italian subjects at the Royal Academy. He was Clerk of Works for the districts of St James, Whitehall and Westminster from 1794 and was appointed architect to the General Post Office in 1807
Bath House, Bath Square, Tunbridge Wells, Kent, *c.* 1804 (mutilated)

Gummow, Benjamin
Brogyntyn, near Oswestry, Shropshire; portico, 1814

Gwilt, George senior (1746–1807)
Surveyor of Surrey *c.* 1770, district surveyor of St George's, Southwark, 1774 and surveyor to Surrey Sewers Commission *c.* 1777; he was patronised by Henry Thrale the brewer and was architect to the West India Dock Company
London Fire Brigade Training Centre (formerly workhouses), Southwark Bridge Road, Southwark, London, 1777

Gwynn, John (*d.* 1786)
He was also known as Gwyn or Gwynne. Along with S Wale, in 1749 he published *Wren's Plan for rebuilding the City of London after the Great Fire in 1666.* A member of the committee for creating the Royal Academy in 1755, he became an original member in 1768; he was also the surveyor of Oxford and a friend of Dr Johnson, who assisted with several of his writings
Severn Bridge, Atcham, Shropshire, 1769–71
English Bridge, Shrewsbury, Shropshire, 1769–74 (altered 1926)
Severn Bridge, Worcester, Hereford and Worcester, 1771–80
Magdalen Bridge, Oxford, Oxfordshire, 1772–90

The Covered Markets, Oxford, Oxfordshire, 1773–74 (reconstructed 1839)

Habershon, Matthew (1789–1852)
St Peter's Church, Belper, Derbyshire, 1824

Hague, Daniel
St Paul's Church, Portland Square, Bristol, Avon, 1789–95 (in disrepair) *below*

Hakewill, Henry (1771–1830)
The eldest son of painter and decorator John Hakewell (1742–91), who had worked on the decorations at Blenheim
Rugby School, Rugby, Warwickshire; quadrangle, 1809–16
Holy Trinity Church, Old Wolverton, Buckinghamshire, 1810–15 (altered *c.* 1870)
Packington Hall, West Midlands; external terraces, 1812
Judge's Lodging, Northgate Street, Warwick, Warwickshire, 1814
St Peter's Church, Eaton Square, London, 1824–27
Wormington Grange, Gloucestershire; enlargement, 1826–27

Halfpenny, William
Thought to have been a carpenter by training, he moved to Bristol *c.* 1740, where he succeeded to the practice of John Strahan. He is best known for his *Companions*, or pattern books, of which there are about 20, covering rococo and gothic styles

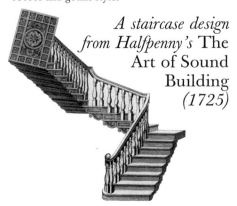

A staircase design from Halfpenny's The Art of Sound Building *(1725)*

Coopers' Hall, King Street, Bristol, Avon, 1743
Stout's Hill, near Stroud, Gloucestershire, 1743
(thought to be by)
with John Strahan
Redland Chapel, Redland Green, Bristol, Avon,
1740–43

Hall, John
Terrace (on the Green), Beaumaris, Anglesey,
Gwynedd, 1824

Hamilton, David (1768–1843)
Hutcheson's Hospital, Ingram Street, Glasgow,
Strathclyde, 1802–05
Airth Castle, central Scotland; new entrance
front, 1807–09
Kincaid Castle, central Scotland; remodelling,
c. 1812
Town Steeple, Falkirk, central Scotland, 1814
Castle Toward, Toward Point, Cowal,
Strathclyde, 1820–21
Church, Bothwell, Strathclyde, c. 1825–33
Stirling's Library (formerly Royal Exchange),
Royal Exchange Square, Glasgow, Strathclyde,
1827–29
Keir, central Scotland; enlargement, 1829–34

Hamilton, James
Gloucester Row, Weymouth, Dorset; southern
end of terrace, c. 1790
St Mary's Church, St Mary Street, Weymouth,
Dorset, 1815–17

Hamilton, Thomas (1784–1858)
Burns Monument, Alloway, Strathclyde,
1820–23
Royal High School, Regent Road, Calton Hill,
Edinburgh, 1825–29
Town Hall, Ayr, Strathclyde, 1828–30 (Wallace
Tower added 1831–34)

Hamilton, William
St Andrew's Square, Glasgow, Strathclyde,
c. 1786 (houses now much altered)

Hanbury-Tracy, Charles (Lord Sudeley)
(1778–1858)
Toddington Manor, near Cheltenham,
Gloucestershire, 1820–35

Hannaford, Joseph
with John Kent
St James's Church, Poole, Dorset, 1819–21

Hannan, Nicholas and William
Court House, Limerick, Co. Limerick, Ireland,
1810

Hansom & Welch
Joseph Aloysius Hansom (1803–82) and Edward
Welch (1806–88)
Gaol, Beaumaris, Anglesey, Gwynedd, 1828–29
Victoria Terrace, Beaumaris, Anglesey,
Gwynedd, 1830–35
Bodelwyddan Hall, Clwyd, c. 1830–40

Hardwick, Philip (1792–1870)
Youngest son of Thomas Hardwick, he exhibited
drawings at the Royal Academy including his
buildings at St Katherine's Docks, London,
Euston Railway Station and designs for
Lincoln's Inn. He was vice-president of the
Institute of British Architects in 1839 and 1841,
and treasurer of the Royal Academy, 1850–61
Holy Trinity Church, Trinity Street, Bolton,
Greater Manchester, 1823–25
Christ Church, Cosway Street, London, 1824–25
Babraham Hall, Cambridgeshire, 1829–32
Goldsmiths' Hall, Foster Lane, City of London,
1829–35

Hardwick, Thomas (1752–1829)
Pupil and biographer of Sir William Chambers,
he exhibited at the Royal Academy 1772–1805
St Mary's Church, Wanstead, London, 1787–90
Bromley College, College Road, Bromley,
London; quadrangle, 1794–1805

Shire Hall, High West Street, Dorchester,
Dorset, 1795–97
St John the Baptist's Church, St John's Wood
Road, St John's Wood, London, 1813
St Mary's Church, Marylebone Road,
Marylebone, London, 1813–17
St John's Church, Washington Street,
Workington, Cumbria, 1822–23 (tower added
later)
St Barnabas' Church, King Square, Finsbury,
London, 1822–26
Holy Trinity, Trinity Street, Bolton, Greater
Manchester, 1823–25
with T Wood
Nelson Column, Castle Green, Hereford,
Hereford and Worcester, 1806–09

Hardy, W
Letheringsett Hall, Holt, Norfolk; remodelling,
1808

Hargrave, Abraham
Dunkathel (also known as Dunkettle),
Glanmire, Co. Cork, Ireland, c. 1785 (thought
to be by)
Protestant Church, Fermoy, Co. Cork, Ireland,
1802

Hargrave, John
Gaol, Trim, Co. Meath, Ireland, c. 1827
Court House, Dungannon, Co. Tyrone, Ireland,
1830

Harris, Daniel (d. c. 1835)
Braziers Park, near Ipsden, Oxfordshire, 1799

Harrison, Henry (c. 1785–c. 1865)
Richmond Terrace, Whitehall, London,
1822–25
Bignor Park, West Sussex, 1826–28
General Lying-in Hospital, York Road, Lambeth,
London, 1828
Port Eliot, near Saltash, Cornwall; entrance hall
and porch, 1829

Harrison, Thomas (1744–1829)
Studied in Rome; he was admitted to the
Academy of St Luke and was decorated by
Pope Clement XIV
Skerton Bridge, Lancaster, Lancashire, 1783–88
St John's Church, North Road, Lancaster,
Lancashire; tower, 1784
Lancaster Castle, Lancashire, reconstruction
1788–1802; further reconstruction 1802–23 by
J M Gandy
County Court, Prison, Armoury and Barracks,
Chester, Cheshire, 1788–1822 (within castle)
Stramongate Bridge, Kendal, Cumbria, 1793–94
Quernmore Park Hall, near Lancaster,
Lancashire, 1795–98 (thought to be by)
Broomhall, Fife, 1796–99
Lyceum Club, Bold Street, Liverpool,
Merseyside, 1800–02
Portico Library (now Lloyd's Bank), Mosley
Street, Manchester, 1802–06
News Room, Northgate Street, Chester,
Cheshire, 1808
North Gate, Chester, Cheshire, 1808–10
Gredington, near Hanmer, Clwyd, 1810–15
Woodbank Park, Woodbank, Stockport, Greater
Manchester, 1812
Allerton (or Grove) House, Liverpool,
Merseyside, c. 1815 (gutted)
Anglesey Column, Anglesey, Gwynedd, 1816
St Martin's Lodge, Castle Esplanade, Chester,
Cheshire; for himself, c. 1820
Watergate House, Watergate Street, Chester,
Cheshire, 1820
Memorial Arch, Holyhead, Anglesey, Gwynedd,
1824
Hawkstone Park, Shropshire; citadel in the
grounds, 1824–25
Grosvenor Bridge, Chester, Cheshire, 1827–33

Harvey, John
Shire Hall, Market Place, Stafford, Staffordshire;
to plan supplied by Samuel Wyatt, 1794–99

Harvey, JT
Higher Terrace, Torquay, Devon, c. 1811
Park Place, Park Crescent and Vaughan Parade,
Torquay, Devon, c. 1830
Beacon Terrace, Torquay, Devon, date unknown

Hawksmore, Nicholas (1661–1736)
Employed by Wren as deputy surveyor of
Chelsea Hospital, 1682–90, clerk of works at
Greenwich Hospital, 1698, and of Kensington
Palace, 1691–1715; as secretary to the Board of
Works and deputy surveyor, he assisted Wren
at St Paul's, 1678–1710, and Vanbrugh at Castle
Howard (1702–14) and Blenheim, 1710–15. He
erected the library at Queen's College, Oxford,
1700–59, and the south quadrangle, 1710–59;
he was appointed Surveyor-General of
Westminster Abbey in 1723. The most
fascinating of all English architects for his
expression of strong, even violent, emotion in
his buildings; his obsessive love of stone and of
the stern grandeur of ancient Roman architecture;
his integration of the old gothic tradition with
classicism; his eccentricity and the intensity
which enabled his genius to emerge from the
shadow of Wren and Vanbrugh
Clarendon Building, Oxford, Oxfordshire,
1711–15 *below*

St Alfege's Church, Greenwich High Road,
Greenwich, London, 1711–18
St George-in-the-East Church, Cannon Street
Road, Whitechapel, London, 1714–29 (gutted)
Christ Church, Fournier Street, Spitalfields,
London, 1714–29
St Anne's Church, Newell Street, Limehouse,
London, 1714–30
St Michael's Church, Cornhill, City of London;
tower, 1715–22
St Mary Woolnoth Church, Lombard Street,
City of London, 1716–27 (interior altered 1875)
St George's Church, Bloomsbury Way,
Bloomsbury, London, 1716–31
All Souls College, Oxford, Oxfordshire;
extensions to North Quadrangle, 1716–35 *below*

Blenheim Palace, Oxfordshire, begun by
  Vanbrugh, 1722–23 *above, reproduced by kind
  permission of His Grace the Duke of Marlborough*
2 Fournier Street, Spitalfields, London, 1726
  (originally a rectory)
Blenheim Palace, Oxfordshire; Chapel, 1726–31
Blenheim Palace, Oxfordshire; Woodstock Gate,
  1727
Castle Howard, near Malton, North Yorkshire;
  mausoleum, 1729
10 Fair Street (former rectory), Bermondsey,
  London, 1730–35 (thought to be by)
Westminster Abbey, London; addition of west
  towers and gable, 1734–45
with John James
St Luke's Church, Old Street, Finsbury, London,
  1727–33

Haycock, Edward (1790–1870)
Royal Salop Infirmary, St Mary's Place,
  Shrewsbury, Shropshire, 1826 (in consultation
  with **Sir Robert Smirke**)
Shire Hall, Monmouth, Gwent, 1829–30
St George's Church, Drinkwater Street,
  Frankwell, Shropshire, 1829–32
St David, Barmouth, Gwynedd, 1830
Clytha Park, near Abergavenny, Gwent, c. 1830

Haycock, John Hiram (1759–1830)
Millington's Hospital, Frankwell, Shrewsbury,
  Shropshire, 1785
Allat's School (now a Health Centre),
  Shrewsbury, Shropshire, c. 1799–1810
Sweeney Hall, Shropshire, 1805
Gunley Hall, Forden, Powys, 1810
with Thomas Telford
County Gaol, Howard Street, Shrewsbury,
  Shropshire, 1787–93

Hayward, Abraham
Disney Place, Eastgate, Lincoln, Lincolnshire,
  1736

Hayward, William
Judge's Lodging, Castle Hill, Lincoln,
  Lincolnshire, c. 1810

Hemsley, Henry
St George's Church, Church Hill, Ramsgate,
  Kent, 1824–27

Henderson, John (1804–62)
Assembly Rooms, George Street, Edinburgh,
  1784–87
Stable, Amisfield Mains, Lothian, 1785

Henderson (alias Anderson), William
Wilford Hall, near West Bridgford,
  Nottinghamshire, 1781

Hesketh, Lloyd Bamford
Gwrych Castle, near Abergate, Clwyd, c. 1814

Hiorne, David (d. 1758)
Holy Cross Church, Daventry,
  Northamptonshire, 1752–58
Foremark Hall, near Swadlincote, Derbyshire,
  1759–61
with William Hiorne
Wolverley House, Wolverley, Hereford and
  Worcester, 1749–52

Hiorne, Francis (1774–88)
Son of William Hiorne, he was an exponent of
  the gothic style; he was appointed Mayor of
  Warwick three times
see also **Sanderson Miller** and **Committee of
taste**
St Mary's Church, Tetbury, Gloucestershire;
  nave, 1771–81
St Giles's Church, Stony Stratford,
  Buckinghamshire; nave, 1776–77
St Bartholomew's Church, Tardebigge, near
  Bromsgrove, Hereford and Worcester, 1777
Hiorne's Tower, Arundel Park, Arundel, West
  Sussex, c. 1790 *below*

Hiorne, William (1715–76)
He became the principal builder in Warwick,
  following the death of Francis Smith and his
  son. His father, John Hyorn, was Francis
  Smith's mason at Ditchley
Holy Trinity Church, Stratford-upon-Avon,
  Warwickshire, 1763

Holl, Edward (d. 1824)
Dock Chapel, Chatham Docks, Chatham, Kent,
  1808–11

Holland, Henry (1745–1806)
Claremont, Esher, Surrey, 1771 (with Lancelot
  Brown)
Benham Park, near Newbury, Berkshire, 1774
  (with Lancelot Brown, altered 1870)

Brooks's Club, 60 St James's Street, London,
  1776–78
Berrington Hall, near Leominster, Hereford and
  Worcester, 1778–81
Crown Inn, Stone, Staffordshire; new front, 1779
Dover House, Whitehall, London; Whitehall
  portion, 1787
Althorp, Northamptonshire; remodelling
  exterior and part interior, 1787–91
Broadlands (house), near Romsey, Hampshire;
  alterations and redecoration, 1788–92
Woburn Abbey, Woburn, Bedfordshire;
  alterations to the south wing including
  remodelling the interiors, 1788–1802
George Inn (now Bedford Arms Hotel),
  Woburn, Bedfordshire; remodelling, 1790
Woburn Abbey, Woburn, Bedfordshire; Chinese
  Dairy, c. 1791
Avenue House, Church Street, Ampthill,
  Bedfordshire; extensions to 1780 house,
  1792–95
Hale House, Hale, near Salisbury, Hampshire;
  rebuilding, c. 1792
Swan Hotel, Bedford, Bedfordshire, 1794
Southill Park, near Biggleswade, Bedfordshire,
  begun in 1795
Eastern Courtyard, New Street, City of London;
  extensions, 1800 (part elevations only survive)
Albany (originally Melbourne House), off
  Piccadilly, Piccadilly, London; enlargement and
  conversion, 1802–04

Hollis, Charles
All Saints' Church, East India Dock Road,
  Poplar, London, 1821–23

Hope, John
Holy Trinity Church, Church Road, Wavertree,
  Liverpool, Merseyside, 1794 (altered 1911)

Hopper, Thomas (1776–1856)
Leigh Court, Abbots Leigh, Avon, 1814
Terling Place, near Witham, Essex; wings,
  1818–21
Gosford Castle, Markethill, Co. Armagh,
  Ireland, 1819–20
County Gaol, Springfield Road, Chelmsford,
  Essex, 1822–26 (extended)
Woolverstone Hall, near Ipswich, Suffolk;
  addition of wings, 1823
Penrhyn Castle, near Bangor, Gwynedd,
  1825–44
Carlton Club (originally Arthur's), St James's
  Street, Westminster, London, 1826–27
Guildhall, Market Place, Salisbury, Wiltshire;
  enlargements and portico, 1829
Margam Abbey, West Glamorgan, 1830–35
  (gutted)

Horne, James
Holy Trinity Church, Guildford, Surrey, 1763

Humphrey, Charles (1772–1848)
Cold Brayfield House, Buckinghamshire, 1809
Maid's Causeway, Cambridge, Cambridgeshire;
  six houses, 1815–26
Willow Walk, Cambridge, Cambridgeshire;
  houses, 1815–26
Short Street, Cambridge, Cambridgeshire;
  houses, 1815–26
Fair Street, Cambridge, Cambridgeshire; houses,
  1815–26
Shire Hall and Gaol, Lynn Road, Ely,
  Cambridgeshire, 1821–22

Left: *the Corinthian portico of
Carlton House, Pall Mall,
London, converted into a palace
in 1783–96 by Holland for the
Prince of Wales; it was
demolished in 1826*

Hunt, Thomas Frederick (*c.* 1791–1831)
Burns Mausoleum, St Michael's Churchyard, Dumfries, Dumfries and Galloway, 1815
Old Episcopal (now Wesleyan) church, Buccleuch Street, Dumfries, Dumfries and Galloway, *c.* 1815

Hurst, William
Christ Church, Thorne Road, Doncaster, South Yorkshire, 1827–29

Hutt, John
13–21 Clapham Common North Side, Clapham, London, 1714–20

Ingleman, Richard (1777–1838)
Lawn Asylum, Union Road, Lincoln, Lincolnshire, 1819–20

Inwood, William (1771–1843) and **Henry William** (1794–1843)
William was both an architect and surveyor, and published *Tables for the purchasing of Estates* in 1811. Henry William was much travelled, and published many archaeological works
St Pancras Parish Church, Upper Woburn Place, Bloomsbury, London, 1819–22
All Saints' Church, Camden Street, Camden Town, London, 1822
St Mary's Church, Eversholt Street, Somers Town, St Pancras, London, 1822–24

Ireland, Joseph (*c.* 1780–1841)
All Saints' Roman Catholic Church, Hassop, Derbyshire, 1816–18
St Mary's Roman Catholic Church, Vicarage Walk, Walsall, West Midlands, 1825–37
St Peter and St Paul's Roman Catholic Church, North Street, Wolverhampton, West Midlands, 1827–28
St John the Baptist's Roman Catholic Church, Haywood, Staffordshire, 1828 (moved to existing site from Tixall in 1845)

Ireson, Nathaniel (1687–1769)
Variously described as architect, sculptor, builder, designer, quarry owner, land owner, money lender and potter
Ireson House, Grant's Lane, Wincanton, Somerset, *c.* 1726 (altered *c.* 1850)
Ven House, near Sherborne, Somerset, *c.* 1730 (altered and redecorated 1835)
Crowcombe Court, Somerset, 1734 (damaged by fire 1963)
St Mary's Church, Bruton, near Wincanton, Somerset, 1743

Ivory, Thomas
Octagon Chapel, Colegate, Norwich, Norfolk, 1754
Assembly Rooms, Theatre Street, Norwich, Norfolk, 1754
29–35 Surrey Street, Norwich, Norfolk, 1761
Carton, Maynooth, Co. Kildare, Ireland; bridge in grounds, 1763
25 and 27 Surrey Street, Norwich, Norfolk, *c.* 1770
Kilcarty, Kilmessan, Co. Meath, Ireland, *c.* 1770–80
Bluecoat School (former), Blackhall Place, Dublin, Ireland, 1773–80
Westport House, Westport, Co. Mayo, Ireland; additional block, 1778 (thought to be by)
Newcomen's Bank, Castle Street, Dublin, Ireland, *c.* 1780 (enlarged)

Jacobsen, Theodore (*d.* 1772)
Royal Naval Hospital, Gosport, Hampshire, 1745
West Front, Trinity College, College Green, Dublin, Ireland, begun in 1752

Jaffray, George
Old Aberdeen Town House, High Street, Aberdeen, 1788

James, John (1672–1746)
Clerk of works at Greenwich Hospital 1705–46;

he was the surveyor of St Paul's Cathedral, London, Westminster Abbey and, from 1716, the fifty new churches. He was made Master of the Carpenters Company in 1734
St Mary's Church, Church Street, Twickenham, London; body, 1714–15 (interior since altered)
St Lawrence's Church, Whitchurch Lane, Little Stanmore, Harrow, London, 1714–16
St George's Chapel, Tiverton, Devon, 1714–33
Parkhall, Chesterfield Walk, Greenwich, London; own house, 1716–24
St George's, Hanover Square, London, 1720–25
Warbrook house, near Wokingham, Hampshire; own house, 1724
St Alfege's Church, Greenwich High Road, Greenwich, London; steeple, 1730

Jarrat, Major
Old Town Hall (now a museum), Market Street, Lancaster, Lancashire, 1781–83

Jelfe, Andrews
Town Hall, Market Street, Rye, East Sussex, 1743

Jelly, Thomas
North Parade Buildings, Bath, Avon, *c.* 1750
below

King Edward's School, Broad Street, Bath, Avon, 1752–54 *below*

Bladud Buildings, London Road, Bath, Avon, 1755
St James Parade, Bath, Avon, 1768

Jenkins, Edward
St James's Church, Suffolk Square, Cheltenham, Gloucestershire, 1825

Jenkins, the Revd William (*c.* 1763–1844)
Methodist Church, Carver Street, Sheffield, South Yorkshire, 1804
Methodist Church, St Peter's Street, Canterbury, Kent, 1811
Methodist Church, Bondgate, Darlington, Co. Durham, 1812
Walcot Methodist Chapel, London Road, Bath, Avon, 1815–16

Jessop, William
High Peak Canal Junction, Cromford, Derbyshire; aqueduct over River Derwent, 1792
with Benjamin Outram
Cromford Canal, Cromford, Derbyshire, 1793

Johnson, Francis
Armagh Palace, Armagh, Co. Armagh, Ireland; additions, 1786
Townley Hall, Drogheda, Co. Louth, Ireland, 1794
Charleville Forest (or Castle), Tullamore, Co. Offaly, Ireland, *c.* 1795–1800
Galtrim House, Summerhill, Co. Meath, Ireland, *c.* 1802–05
St George's Church, Hardwicke Place, Dublin, Ireland, 1802–13
Chapel Royal, Lower Castle Yard, Dublin Castle, Dublin, Ireland, 1807–14
Court House, Armagh, Co. Armagh, Ireland, 1809
Dobbin House, Scotch Street, Armagh, Co. Armagh, Ireland, *c.* 1810
General Post Office, O'Connell Street, Dublin, Ireland, 1814 (gutted 1916, since rebuilt)
St Catherine's Protestant Church, Tullamore, Co. Offaly, Ireland, 1818

Johnson, James (*d.* 1807)
Royal Mint, Tower Hill, Whitechapel, London; completed by Smirke, 1807–12

Johnson, Joel
St John's Church, Scandrett Street, Wapping, London, 1756
with Boulton Mainwaring
London Hospital, Whitechapel Road, Whitechapel, London, begun 1752 (original survives as core of the extensively revised existing building)

Johnson, John (1754–1814)
County Surveyor of Essex
Terling Place, near Witham, Essex, 1772–78
Woolverstone Hall, near Ipswich, Suffolk, *c.* 1776
Bridge, Chelmsford, Essex, 1787
Shire Hall, Chelmsford, Essex, 1789–91
Bradwell Lodge, Bradwell-on-Sea, Essex; wing only, 1781–86
County Rooms, Hotel Street, Leicester, Leicestershire, 1792–1800
Braxted Park, near Witham, Essex; rebuild of north front, 1804–06
County Hall, High Street, Lewes, East Sussex, 1808

Johnson, Thomas (*d.* 1814)
County Gaol, Northgate Street, Warwick, Warwickshire, 1779–82
St Mary's Church, Hanbury, near Droitwich, Hereford and Worcester, 1792–95 (rebuilding of earlier church which was then later rebuilt in 1860)
Holy Trinity Church, Harrison Road, Halifax, West Yorkshire, 1795
Leeds Library (former), Commercial Street, Leeds, West Yorkshire, 1808
St Nicholas's Church, Banbury Road, Warwick, Warwickshire; tower and spire, date unknown
with Job Collins
St Nicholas's Church, Banbury Road, Warwick, Warwickshire; nave, 1779–80

Jones, Richard
Prior Park, Combe Down, Avon; east wing and building of main house to design of Wood the Elder, 1735–48

Jones & Clark
A practice established in Birmingham
Wollaton Hall, Nottingham, Nottinghamshire; Camellia House in grounds, 1823

Jones, Thomas (*c.* 1794–1859)
Talacre Hall, Clwyd, 1824–27

Jopling, Joseph
Pantechnicon (now Sotheby's, Belgravia), Motcombe Street, London, *c.* 1830

Joy, Robert
Clifton House (originally Poor House), Donegall Street, Belfast, Co. Antrim, Ireland, 1774

Joynes, Henry
Carshalton House, Carshalton, London; water
tower in grounds, c. 1720 (thought to be by)
57 and 58 Lincoln's Inn Fields, Holborn,
London, c. 1730 *below*

Barrington Park, near Witney, Gloucestershire,
1734 (thought to be by)
Linley Hall, near Montgomery, Shropshire,
1743–46

Jupp, Richard (d. 1799)
Chief architect and surveyor to the East India
Company, he was an original member of the
Architects Club, in 1791
Old Bengal Warehouse, New Street, City of
London, 1769
Manor House (now public library), Old Road,
Lee, Lewisham, London, 1771–72
Guy's Hospital, St Thomas Street, Southwark,
London; west wing, 1774–80
Painshill Park, near Weybridge, Surrey, c. 1778
(house thought to be by)
Western Courtyard, New Street, City of
London, 1792–94 (elevations only survive)
Eastern Courtyard, New Street, City of London,
1796–97 (part elevations survive)

Jupp, William (d. 1788)
Brother of Richard Jupp
Severndroog Castle, off Castlewood Drive,
Shooters Hill, London, 1784
Skinners' Hall, Dowgate Hill, City of London,
c. 1801–03 (façade)

Jupp, William the Younger (d. 1839)
Architect to the Skinners and other companies
Merchant Taylors' Almshouses, Lee High Road,
Lee, Lewisham, London, 1826

Kay, Joseph (1775–1847)
Pelham Crescent, Hastings, Hampshire,
1824–28
St Mary-in-the-Castle Church, Pelham Crescent,
Hastings, Hampshire, c. 1826
College Approach, Nelson Road and King
William Walk, Greenwich, London, c. 1829–30

Keck, Anthony
Royal Infirmary, Castle Street, Worcester,
Hereford and Worcester, 1767–70 (altered)
St Martin's Church, Cornmarket, Worcester,
Hereford and Worcester, 1768–72
Moccas Court, near Hereford, Hereford and
Worcester, 1775–81
Margam Abbey, West Glamorgan; orangery,
1787–89

Keene, Henry (1726–76)
He played a notable part in the transition of
rococo classicism into gothic. He was appointed
Surveyor of Westminster Abbey by the Dean
and Chapter at the age of 20, and appointed
Architect of HM Works, Ireland, in 1761
St Mary's Church, Lower Hartwell,
Buckinghamshire, 1753–55 (ruin)
Guildhall, High Wycombe, Buckinghamshire, 1757
Hartwell House, near Aylesbury,
Buckinghamshire; reconstruction of east front,
1759–61
Radcliffe Observatory, Woodstock Road,
Oxford, Oxfordshire, begun in 1772 *top right*

Provost's Lodgings, Worcester College, Oxford,
Oxfordshire, 1773–76
Worcester College, Oxford, Oxfordshire;
quadrangle, north range, completion c. 1775

Kendall, Henry Edward (1776–1875)
Session House and House of Correction,
Spilsby, Lincolnshire, 1824–26
Sessions House, Market Place, Sleaford,
Lincolnshire, 1830
Carr's Hospital, Eastgate, Sleaford, Lincolnshire,
1830 and 1841–46

Kent, William (c. 1685–1715)
Born in Bridlington, East Yorkshire, he was sent
to Italy in 1709 where, working as an artist, he
met the Earl of Burlington in 1719 and returned
to live with him at Burlington House in
London. He edited Burlington's *The Designs of
Inigo Jones,* which was published in 1727. He
was then involved in architecture, landscape
design and interior decoration from the 1730s,
and his tenure on the Board of Works brought
him the commission for the new Horse Guards
block
Odsey House, near Royston, Cambridgeshire,
1722–29
Esher Place, Esher, Surrey; rebuilding, c. 1729
1 Savile Row, Piccadilly, London; interior,
c. 1731
Treasury (facing Horse Guards Parade),
Whitehall, London, 1733–36
Rousham House, near Woodstock, Oxfordshire;
alterations, 1738–41
Wimborne House, 22 Arlington Street,
Piccadilly, London, 1740
44 Berkeley Square, London, 1742–44
Horse Guards, Whitehall, London, c. 1745–48
(built by Vardy c. 1750–60 after Kent's death)
centre right
Wakefield Lodge, Potterspury,
Northamptonshire, 1748–50
Holkham Hall, near Wells-next-the-Sea, Norfolk;
arch in grounds, c. 1740
Badminton House, Avon; alterations c. 1740,
staircase c. 1760
Badminton House, Avon; Worcester Lodge in
the grounds, 1746
with Lord Burlington
Holkham Hall, near Wells-next-the-Sea, Norfolk,
c. 1731

Right: *three buildings that
illustrate Kent's diverse repertoire*

Above: *the Treasury building
entrance, Whitehall;* below,
Horseguards Parade; bottom,
the façade of 44 Berkeley Square

Kirby, John Joshua (1716–74)
Clerk of works at Kensington Palace, he
published the *Perspective of Architecture* in 1761
St Anne's Church, Kew Green, Kew, Richmond-
upon-Thames, London; enlargement of nave,
1768 (altered nineteenth and twentieth
centuries)

Knight, Richard Payne
Downton Castle, near Ludlow, Hereford and
Worcester, begun in 1772

Knight, William
Sebright School, Wolverley, Hereford and
Worcester, c. 1829 (thought to be by)

Laing, David (1774–1856)
Articled to Sir John Soane c. 1790, he was
appointed surveyor of buildings at the Customs
House, London, in 1811
Custom House, Plymouth, Devon, 1810
Custom House, Lower Thames Street, City of
London 1813–17 (centre rebuilt 1825)

Lane, John
Paymaster General's Office, Whitehall, London,
1732–33

Lane, Richard
Tiviot Dale Wesleyan Methodist Chapel,
Stockport, Greater Manchester, 1825–26
Town Hall and Assembly Room, Bexley Square,
Salford, Greater Manchester, 1825–27
St Mary's Church, Church Street, Oldham,
Greater Manchester, 1827–30
Blue Coat School, Horsedge Street, Oldham,
Greater Manchester, 1829–34
Regional College of Art, Grosvenor Square,
Chorlton-on-Medlock, Manchester, 1830
with Francis Goodwin
St Thomas, Broad Street, Pendleton, 1829–31

Lapidge, Edward (1779–1860)
Surveyor of bridges and public works for Surrey
Hildersham Hall, Cambridgeshire, 1814
St Peter's Church, Black Lion Lane,
Hammersmith, London, 1827–28
St John the Baptist's Church, St John's Road,
Hampton Wick, London, 1829–31

Latrobe, Benjamin Henry (1764–1820)
Hammerwood House, near East Grinstead, East
Sussex, 1790–92
Ashdown House (near Forest Row), East Sussex,
1793–94

Leadbetter, Stiff
Nuneham Park, Nuneham Courtenay,
Oxfordshire, 1756–64 (altered)
Shardeloes, near Beaconsfield, Buckinghamshire,
reconstruction 1758–66
Elvills, near Egham, Surrey, 1766
Radcliffe Infirmary, Woodstock Road, Oxford,
Oxfordshire, 1766–70 *below*

Langley Park, near Slough, Buckinghamshire,
1775–78 (altered c. 1855)
with Luke Singleton
Royal Infirmary, off Southgate Street,
Gloucester, Gloucestershire, 1758–61 (enlarged
1827)

Lee, Thomas (1794–1834)
Arlington Court, Devon, 1820–23
Guildhall, High Street, Barnstaple, Devon,
1826–28
with Thomas Ingleman
St Clement's Church, Henwick Road,
Worcester, Hereford and Worcester, 1822–23
(altered in 1879)
All Saints' Church, Vicar Lane, Sedgley, West
Midlands, 1826–29

Legg, William Daniel (d. 1806)
Hopkin's Hospital, St Peter Street, Stamford,
Lincolnshire, c. 1770 (thought to be by)
Town Hall, St Mary's Hill, Stamford,
Lincolnshire, 1777 (thought to be by Legg or
Lovell)
Library (formerly Market), High Street,
Stamford, Lincolnshire, 1804

Leigh, Charles
Adlington Hall, near Wilmslow, Cheshire; main
entrance in west range, c. 1750; his portico was
not added until 1757

Leoni, Giacomo (c. 1686–1746)
Born in Venice, he is said to have been employed
by the Elector Palatine before reaching England
in c. 1713. He spent several years studying and
preparing drawings of Palladio's buildings,
publishing *The Architecture of Andrea Palladio* in
1715. His buildings decisively influenced
English architecture and show a considerable
appreciation of national factors
7 Burlington Gardens (now Bank of Scotland),
Piccadilly, London, 1721–23 (altered 1785)
Argyll House, 211 King's Road, Chelsea,
London, 1723
Lyme Park, near New Mills, Cheshire;
alterations, 1725–35
Clandon Park, Guildford, Surrey, c. 1730–33
Alkrington Hall, near Heysham, Lancashire,
1735
Cliveden, near Maidenhead, Buckinghamshire;
Blenheim Pavilion in grounds, c. 1735
21 Arlington Street, Piccadilly, London, 1738
(altered 1769)
Cliveden, near Maidenhead, Buckinghamshire;
gazebo in grounds, c. 1740

Leroux, Jacob
Cams Hall, Portsmouth Road, Fareham,
Hampshire, 1771
Canonbury Square, Canonbury, Islington,
London, begun c. 1800
Compton Terrace, Canonbury, Islington,
London, begun c. 1806

Leverton, Thomas (1743–1824)
Exhibited at the Royal Academy 1771–1803
65 Lincoln's Inn Fields, Holborn, London, 1772
right
Boyles Court, near Brentwood, Essex, 1776
Woodhall Park, near Hertford, Hertfordshire,
1777 (extended 1795)
Bedford Square, Bloomsbury, London, 1776–86
(thought to have been laid out by Leverton)
Quernmore School, London Lane, Bromley,
London, c. 1778 (thought to be by)
Scampston House, near Pickering, Humberside;
additions, 1803

Lewis, James (c. 1751–1820)
Lavington House, East Lavington, West Sussex,
1790–94
Hackthorn House, Lincolnshire, c. 1798
14 New Bridge Street, City of London, 1802
Imperial War Museum (former Bethlehem
Hospital), Lambeth Road, Southwark, London,
1812–15

Lightoler, Timothy
Burton Constable Hall, near Kingston-upon-
Hull, Humberside; alterations including
entrance hall, 1760
Octagon Chapel behind Milsom Street, Bath,
Avon, 1767
Town Hall, Sheep Street, Stratford-upon-Avon,
Warwickshire 1767 (thought to be by Lightoler
and / or Robert Newman)

Lindley, William (c. 1739–1818)
Owston Hall, South Yorkshire, 1794–95

Logan, David
Parish Church, Montrose, Tayside, 1791; tower
and spire, 1832
Academy, Montrose, Tayside, 1815

Loudon, John Claudias (1783–1843)
A landscape gardener and horticultural writer,
he published *Encyclopedia of Gardening* in 1822,
Encyclopedia of Agriculture in 1825, and
Encyclopedia of Plants in 1829
3–5 Porchester Terrace, Paddington, London;
own house, 1823–24

Lucas, Thomas
Albury Street, Deptford, London, c. 1706–17
(some houses remain)

Lugar, Robert (c. 1773–1855)
Dunstall Priory (formerly Gold Hill), near
Sevenoaks, Kent, 1806
Balloch Castle, Strathclyde, 1809
The Ryes, Little Henny, Essex, 1810
Yaxham Rectory, Norfolk, 1820–22
Glenlee, Dumfries and Galloway, 1823
Cyfarthfa Castle near Merthyr Tydfil, mid-
Glamorgan, 1825
Newlaithes Hall, Horsforth, West Yorkshire,
c. 1825
Hensol, near Castle Douglas, Dumfries and
Galloway, c. 1825

Lumby, William
Bluecoat School (now Lincoln School of Art),
Christ's Hospital Terrace, Lincoln,
Lincolnshire, 1784

Lumley, John
Emmanuel College, Cambridge,
Cambridgeshire; Westmoreland Building,
1719–22

Mack, Robert
Powerscourt House, South William Street,
Dublin, Ireland, 1771

Madden, Dominick
Ballyfin, Mountrath, Co. Laois, Ireland (begun
by), 1821–26
Roman Catholic Cathedral, Tuam, Co. Galway,
Ireland, 1827
Roman Catholic Cathedral, Ballina, Co. Mayo,
Ireland, 1829 (thought to be by)

Marshall, William
St Lawrence's Church, Bourton-on-the-Water,
Gloucestershire; tower, 1784

Martin, James
St Macartan's Church of Ireland Cathedral,
Clogher, Co. Tyrone, Ireland, 1744 (thought to
be by; altered 1818)

Masters, Charles Harcourt (1759–?)
Sydney Gardens, Bathwick, Avon, date
unknown
Sydney Hotel (now Holbourne Museum), Great
Pulteney Street, Bath, Avon, 1796
Widcombe Terrace, Bath, Avon, 1805
Widcombe Crescent, Bath, Avon, 1805

Mead, John Clement (1798–1839)
Observatory, Madingley Road, Cambridge,
Cambridgeshire, 1822–23

Meade, William
Clock Gate, South Main Street, Youghal,
Co. Cork, Ireland, 1771

Medworth, Joseph
The Crescent, Wisbech, Cambridgeshire,
c. 1808
Town Hall, North Brink, Wisbech,
Cambridgeshire, 1810

Middleton, William (1730–1815)
Beverley Arms Hotel, North Bar Within,
Beverley, Humberside, 1744

Miller, Sanderson (1717–80)
Educated at St Mary's Hall, Oxford; he
inherited Radway Grange in 1737 and began
landscaping the scene c. 1739, erecting a gothic
castle and a thatched cottage. The classical
Shire Hall, Warwick, was designed by him but
was built by Hiorne. He enjoyed an enormous
reputation as a gentleman architect and showed
a precocious technical appreciation of gothic;
his classical buildings are among the most
notable of the rococo phase
Cottage, adjacent to Edge Hill Tower, Edge Hill,
Warwickshire, 1743
Radway Grange, near Banbury, Warwickshire,
1744
Edge Hill Tower, Edge Hill, Warwickshire, 1745
All Saints' Church, Wroxton, Oxfordshire;
tower, 1747
Hagley Hall, near Kidderminster, Hereford and
Worcester; Castle Folly in the grounds, 1747–48
Wimpole Hall, near Cambridge,
Cambridgeshire; castle in the grounds, 1749–50
Adlestrop Park, Adlestrop, Gloucestershire, 1750
Shire Hall, Northgate Street, Warwick,
Warwickshire, 1754–58
Hagley Hall, near Kidderminster, Hereford and
Worcester, 1754–60
Lacock Abbey, near Chippenham, Wiltshire;
additions, c. 1754
Ecton Hall, near Northampton,
Northamptonshire, 1756 (thought to be by)
Church and Hillsborough Fort, Hillsborough,
Co. Down, Ireland, c. 1760 (thought to be by)
**with Henry Keene, William Hiorne and
others as the 'Committee of taste'**
Arbury Hall, Warwickshire, c. 1750

Milne, James
St Bernard's Crescent, Raeburn Estate,
Edinburgh, 1824

Mitchell, Robert (d. 1800)
Exhibited at the Royal Academy 1782–98
Preston Hall, Lothian, 1791–94

Monck, Sir Charles (1779–1867)
Changed his name from Middleton in 1799, to
satisfy the terms of his maternal grandfather's will
Belsay Hall, Northumberland; own house,
1806–17 *below*

Linden House, near Long Horsley,
Northumberland, 1812–13

Moneypenny, George (1768–?)
11A Jewry Street, Winchester, Hampshire, gaol,
1805 (some remains)
Session House and House of Correction, Toft
Road, Knutsford, Cheshire, 1817–19
Crown Court (formerly Assize Court) and Gaol,
Durham, Co. Durham, date unknown

Montier, John
St Alban, Frant, East Sussex, 1819–22

Morgan, James
St George's Church, Bilston Road,
Wolverhampton, West Midlands, 1828–30

Morison, David
Marshall Monument, George Street, Perth,
Tayside, 1822 (remodelled 1854)

Morris, Roger (1695–1749)
Began his working life as a bricklayer and joiner,
before winning commissions with the help of
Henry Herbert, ninth Earl of Pembroke. These
included Marble Hill, which was built for the
mistress of the future George II, and Royal
Lodge (now known as White Lodge) in
Richmond Park. He was carpenter and
principal engineer of the Board of Ordnance
and a friend and protegé of the second Duke of
Argyll, who was Master-General of Ordnance
between 1725–30 and in 1742, and for whose
successor he designed Inverarary Castle
Marble Hill House, Twickenham, London, 1724
(may have been with Lord Pembroke)
Combe Bank, near Sevenoaks, Kent, 1725 (villa
later altered)
Clearwell Castle, near Monmouth,
Gloucestershire, 1725–30
Hunting Lodge, Fox Hall, near Chichester, West
Sussex, 1730
Blenheim Palace, Oxfordshire; Column of
Victory, 1730
61 Green Street, London; own house, 1730
Council House, Chichester, West Sussex,
1731–33
Althorp, Northamptonshire; stable, 1732
Trafalgar House (originally Standlynch), near
Salisbury, Wiltshire, 1733
Althorp, Northamptonshire; entrance hall, 1733
Inverarary Castle, Inveraray, Strathclyde,
1745–60
with Lord Pembroke
White Lodge, Richmond Park, Richmond-upon-
Thames, London, 1727–30 (now the Royal
Ballet School)
Wilton House, Wilton, Wiltshire; Palladian
bridge in the grounds, 1736–37

Morrison, John
Kingston College (almshouses), Kingston
Square, Mitchelstown, Co. Cork, Ireland,
1771–75

Morrison, Sir Richard (1767–1849)
Knighted in 1841
Ballingarrane, Clonmel, Co. Tipperary, 1797
(thought to be by)
Mount Henry, Portarlington, Co. Laois, Ireland,
c. 1800
Castlegar, Ahascragh, Co. Galway, Ireland,
c. 1803
Castle Howard, Avoca, Co. Wicklow, Ireland,
1811
Court House, Port Laoise, Co. Laois, Ireland,
1812
Carton, Maynooth, Co. Kildare, Ireland;
alterations, c. 1815
Fota Island, Carrigtwohill, Co. Cork, Ireland;
enlargement, c. 1820
Kilruddery, Co. Wicklow, Ireland, c. 1820
(partly demolished)
with W V Morrison
Ballyheigue Castle, near Tralee, Co. Kerry,
c. 1760 (now a ruin)
Borris House, Borris, Co. Carlow, Ireland,
c. 1820

Morrison, William Vitruvius (1794–1838)
Son of Sir Richard Morrison, to whom he
became an assistant; travelled extensively in
Europe from 1821
Court House, Tralee, Co. Kerry, Ireland, early
nineteenth century
Mount Stewart, Newtownards, Co. Down,
Ireland; enlargement, 1825–28
Court House, Carlow, Co. Carlow, Ireland,
1830

Mountain, Charles
Court House, Wood Street, Wakefield, West
Yorkshire, 1807–10
White Hall, Winestead, Humberside, c. 1815
(thought to be by)
Wood Hall, near Kingston-upon-Hull,
Humberside, 1820

Mountain, Charles the Younger (1773–1839)
Hall Garth (formerly Rectory), Goodmanham,
Humberside, 1823–25
Trinity Almshouses, Postern Gate, Kingston-
upon-Hull, Humberside, 1828
Whitefriars Gate, Kingston-upon-Hull,
Humberside; south side terrace, 1829–30
with Richard Sharp
Assembly Rooms (now New Theatre), Kingston
Square, Kingston-upon-Hull, Humberside,
1830

Moyle, John
Powderham Castle, near Dawlish, Devon,
remodelling, 1710–27 (later altered)

Moyser, Colonel
Norstell Priory, near Wakefield, West Yorkshire,
c. 1735

Moyser, James
Bretton Hall, near Barnsley, West Yorkshire,
1730
Ann Routh's Hospital, 28 Keldgate, Beverley,
Humberside, 1748

Mulholland, Roger
Presbyterian Church, Rosemary Street, Belfast,
Co. Antrim, Ireland, 1783 (front altered
c. 1823)

Myers, Graham
Dunsink Observatory, Castleknock, Dublin,
Ireland, 1782

Mylne, Robert (1733–1811)
Architect and engineer, the son of Thomas
Mylne; he studied in Rome, 1754–58, and
travelled throughout Switzerland and Holland

before returning to England, where he was made Surveyor of St Paul's Cathedral, London, in 1766, and engineer to the New River Company 1770–1811. He was an original member of the Architects Club

King's Weston, Bristol, Avon; internal alterations, 1763–68

St Cecilia's Hall, Niddry Street, Edinburgh, 1761

Union Fire Office, Surrey Street, Norwich, Norfolk, 1764

Blaise Castle House, Henbury, near Bristol, Avon; tower, 1766

Wormleybury House, near Cheshunt, Hertfordshire, 1767–69

St George's Circus, Southwark, London; c. 1770 (laid out by)

Woodhouse, near Ellesmere, Shropshire, 1773–74

Addington Palace (now Royal School of Church music), Croydon, London, 1773–79

Tern Bridge, Atcham, Shropshire, 1774

Arkland Road and Relief Road, Inveraray, Strathclyde; tenements, 1774–76

The Wick, Richmond Hill, Richmond-upon-Thames, London, 1775

Custom House and Inn, Tobermory, Strathclyde, 1789

Amwell Grove, Great Amwell, Hertfordshire; own house, 1794–97

Wandle House, Riverside Drive, Merton, London, c. 1795 (thought to be by)

Church, Inveraray, Strathclyde, 1796

Stationers' Hall, Stationers' Hall Court, City of London; east front, 1800–01

Mylne, Robert William (1817–90)

Architect, engineer and geologist, the son of William Chadwell Mylne, and engineer to the Limerick Water Works

Doldowlod House, Rhayader, Powys, 1827 (additions 1878)

Mylne, William Chadwell (1781–1863)

An engineer and architect, he was the son of Robert Milne, and engineer to the New River Company, 1811–61

St Mark's Church, Myddleton Square, Finsbury, London, 1826–28

Nash, John (1752–1835)

Brought up in Lambeth, London, the son of a millwright, Nash was a pupil of Sir Robert Taylor before establishing his own practice in 1793. He was made bankrupt in 1783, partly as the result of the extravagant milliner's debts incurred by his first wife. After this, Nash went to ground in Wales, from where his mother had originated, before becoming involved in a growing practice in Carmarthen. He later met and employed a refugee from the French Revolution, Auguste Charles de Pugin, a brilliant draughtsman and father of the great Pugin. Nash re-established his practice in London in 1795, when he entered into partnership with Humphrey Repton. He was the great English exponent of the romantic picturesque movement in building; although his works are often criticised on the grounds of impure style, as large-scale urban design they often achieve a sublime picturesque splendour

3–6 Great Russell Street, Bloomsbury, London, c. 1778

17 Bloomsbury Square, Bloomsbury, London; reconstruction, c. 1782

Six Bells Inn, Carmarthen, Dyfed, 1785 (now a row of houses)

Nolton House, Orchard Street, Carmarthen, Dyfed, 1785

Clytha Castle, Gwent, 1790

Ffynone, Dyfed, 1792–96 (altered 1904)

Foley House, Goat Street, Haverfordwest, Dyfed, 1794

Whitson Court, Gwent, 1794 (altered)

Llanaeron, Dyfed, c. 1794

Kentchurch Court, near Hereford, Hereford and Worcester; remodelling, c. 1795

County Gaol, Commercial Road, Hereford,

Three Nash buildings, on different scales; above, *17 Bloomsbury Square;* below, *Luscombe Castle; and* bottom, *the Royal Pavilion, Brighton*

Hereford and Worcester, 1795–96 (largely demolished in 1929)

Clytha Castle, near Abergavenny, Gwent; folly in park grounds, c. 1795

Grovelands House, Southgate, London, 1797

Corsham Court, Corsham, Wiltshire; alterations, 1797–98

Luscombe Castle, near Totnes, Devon, 1799–1804

Cronkhill, near Shrewsbury, Shropshire, 1802

Longner Hall, near Shrewsbury, Shropshire, c. 1805

Sandridge Park, Stoke Gabriel, Devon, c. 1805

Market House, North Street, Chichester, West Sussex, 1807–08

Attingham Hall, Shropshire; picture gallery with cast-iron roof, 1807–10

Southborough Place, Ashcombe Avenue, Surbiton, Surrey, 1808

Caerhayes Castle, near St Austell, Cornwall, c. 1808

Caledon, near Armagh, Co. Tyrone, Ireland; alterations to a house, 1808–10

West Grinstead Park, West Sussex, c. 1809 (enlarged 1865; a ruin)

Charborough Park, Dorset; extensions, c. 1810

Blaise Hamlet almshouses, Henbury, near Bristol, Avon, 1811

Literary Institute (now Country Club), St James's Square, Newport, Isle of Wight, 1811

Lough Cutra Castle, Gort, Co. Galway, Ireland, 1811

Rheola, West Glamorgan; house enlargement, c. 1812

Park Crescent, Regent's Park, Marylebone, London, 1812–22

'Swiss Cottage', Cahir, Co. Tipperary, Ireland; *cottage orné* c. 1814 (thought to be by)

Wood Hall, Swine, near Burton Constable, Humberside, 1814–15

Guildhall, corner of High Street and Quay Street, Newport, Isle of Wight, 1814–16

Royal Pavilion, Old Steine, Brighton, East Sussex, 1815–21

St Mary's Church, West Cowes, Isle of Wight; west tower, 1816

Royal Opera Arcade, Pall Mall, Westminster, London, 1816–18

Protestant Church, Cahir, Co. Tipperary, Ireland, 1817 (thought to be by)

Suffolk Place and Suffolk Street, Trafalgar Square, London, 1820–23

Theatre Royal, Haymarket, Trafalgar Square, London, 1821

Sussex Place, Regent's Park, Marylebone, London, 1822

York Terrace East and West, Regent's Park, Marylebone, London, 1822

Hanover Terrace, Regent's Park, Marylebone, London, 1822–23

All Souls' Church, Langham Place, Marylebone, London, 1822–24

Park Square, Regent's Park, Marylebone, London, 1823; west side, 1823–25

St Andrew's Place, Regent's Park, Marylebone, London, 1823–26

Ulster Terrace, Regent's Park, Marylebone, London, 1824

Chester Terrace and Cambridge Terrace, Regent's Park, Marylebone, London, 1825 *below*

Clarence House, St James's, Westminster, London, 1825–27 (enlarged in 1873)
Buckingham Palace, St James's, Westminster, London; remodelling of earlier house, 1825–30 (entrance front 1913)
Aroid House No. 1, Royal Botanic Gardens, Kew, Richmond-upon-Thames, London, c. 1825–30
Kent Terrace, Regent's Park, Marylebone, London, 1826
United Services Club, Pall Mall, St James's, Westminster, London, 1826–28
Gloucester Gate, Regent's Park, London, 1827
Carlton House Terrace, off The Mall, St James's, Westminster, London, 1827–33
St Martin's School, St Martin's Place, Trafalgar Square, London, c. 1830
with James Thomson
Cumberland Terrace, Regent's Park, London, 1825 *below*

Nasmith, Alexander
Steading, Rosneath Castle, near Helensburgh (across Gare Loch), Strathclyde 1800

Nasmith, Robert (*d.* 1793)
Stoke Park, Stoke Poges, Buckinghamshire, 1789

Neave, David (1773–1841)
South Tay Street, Dundee, Tayside, 1792
7–19 King Street, Dundee, Tayside, 1815–19 (thought to be by)
St David's Church, Dundee, Tayside, 1822–24
County Buildings, Forfar, Tayside, 1823–24
Thistle Hall, Union Street, Dundee, Tayside, 1826–29
Union Street, Dundee, Tayside, 1828
St Ninian's Church, Methven Street, Dundee, Tayside, 1829–30

Nelson, S
Pavilion, Mote Park, off Mote Road, Maidstone, Kent, 1801

Newton, William (1739–90)
Appointed assistant to James Stuart and clerk of works at Greenwich Hospital in 1782; he completed Stuart's *Antiquities of Athens*, published in 1787, and translated *Vitruvius*, published in 1791
St Ann's Chapel, City Road, Newcastle-upon-Tyne, Tyne and Wear, 1764–68
Highams, Woodford Green, Woodford, London, 1768
Assembly Rooms, Westgate, Newcastle-upon-Tyne, Tyne and Wear, 1774

Nicholson, Peter (1765–1844)
Carlton Place, Glasgow, Strathclyde, 1802 *below*
Princes Street and Montgomerie Street, Ardrossan, Strathclyde, 1806 (for Earl of Eglinton)
Corby Castle, Cumbria, 1812–17

with W Reid
Castletown House, near Rockcliffe, Cumbria, 1811

Nicholson, William Adams (1803–53)
Articled to John Buonarotti Papworth; he established his own practice in Lincoln in 1828

Nisbet, James
Twizell Castle, near Berwick-upon-Tweed, Northumberland, c. 1770 (ruin)
with John Laidlaw and Robert Purves
Church, Kelso, Borders, 1773

Norfolk, Duchess of
Castle Farm, near Worksop, Nottinghamshire, c. 1760

Norfolk, eleventh Duke of (Howard Charles, 1746–1815)
Greystoke Castle, near Penrith, Cumbria; Fort Putnam and Bunker Hill in grounds, c. 1778

Novosielski, Michael (1759–95)
Fortfield Terrace, Sidmouth, Devon, begun c. 1790

Pace, Richard (c. 1760–1838)
Salperton Park, Gloucestershire; alterations, 1817

Page, E
11 Cross Street, Beverley, Humberside, c. 1830

Page, Joseph
Maisters House, 160 High Street, Kingston-upon-Hull, Humberside, 1744
Blaydes House, 6 High Street, Kingston upon-Hull, Humberside, c. 1760
9–12 King Street, Kingston-upon-Hull, Humberside, 1771 (thought to be by)
Trinity House, Kingston-upon-Hull, Humberside; courtroom, 1773

Page, Samuel Flood (1796–1854) and **Philip Flood Page** (1798–?)
Portis College almshouses, Weston, Avon 1825–27

Pain, George Richard (1793–1838)
St Mary's Pro-Cathedral (known as North Chapel), Shandon, Cork, Co. Cork, Ireland; remodelling, c. 1827
with James Pain
Male prison, Cork, Co. Cork, Ireland, 1818–23
Dromoland Castle, Newmarket-on-Fergus, Co. Clare, Ireland, 1826
Prison, Port Laoise, Co. Laois, Ireland, c. 1830 (thought to be by)

Paine, James (1714–87)
Paine was a pupil of St Martin's Academy, and a disciple of Burlington. He was the outstanding country-house architect of the mid-century. He was put in charge of Norstell Priory in 1733 by Sir Rowland Winn, who retained his services for ten years. In 1740, he won the competition for the Assembly Rooms, Doncaster, and by 1760 was established, with a large country-house practice in the north of England, before extending his operations to the south. His treatment of walls, ceilings and also chimneypieces admitted wholly rococo decoration or its naturalistic variants, derived from Palladian models, within his architectural framework. A pilaster with an expanding shaft, like an inverted obelisk, is a favourite motif of his. After 1760 he was influenced by Piranesi and neoclassicism

Heath House, Heath, West Yorkshire, 1744–45
Mansion House, Doncaster, South Yorkshire, 1745–48
Wadworth Hall, near Tickhill, South Yorkshire, c. 1750
Ormsby Hall, near Horncastle, Lincolnshire, 1752–55
Wallington Hall, near Morpeth, Northumberland; bridge in the grounds, 1755
Park Farm, Raby Castle, near Bishop Auckland, Co. Durham, c. 1755
Dover House, Whitehall, London; rear portion, 1755–58
Stockeld Park, near Harrogate, North Yorkshire, 1758–63
Kedleston, near Derby, Derbyshire; north-west wing, 1759–60
Bywell Hall, near Prudhoe, Northumberland, c. 1760
Chapel, Gibside, Tyne and Wear, 1760–66
The Hall, Gibside, Tyne and Wear; column in the grounds, 1760
Brocket Hall, near Welwyn Garden City, Hertfordshire, 1760–75
Sandbeck Park, near Tickhill, South Yorkshire, 1763–68
Thorndon Hall, near Brentwood, Essex, 1764 (gutted 1878; rebuilt)
Weston Park, near Oakengates, Staffordshire; Temple of Diana and Roman bridge in the grounds, 1765
Home Farm, Weston Park, near Oakengates, Staffordshire; barn, 1768 (thought to be by)
Hare Hall, Brentwood Road, Romford, London, 1769–70 (inside since altered)
Parish workhouse, 14 Manette Street, Soho, London, 1770 (much altered)
Wardour Castle (now Cranborne Chase School), near Shaftesbury, Wiltshire, 1770–76
Lodge and entrance screen, in the grounds of Brocket Hall, Hertfordshire, c. 1770
Bridge, in the grounds of Brocket Hall, Hertfordshire, 1772–74
37 King Street, Covent Garden, London, c. 1775 (thought to be by)

Palmer, John (c. 1738–1817)
St Swithin's Church, London Street, Walcot, Bath, Avon, 1777–80 *below*

Lansdown Crescent, Bath, Avon, 1789–93
Norfolk Crescent, Bath, Avon, c. 1790–1810 (thought to be by)
St James's Square, Bath, Avon, 1791–94
Great Pump Room, Abbey Churchyard, Bath, Avon, 1793–96 (begun by Thomas Baldwin)

Palmer, John (1785–1846)
St Mary and St John Baptist Roman Catholic
  Church, Pleasington, Lancashire, 1816–19
St Peter's Church, St Peter's Street, Blackburn,
  Lancashire, 1819–21
St Mary's Cathedral, St Peter's Street,
  Blackburn, Lancashire, 1820–26

Papworth, John Buonarotti (1775–1847)
Architect and designer, he contributed to the
  Royal Academy exhibitions 1794–1841. He was
  an original member of the Associated Artists in
  Watercolours, 1807, and of the Institute of
  British Architects, 1834
Laleham Park, Surrey, 1803–06, 1827 and 1839
St Julian's Underriver, near Sevenoaks, Kent,
  1818–20 (enlarged by him 1835)
Alton Towers, Staffordshire; garden buildings
  for fifteenth Earl of Shrewsbury, including
  bridge and temples, 1818–22
Montpellier Parade, Cheltenham,
  Gloucestershire, c. 1823
Suffolk Square, Cheltenham, Gloucestershire,
  c. 1825
Montpellier Pump Rooms and Rotunda,
  Cheltenham, Gloucestershire; enlargements,
  1825 (now Lloyds Bank)
Lansdown Place and Lansdown Crescent,
  Cheltenham, Gloucestershire, 1825–29
St James's Church, Suffolk Square, Cheltenham,
  Gloucestershire; completion, 1826–32
Denford House, Berkshire; alterations,
  1827–28
Park Hill (now St Michael's Convent), off
  Streatham Common North, Streatham,
  London, begun c. 1830
Lansdown Terrace, Cheltenham,
  Gloucestershire, c. 1830 (thought to be by)
Cranbury Park, near Eastleigh, Hampshire;
  additions, 1830s
The Jearrads, Cheltenham, Gloucestershire, date
  unknown (thought to be by)

Park, Edward
with William Murray
Royal College of Surgeons, St Stephen's Green,
  Dublin, Ireland, 1806
with John Bowden
Court House, Dundalk, Co. Louth, Ireland,
  c. 1820

Parker, Charles (1799–1881)
Published *Villa Rustica*, 1832
Unitarian Chapel, Stamford Street, Southwark,
  London, 1823 (only portico survives)
Hoare's Bank, Fleet Street, City of London,
  1829–32

Parker, William
General Hospital, Nelson Street, Hereford,
  Hereford and Worcester, 1781–83 (since
  enlarged)

Parkinson, Joseph (1783–1855)
Bryanston Square, Marylebone, London, 1811

Parkyns, Sir Thomas (1662–1741)
He was educated at Trinity College, Cambridge
  and at Gray's Inn, and was a Justice of the
  Peace in Leicestershire and Nottinghamshire,
  1684–1741
Bunny Hall, near Nottingham, Nottinghamshire,
  c. 1723

Parsons, William (1796–1857)
Caythorpe Hall, Lincolnshire, 1824–27
Gaol, Welford Road, Leicester, Leicestershire,
  1825–28 (enlarged 1844–46)

Paterson, John (d. 1832)
Monzie Castle, Tayside, c. 1795–1800 (restored
  after fire in 1908)
St Paul's Church, Perth, Tayside, 1800–07
Barmoor Castle, Northumberland, 1801
Milbourne Hall, Penteland, Northumberland,
  1807–19
Fetteresso, Grampian, 1810–12

Patey, Andrew (d. 1834)
St Michael, East Teignmouth, Devon, 1822–23
Den Crescent, East Teignmouth, Devon, 1826

Patience, John Thomas
Friends' Meeting Place, Upper Goat Lane,
  Norwich, Norfolk, 1826

Paty, James
Theatre Royal, King Street, Bristol, Avon,
  1764–66 *below*

Paty, Thomas
Boyce's Buildings, Clifton, Avon, 1763
Prospect House, Clifton, Avon, c. 1765

Paty, William (1758–1800)
St Michael's Church, St Michael's Hill, Bristol,
  Avon; nave, 1774
Christ Church, Broad Street, Bristol, Avon,
  1786–90 *below*

Cornwallis Crescent, Clifton, Bristol, Avon, 1790
with John Nash
Blaise Castle House, Henbury, near Bristol,
  Avon, c. 1795

Paul, Sir John Dean (1802–68)
Chapels, Kensal Green Cemetery, London,
  c. 1835

Pearce, Sir Edward Lovett (d.1733)
MP for Ratoath in the Irish Parliament, 1727
King's House, Boyle, Co. Roscommon, Ireland,
  c. 1720–30 (attributed to office of)
Castletown, Celbridge, Co. Kildare, Ireland;
  completion, c. 1726
Drumcondra House (now All Hallows College),
  Drumcondra, Co. Dublin, Ireland; south front,
  1727–30
Parliament House (now Bank of Ireland),

College Green, Dublin, Ireland, 1729 (extended
  1782)
9 Henrietta Street, Dublin, Ireland, c. 1729
10 Henrietta Street, Dublin, Ireland, c. 1730
Ballamont Forest, Cootehill, Co. Cavan, Ireland,
  c. 1730
Cashel Palace, Cashel, Co. Tipperary, Ireland,
  1730–32
Woodlands, Santry, Co. Dublin, Ireland,
  c. 1730–35 (thought to be by)
Stillorgan House (demolished), Stillorgan, Co.
  Dublin, Ireland; grotto and obelisk in the
  grounds, c. 1732
Southwell School and Almshouses,
  Downpatrick, Co. Down, Ireland, 1733
  (thought to be to design of)

Penn, Thomas
Hospital, Stoke Poges, Buckinghamshire, 1765

Pentland, George
Dysart, Delvin, Co. Westmeath, Ireland, 1757

Pentland, John
Wilson's Hospital School, Multyfarnham,
  Co. Westmeath, Ireland, c. 1760

Pickernell, Jonathan
Town Hall, between Church Street and Market
  Place, Whitby, North Yorkshire, 1788

Pickford, Joseph
The Mansion, Church Street, Ashbourne,
  Derbyshire, 1764 (thought to be by)
41 Friar Gate, Derby, Derbyshire, 1768 (thought
  to be by)
44 Friar Gate, Derby, Derbyshire, c. 1770
Lloyds Bank, Compton Street, Ashbourne,
  Derbyshire, c. 1775 (thought to be by)

Pilkington, William (1758–1848)
He established a large practice in London and
  was employed at Salisbury as surveyor and
  architect by the Earl of Radnor
Otterden Place, near Faversham, Kent, 1802
Royal Naval (now St Nicholas) Hospital, Great
  Yarmouth, Norfolk, 1809–11 (thought to be by
  Pilkington or by **Edward Holl**)

Pinch, John (c. 1770–1827)
New Sydney Place, Bathwick, Avon, 1808
Cavendish Place, Bath, Avon, 1808–16
St Mary's Church, Raby Place, Bathwick, Avon,
  1814–20 (chancel 1873)
Cavendish Crescent, Bath, Avon, c. 1814–30
Sion Hill Place, Bath, Avon, date not known

Pitt, Stephen
Cricket Court, near Ilminster, Somerset, 1811

Pitt, Thomas
Stratfield Saye House, near Reading,
  Hampshire; St Mary's Church in the grounds,
  1754–58 (thought to be by)
Hagley Hall, near Kidderminster, Hereford and
  Worcester; Palladian bridge in the grounds,
  1764
Stowe, near Buckingham, Buckinghamshire;
  Corinthian arch in the grounds, 1766

Platt, John
Moorgate Hall, Moorgate Road, Rotherham,
  South Yorkshire, 1768
Charity School (Feoffes), The Crofts,
  Rotherham, South Yorkshire, 1776

Plaw, John (c. 1745–1820)
Architect and master builder, established in
  Westminster, London, he published several
  professional works
House on Belle Isle (on Lake Windermere),
  Cumbria, c. 1775
St Mary's Church, Paddington Green, London,
  1788–91

Playfair, James (1755–94)
Town Hall, Forfar, Tayside, 1786

Melville Castle, near Dalkeith, Lothian, 1786–91
Model Farm, Burley-on-the-Hill, Leicestershire, 1788
Cairness House, near Fraserburgh, Grampian, 1791–97
Mausoleum, Methven, Tayside, 1793

Playfair, William Henry (1790–1857)
Practised in Edinburgh, where between 1815–20 he laid out part of the New Town. Between 1817–24 he was engaged in the rebuilding and enlarging of the university buildings. His classical buildings are predominant in any view of Edinburgh and have gained for it the soubriquet of the 'modern Athens'
University, Chambers Street, Edinburgh, after 1817 (completion with Robert Reid)
Observatory, Calton Hill, Edinburgh, 1818
Dollar Academy, Dollar, central Scotland, 1818–20
Royal Terrace, Edinburgh, 1821
Hillside Crescent, Edinburgh, 1823
St Stephen, St Vincent Street, Edinburgh, 1827–28 (interior altered)
Preston Grange, Prestonpans, Lothian; remodelling, 1830
Dugald Stewart Monument, Calton Hill, Edinburgh, c. 1830

Poole, the Revd Henry (c. 1785–1857)
St Paul's Church, Parkend, Forest of Dean, Gloucestershire, 1822

Pope, Alexander (1688–1744)
Alfred's Hall, Cirencester, Gloucestershire, 1721

Porden, Charles Ferdinand (1790–1863)
St Matthew's Church, Brixton, London, 1822–24

Pope, Richard Shackleton (c. 1792–1854)
Court of Justice, Bristol, Avon, 1827–28

Potter, Joseph (c. 1756–1842)
Newton's College, Cathedral Close, Litchfield, Staffordshire, 1800
Plas Newydd, near Menai Straits, Anglesey, Gwynedd; completion, 1823

Poynter, Ambrose (1796–1886)
Established an architectural practice in Westminster, London, in 1821 and was a founding member of RIBA
St Katharine's Royal Hospital, Regents Park, London, 1826–28

Price, John (d. 1736)
St George's Church, Great Yarmouth, Norfolk, 1714–16
Barnsley Park, near Cirencester, Gloucestershire, 1720–21 (thought to be by)
St George the Martyr's Church, Borough High Street, Southwark, London, 1734–36 (interior since altered)

Price, William
St Bartholomew's Hospital, Westgate Street, Gloucester, Gloucestershire, 1788

Priestly, Michael
Court House, Lifford, Co. Donegal, Ireland, 1745
Port Hall, Lifford, Co. Donegal, Ireland, 1746
St John's Church, Ballymore, near Sheephaven, Co. Donegal, Ireland, 1752 (thought to be by)

Prince, John
Cound Hall, near Shrewsbury, Shropshire, 1704

Pritchard, Thomas F
St Julian's Church, Wyle Cop, Shrewsbury, Shropshire; rebuilding, 1749–50 (altered in the nineteenth century)
Brockhampton Park, near Bromyard, Hereford and Worcester, c. 1750
Hosyer's Almshouses, Ludlow, Shropshire, 1758
Foundling Hospital (now Shrewsbury School),

over Frankland Bridge, Shrewsbury, Shropshire, 1759–63 (remodelled in 1878)
Swan Hill Court, Swan Court, Shrewsbury, Shropshire, 1764
Hatton Grange, near Ludlow, Shropshire, c. 1764–68
Croft Castle, near Leominster, Hereford and Worcester; alterations, 1765
10–11 High Street, Shrewsbury, Shropshire, 1766
Guildhall, Mill Street, Ludlow, Shropshire; rebuilding, 1774–76
Iron Bridge, Ironbridge, Shropshire, 1777–79

Pritchett, JP
Assembly Rooms, Blake Street, York, North Yorkshire; rebuilding of façade, 1828

**Probert, Benjamin
with Robert Comfort**
Dowry Parade, Bristol, Avon, 1764

Prowse, Thomas
Church of St Mary the Virgin, Berkley, Somerset, 1751
Kimberley Hall, near Wymondham, Norfolk; alterations, c. 1755
St John the Evangelist's Church, Wicken, Northamptonshire, 1758–c. 1768

Pycock, George (c. 1749–99)
Customs House Buildings (former Neptune Inn), Whitefriars Gate, Kingston-upon-Hull, Humberside, 1794–96

Raffield, John
St John's Lodge, in Regent's Park, Marylebone, London, c. 1818 (altered)

Rawlinson, Charles
St Aubyn's Church, St Aubyn's Street, Devonport, Devon, 1770–71 (thought to be by)

Rawsthorne, John
Royal Infirmary, Infirmary Road, Sheffield, South Yorkshire, 1793

Read, Thomas
Unitarian chapel, Adrian Street, Dover, Kent, 1819

Rebecca, John Biagio (d. 1847)
Castle Goring, near Worthing, West Sussex, c. 1790
St Paul's Church, Chapel Road, Worthing, West Sussex, 1812
Knebworth House, Hertfordshire, 1813 (remodelled 1844 and 1878)
Beach House, Worthing, West Sussex, 1820
Sea Hotel, Worthing, West Sussex, c. 1826

Reid, Robert (1774–1856)
Salutation Hotel, South Street, Perth, Tayside, c. 1800 (thought to be by)
Marshall Place, Perth, Tayside, 1801
Heriot Row, Edinburgh, 1802
Old Academy, Rose Terrace, Perth, Tayside, 1803–07
New Law Courts, Parliament Square, Edinburgh, 1804–10 and 1825–40
London Street, Edinburgh, 1806
Gaol, Edinburgh Road, Perth, Tayside, 1810–12 (altered 1842)
Upper and Lower Signet Library, Edinburgh, 1810–26 (with Stark, Playfair and Burn)
Custom House, Leith, Edinburgh, 1811–12
St George, Charlotte Square, Edinburgh, 1811–14
Paxton House, Borders; east wing, 1812–13
University, Chambers Street, Edinburgh, after 1817 (completion with William H Playfair)
Register House, Edinburgh; rear wing addition, 1822–30

Reid & Crichton
Bank of Scotland, The Mound, Edinburgh, 1802

Rennie, John (1761–1821)
Studied civil engineering at Edinburgh

University, after which he was employed by James Watt in 1784, before establishing his own practice c. 1791. He enjoyed a great reputation as a constructor of canals, docks, harbours and bridges
Dundas Aqueduct, Limpley Stoke, Wiltshire, c. 1795–97
Wolseley Bridge, Colwich, Staffordshire, 1798–1800
Kelso Bridge, Borders, 1800–03
Bridge, Musselburgh, Lothian, 1803 (widened 1924)
Ladies Bridge, Wilcot, Wiltshire, 1808
Pier, Margate, Kent, 1810–15
Newton Stewart Bridge, Dumfries and Galloway, 1812–13
Sowe Bridge, Stoneleigh, Warwickshire, 1814
Iron Bridge, Chepstow, Gwent, 1815–16
Wellington Bridge, Leeds, West Yorkshire, 1817–19
Bridge, Bridge of Earn, Tayside, 1819–21
Bridge, Cramond, Edinburgh, 1819–23
Ken Bridge, New Galloway, Dumfries and Galloway, 1820–21
Admiralty Pier, Holyhead, Anglesey, Gwynedd, 1821
with Alexander Stevens (c. 1730–96)
Lune Aqueduct (over Caton Road), Lancaster, Lancashire, 1794–97

Rennie, Sir John (1794–1874)
A civil engineer who carried on the business of his father, John Rennie; he completed London Bridge, opened in 1831, and the Plymouth breakwater. He was knighted in 1831, and retired c. 1862
Royal William Victualling Yard, Plymouth, Devon, 1826–32
Bridge, Staines, Surrey, 1829–32
Customs House and Harbour Office, Holyhead, Anglesey, Gwynedd, 1830

Repton, George Stanley (1786–1858)
Son of Humphry Repton, he assisted his father with the design of Brighton Pavilion
Assembly Rooms (now Students Union), Laura Place, Aberystwyth, Dyfed, 1820
Llanerchydol, Welshpool, Powys, 1820 (thought to be by)
Kitley House, near Plymouth, Devon; remodelling, c. 1820–25
Sarsgrove House, Sarsden, Oxfordshire, c. 1825
Sarsden House, Sarsden, Oxfordshire; alterations, c. 1825
Follaton House, near Totnes, Devon, c. 1826–29
Widworthy Court, near Honiton, Devon, 1830
Dumbleton Hall, near Evesham, Gloucestershire, c. 1830

Repton, Humphry (1752–1818)
Having lost his fortune, he became a professional landscape gardener
with John Nash
Sundridge Park, Sundridge, London, c. 1796–99

Repton, John Adey (1775–1860)
The son of Humphry Repton, he assisted his father by preparing architectural designs as adjuncts to landscape gardening. He was a contributor to *Archaeologia*
Stanage Park, Powys; rebuilding, 1803–07
Laxton Hall, near Corby, Northamptonshire, 1805–11
Sheringham Hall, Norfolk, 1813–19
Bourn Hall, near Cambridge, Cambridgeshire; remodelling, 1817–19
Buckhurst Park, Withyham, East Sussex, c. 1830–35

Revett, Nicholas (1720–1804)
The son of a Suffolk squire, he originated the Athens project with James Stuart and made the architectural drawings for *The Antiquities of Athens*
Dower House (originally Rectory), on edge of West Wycombe Park, West Wycombe, Buckinghamshire, 1763

West Wycombe Park, West Wycombe,
Buckinghamshire; Temple of the Four Winds in
the grounds, c. 1770–75 (thought to be by)
Trafalgar House, (originally Standlynch), near
Salisbury, Wiltshire; porch, c. 1766
New St Lawrence's Church, Ayot St Lawrence,
Hertfordshire, 1778
West Wycombe Park, West Wycombe,
Buckinghamshire; Island Temple in the
grounds, 1778–80

Reynolds, Esau
Town Bridge, Trowbridge, Wiltshire, 1777

Rhodes, Henry (d. 1846)
Church of St John the Baptist, Egham, Surrey,
1817–20

Richardson, George (c.1736–1817)
He was in full professional practice in London
until towards the end of the century; he
published works on decorative art and
architecture, but in his old age fell into poverty
Holy Trinity Church, Teigh, Leicestershire;
nave, 1782
St Mary Magdalen's Church, Stapleford,
Leicestershire, 1783 (thought to be by)
St Peter's Church, Saxby, Leicestershire, 1788

Rickman, Thomas (1776–1841)
Established in practice in Liverpool c. 1815; he
published a series of lectures on the English
styles of architecture in 1817
Court House (former), Stanley Street, Preston,
Lancashire, 1825
Royal Infirmary, off Southgate Street,
Gloucester, Gloucestershire; enlargements,
1827
Bank, English Street, Carlisle, Cumbria, 1830
with John Cragg
St George's Church, Heyworth Street, Everton,
Merseyside, 1813

Rickman & Hutchinson
Thomas Rickman and Henry Hutchinson
(1800–31)
St George's Church, St George's Street, Chorley,
Lancashire, 1822
St Peter's Church, St Peter's Square, Preston,
Lancashire, 1822–25
St Peter's Church, Hampton Lacy, near
Stratford-upon-Avon, Warwickshire, 1822–26
St David's (Ramshorn) Church, Ingram Street,
Glasgow, Strathclyde, 1824–26
Estate Church, near Ombersley Court,
Ombersley, Hereford and Worcester, 1825–29
St John's College New Court, Cambridge,
Cambridgeshire, 1825–31
St Mary's Church, Mellor, Lancashire, 1827–29
Holy Trinity Church, Darwen, Lancashire,
1827–29
Oulton Hall, Oulton, West Yorkshire; St John's
Church in the grounds, 1827–29
Holy Trinity Church, Wigton Road, Carlisle,
Cumbria, 1828–30
Midland Bank, Waterloo Street, Birmingham,
West Midlands, 1830
St David, Haigh, Lancashire, 1830

Ripley, Thomas (1683–1758)
Born in Yorkshire, he became master carpenter
to the Crown in 1721, and was appointed
executive architect at Houghton by Sir Robert
Walpole
Admiralty, Whitehall, London, 1723–26
16 Grosvenor Street, London, 1724
Wolterton Hall, near Cromer, Norfolk, 1727–41
Hatchlands, near Guildford, Surrey; west front,
c. 1758 (thought to be by)

Roberts, John
Curraghmore, Portlaw, Co. Waterford, Ireland;
forecourt, c. 1755
Church of Ireland Cathedral, Waterford,
Co. Waterford, Ireland, 1773–79
St Iberius' Church, Wexford, Co. Wexford,
Ireland; rebuilding, c. 1775

Roman Catholic Cathedral, Waterford,
Co. Waterford, Ireland, 1792 (façade nineteenth
century)

Robertson, Daniel
Oriel College, Oxford, Oxfordshire; St Mary's
Quadrangle west side, c. 1825
Clarendon Press, Walton Street, Oxford,
Oxfordshire, 1826–27 *below*

St Clement's Church, Marston Road, Oxford,
Oxfordshire, 1827–28
St Swithin's Church, Kennington, Oxfordshire,
1828

Robertson, William (c. 1786–1841)
Episcopal Church and Parsonage, North Street,
Elgin, Grampian, 1825
Kilkenny Castle, Kilkenny, Co. Kilkenny,
Ireland; reconstruction, 1826

Robinson, Peter Frederick (1776–1858)
One of the first vice-presidents of the Institute of
British Architects, 1835–39
Trelissick, near Truro, Cornwall, 1824

Robinson, Sir Thomas (c. 1700–77)
An amateur architect, who had travelled to Italy
and Greece when young; he married a
daughter of Lord Carlisle. He was left
impoverished following her death in 1742, but
was made Governor of Barbados, returning to
England in 1748, when he was made manager
of Ranelagh Gardens
Rokeby Hall, near Barnard Castle, North
Yorkshire, 1725–50
Claydon House, near Buckingham,
Buckinghamshire, c. 1750 (remodelled c. 1860)
Castle Howard, near Malton, North Yorkshire;
west wing, 1753–59
Bishop's Palace, Bishop Auckland, Co. Durham;
Bishop Trevor's Gothic Gatehouse, 1760
St Mary's Church, Glynde, East Sussex, 1763
St Mary's Church, near Rokeby Hall, North
Yorkshire, consecrated 1778

Rogers, Thomas
Middlesex Sessions House (now Masonic Halls),
Clerkenwell Green, Clerkenwell, London,
1779–82

Roper, David Riddall (c. 1774–1855)
Brockwell Hall, Brockwell Park, Tulse Hill,
London, 1811–16
Grove Chapel, Camberwell Grove, Camberwell,
London, 1819
St Mark's Church, Clapham Road, Lambeth,
London, 1822–24
Shoreditch Training College, Pitfield Street,
Shoreditch, London, 1825

Rose, Henry
Licensed Victuallers' Benevolent Institution
Almshouses, Asylum Road, Peckham, London,
1827–31

Ross, Charles
Wentworth Castle (formerly Stainworth Hall),
near Barnsley, South Yorkshire; south front,
1759–64

Rothery, John
Mount Ievers Court, Sixmilebridge, Co. Clare,
Ireland, begun c. 1736

Rouchead, Alexander
Royal Naval Hospital, Plymouth, Devon,
1756–69 (since enlarged)

Rowland, Samuel (d. c. 1845)
St Bride, Percy Street, Liverpool, Merseyside,
1830–31

Salmon, Robert (1763–1821)
Clerk of works under Henry Holland and
architect to Francis Russell, fifth Duke of
Bedford at Woburn Abbey 1794–1821. He
invented the first haymaking machine in 1814
and was a silver medallist of the Society of Arts
Woburn Park Farm, Woburn, Bedfordshire,
1795
Tithe Farm, Eaton Socon, Cambridgeshire, 1797

Salvin, Anthony (1799–1881)
A pupil of John Nash, he practised in London
and executed restoration work to the Tower of
London, Windsor and other castles. He was
vice-president of the Royal Institute of British
Architects in 1839; a gold medallist in 1863,
and an exhibitor at the Royal Academy 1823–36
Moreby Hall, near York, North Yorkshire,
1828–33
Mamhead House, near Topsham, Devon, 1828–38

Sambell, Philip (1798–1874)
St John's Church, Truro, Cornwall, 1827–28
(altered)

Sanders, John (1768–1826)
Soane's first pupil
Beoley Hall, Hereford and Worcester;
remodelling, 1791
Duke of York's Headquarters, King's Road,
Chelsea, London, 1801–03
Royal Military Academy, Sandhurst, Berkshire,
1807–12

Sanderson, James (c. 1791–1835)
Town Hall, Lind Street, Ryde, Isle of Wight,
1830

Sanderson, John (d. 1783)
In 1733 he surveyed Woburn Abbey for the
third Duke of Bedford. Although he produced
designs for its rebuilding, he was replaced with
Henry Flitcroft by the fourth Duke
St John's Parish Church, Church Row,
Hampstead, London, 1744–47
Pusey House, near Faringdon, Oxfordshire,
1753
Radcliffe Infirmary, Woodstock Road, Oxford,
Oxfordshire; completion, 1766–70

Sands, William the Elder
St James's Chapel, Moulton Chapel,
Lincolnshire, 1722

Sands, William the Younger
4 Cowbit Road, Spalding, Lincolnshire,
c. 1760–70 (thought to be by)
3 Cowbit Road, Spalding, Lincolnshire, date not
known
Westbourne Lodge, Cowbit Road, Spalding,
Lincolnshire, c. 1765
Holland House, High Street, Spalding,
Lincolnshire, 1768

Sandys, Francis
Finborough Hall, Suffolk, 1795
Worlingham Hall, Suffolk, c. 1800
Athenaeum, Angel Hill, Bury St Edmunds,
Suffolk, 1804
with Marco Asprucci
Ickworth, near Bury St Edmunds, Suffolk,
begun c. 1795

Savage, James (1779–1852)
Studied at the Royal Academy, where he
exhibited between 1799–1832. He was architect
to the Society of Middle Temple, 1830, and
published *Observations on Styles in Architecture* in
1836

St Luke's Church, Sydney Street, Chelsea,
London, 1820–24
All Saints' Church, Beulah Hill, Upper
Norwood, London, 1827–29
St James's Church, Thurland Road,
Bermondsey, London, 1827–29
Holy Trinity Church, Tottenham Green,
Tottenham, London, 1828–30
St Mary's Church, High Road, Ilford, London,
1829–31

Saxon, Samuel (1757–?)
General Infirmary, Billing Road, Northampton,
Northamptonshire, 1791–93
Courteenhall Hall, near Northampton,
Northamptonshire, 1791–94

Searles, Michael (1750–1813)
31 Blackheath Road, Greenwich, London,
c. 1776–80
Gloucester Circus, Greenwich, London,
c. 1790–1807
Clare House, near Maidstone, Kent, 1793
The Paragon, Blackheath Park, London,
1793–1807
Paragon House, off South Row, Blackheath,
London, 1794
155 Old Kent Road, Peckham, London; own
house, 1795
20 Montpelier Row, Blackheath, London,
c. 1803
Colonnade House, South Row, Blackheath,
London, 1804 (thought to be by)

Semple, George (c. 1700–82)
St Patrick's Hospital, Dublin, Ireland, 1746–48
Headfort, Kells, Co. Meath, Ireland, 1760–70
Bridge, Graiguenamanagh, Co. Kilkenny,
Ireland, 1764 (thought to be by)

Semple, John
Black Church (now Chapel of Ease to St
Mary's), St Mary Street, Dublin, Ireland,
c. 1830
Church of Ireland Church, Monkstown,
Co. Dublin, Ireland, c. 1830

Shanahan, Michael
Downhill Castle, near Coleraine,
Co. Londonderry, Ireland; mausoleum in
grounds, c. 1779
Downhill Castle, near Coleraine,
Co. Londonderry, Ireland; Mussenden Temple
in grounds, 1780

Sharp, Richard Hey (c. 1793–1853)
Rotunda Museum, Scarborough, North
Yorkshire, 1828–29
Assembly Rooms (now New Theatre), Kingston
Square, Hull, Humberside, 1830–34

Sharp, Samuel (1808–74)
St James's Church, Thornes, Wakefield, West
Yorkshire, 1829–31

Shaw, John the Elder (1776–1832)
Articled to George Gwilt the Elder, he
established his own practice in 1798 and was
appointed architect to Christ's Hospital,
London
Clock House, Harbour Street, Ramsgate, Kent,
c. 1815
Sudley Lodge, High Street, Bognor Regis, West
Sussex, 1827
St Dunstan-in-the-West Church, Fleet Street,
City of London, 1829–33

Shepherd, Edward (d. 1747)
A London contractor-architect and developer,
and the owner of Shepherd Market, Mayfair.
He built several theatres, including Covent
Garden, 1732. His design project for the north
side of Grosvenor Square, c. 1725, was
conceived as a single grand terrace and is
thought to have inspired Wood's proposal
along the same principles for Bath
72 Brook Street, London, 1726

Above: *72 Brook Street, and
below, 71 South Audley Street*

4 St James's Square, St James's, Westminster,
London, 1726–28 (thought to be by)
Crewe House, 15 Curzon Street, London, 1730
(extensively altered)
71 South Audley Street, London, 1736

Sibbald, William (d. 1809)
St Andrew's Church, George Street, Edinburgh;
tower and portico, 1786–87

Sim, James and **Robert**
Torrington Square, Bloomsbury, London; part
of west side, 1821–25
Woburn Square, Bloomsbury, London; northern
end, 1829

Simons, Samuel
St George's Church, High Street, Deal, Kent,
1716

Simpson, Archibald (1790–1847)
Castle Forbes, Grampian, 1814–15
St Andrew's Cathedral, King Street, Aberdeen,
1816–17
County Assembly Rooms, Aberdeen, 1820–22
Letham Grange, near Arbroath, Tayside,
1825–30
St Giles' Church, High Street, Elgin, Grampian,
1827–28
Stracathro House, Tayside, 1828
Anderson Institution, Elgin, Grampian, 1830–33

Simpson, James (d. 1864)
Brunswick Methodist Church, Brunswick Street,
Leeds, West Yorkshire, 1824

Slater, John
St Patric Roman Catholic Church, Park Place,
Toxteth, Merseyside, 1821–23

Sloane, Charles
St George's Church, Gravesend, Kent, 1731–33

Smalman, John (c. 1783–1852)
Quatford Castle, Shropshire, 1829–30

Smirke, Sir Robert (1780–1867)
Born in London, he was the second son of the
successful painter and Royal Academician
Robert Smirke, 1752–1845. He was educated in
Bedford and became a pupil of Sir John Soane
in 1796, leaving after only a few months to
work as a surveyor. His architectural education
was gained in two years' private tuition from
George Dance the Younger and at the Royal
Academy Schools, from which he won the Gold
Medal in 1799. He spent five years travelling
with his brother and studying in Europe before
returning to London in 1805. Here he set up in
practice, receiving his first major commission
from Lord Lonsdale the following year for
Lowther Castle in Westmorland. He published
Specimens of Continental Architecture in 1806, gained
first prize for his navy memorial of 1817; was
treasurer to the Royal Academy between
1820–50, and received his knighthood in 1832
Wilton Castle, Cleveland c. 1807 (interiors later
altered; additions in 1887)
Assize Court, Court Square, Carlisle, Cumbria,
1810–12
Bentley Priory, Stanmore, London;
enlargements, 1810–18 (now much altered;
damaged by fire 1980)
Eastnor Castle, near Ledbury, Hereford and
Worcester, 1811–20
Kinmount, near Annan, Dumfries and
Galloway, 1812
Boultibrook, Presteigne, Powys, 1812–15
Shire Hall, Westgate Street, Gloucester,
Gloucestershire, 1814–16
The Homend, Stretton Grandison, Hereford and
Worster; entrance front, 1814–21
Somerset House (now Judge's Lodgings),
Gloucester, Gloucestershire, 1815
Luton Hoo, Bedfordshire; remodelling, c. 1815
(later altered 1843 and 1903) *below*, as it is
today

Newton Don, near Kelso, Borders, c. 1815
Shire Hall, St Peter Street, Hereford, Hereford
and Worcester, 1815–17
County Buildings, Tay Street, Perth, Tayside,
1815–19
Worthy House, Kingsworthy, Hampshire, 1816
Somerset House (now Judge's Lodgings),
Gloucester, Gloucestershire, c. 1816
Cholmondley Castle, Cheshire; extensions, 1817
and c. 1829
Whittinghame House, near East Linton,
Lothian, 1817 (altered 1827)
Walberton House, West Sussex, 1817–18
Strathallan Castle, Tayside; enlargement,
1817–18
Haffield House, near Donnington, Hereford and
Worcester, 1817–18
Hardwicke Court, Gloucestershire, 1817–19
Cultoquhey House, Tayside, 1818
Armley House, Gott's Lane, Leeds, West
Yorkshire; remodelling, c. 1818
St Anne's Church, St Anne's Hill, Wandsworth,
London, 1820–24
Kinfauns Castle, near Perth, Tayside, 1820–25

St George's Church, Great George Street,
Bristol, Avon, 1821–23
Oulton Hall, Oulton, West Yorkshire, c. 1822
St Philip's Church, St Philip's Place, Salford,
Greater Manchester, 1822–24
Old Council House, Broad Street, Bristol, Avon,
1822–27
Canada House (formerly Union Club and Royal
College of Physicians), Trafalgar Square,
London, 1822–27 (altered 1925) *below*

St Mary's Church, Wyndham Place,
Marylebone, London, 1823
Assize Courts, Lincoln Castle, Lincoln,
Lincolnshire, 1823–30
British Museum, Great Russell Street,
Bloomsbury, London, 1823–46
Edmond Castle, Hayton, Cumbria, 1824
Custom House, Lower Thames Street, City of
London; rebuilding of centre, 1825
Normanby Park, near Scunthorpe, Humberside,
1825–30 (later altered with additions, 1906)
Sedbury Park, Tidenham, Gloucestershire;
remodelling, 1826 (much altered)
Custom House, Queen Square, Bristol, Avon,
1826
Sessions House (former Shire Hall), corner of
County Road and Lower Boxley Road,
Maidstone, Kent, 1826–27 (enlarged later)
Erskine House, Strathclyde, 1828
Kings College (east wing of Somerset House),
Strand, London, 1829–35

Smith, Charles S (*c*. 1790–?)
Pump Room, Leamington Spa, Warwickshire,
1813 (only colonnade survives)

Smith, Francis (1672–1738)
The father of William Smith the Younger. The
majority of his buildings are of brick with stone
dressings, characteristically with emphasized
keystones and tall columns flanking
chimneypieces. His designs can be said to have
contributed notably to the evolution of the
Georgian synthesis, reflecting first Wren's then
Gibbs' baroque, as well as the simplifying
influence of Palladio, as early as 1726
Cottesbrooke Hall, near Northampton,
Northamptonshire, 1702–13 (thought to be by)
Old Grammar School (now two shops), John
Street, Wolverhampton, West Midlands,
1712–14
Abbotsford House, 10 Market Place, Warwick,
Warwickshire, 1714 (thought to be by)
Stoneleigh Abbey, near Kenilworth,
Warwickshire; west range, 1714–26
Chicheley Hall, near Newport Pagnell,
Buckinghamshire, 1719–21
Hardwick, near Ellsmere, Shropshire, c. 1720
Buntingsdale, near Market Drayton, Shropshire,
1721
Chillington Hall, near Wolverhampton,
Staffordshire; south front, 1724
Sutton Scarsdale, near Chesterfield, Derbyshire,
1724 (now a ruin)
Court House, Jury Street, Warwick,
Warwickshire, 1725–28
Swynnerton Hall, near Stone, Staffordshire,
c. 1725–29 (thought to be by; altered 1811,
1949, 1974)
Davenport House, near Bridgnorth, Shropshire,
1726

St Modwen's Church, Burton-upon-Trent,
Staffordshire; completion, *c*. 1726
Shardeloes, near Beaconsfield, Buckinghamshire,
1726–27 (reconstructed 1758–66)
Mawley Hall, near Bewdley, Shropshire, 1730
Brogyntyn, near Oswestry, Shropshire, 1735

Smith, George
Green's Bridge, Kilkenny, Co. Kilkenny, Ireland,
1764

Smith, George (1783–1869)
St Peter and St Paul's Church, Church Road,
Merton, London, 1819–21
St Peter's Church, London Colney,
Hertfordshire, 1825–26
St Michael's Church, Blackheath Park,
Greenwich, London, 1828–29

Smith, George (1793–1877)
Exchange Coffee Room, corner of Castle Street
and Exchange Street, Dundee, Tayside,
1828–30

**Smith, James
with Alexander MacGill**
Yester House, near Haddington, Lothian,
1699–1728

Smith, John
Nigg Church, Grampian, 1828–29
North Church, King Street, Aberdeen, 1830
South Church, King Street, Aberdeen, 1830–31

Smith, Marmaduke
17–25 Wilkes Street, Spitalfields, London, 1723
4 and 6 Fournier Street, Spitalfields, London,
1726

Smith, William (1705–48)
Catton Hall, near Burton-upon-Trent,
Derbyshire, 1741
with Richard Smith
St Modwen's Church, Burton-upon-Trent,
Staffordshire, 1719–26
with John Sanderson
Kirtlington Park, near Bicester, Oxfordshire,
1742–47
Thame Park, Thame, Oxfordshire; west façade,
c. 1745

Smyth, Grice
Ballynatray, Glendine, Co. Waterford, 1795

Smyth, John
St Catherine's Church, Thomas Street, Dublin,
Ireland, 1769

Soane, Sir John (1753–1837)
Born in the Reading area and the youngest son
of seven children, he was taken into the office
of George Dance the Younger at the age of 15.
He was awarded a Royal Academy silver medal
for an architectural drawing and went to Rome
in 1777 as a travelling student. Following a
wealthy marriage, he was appointed architect of
the Bank of England in 1788, rebuilding the
whole structure and gaining a great reputation
for the work.
  He succeeded Dance as Professor of
Architecture at the Royal Academy in 1806,
and began a collection of paintings, sculptures,
drawings and gems at a home in Lincoln's Inn
Fields, which he presented with its contents to
the nation in 1833. Soane ranks, with a few
others, among the great original designers in
the history of British architecture but his work
has suffered greatly at the hands of the
demolishers. It was very much a part of the
neoclassical revival and of the interest in
ancient Greek, rather than Roman,
architectural forms which swept through
Europe at the end of the eighteenth century. He
used these forms with a brilliant inventiveness
fascinating those interested in the penetration of
solid forms by space, the enclosure of space in
interiors, and the use of subtle daylighting

Malvern Hall, Solihull, West Midlands;
alterations, *c*. 1780
Petersham Lodge, River Lane, Petersham,
Richmond-upon-Thames, London;
redecoration and repair, 1781
Barn Hall, near Durham, Co. Durham;
cowshed, 1783
Blackfriars Bridge, St George Street, Norwich,
Norfolk, 1783 (since widened)
Letton Hall, near Swaffham, Norfolk, 1783–89
Rectory, Saxlingham Nethergate, Norfolk,
1784–87
Lodges, Langley Park, near Norwich, Norfolk,
1784–90
Shotesham Park, near Norwich, Norfolk, *c*. 1785
Blundeston House, near Lowestoft, Suffolk,
1785–86
Chillington Hall, near Wolverhampton,
Staffordshire; alterations, 1785–89
Piercefield, Chepstow, Gwent, 1785–93 (ruin)
Bentley Priory, Stanmore, London; additions,
1788–1801 (now much altered, and damaged
by fire 1980)
Bank of England, Threadneedle Street, City of
London; completion, 1788–1833 (rebuilt
1921–37)
82 Guildhall Street, Bury St Edmunds, Suffolk;
extensions, 1789
Sydney Lodge, near Southampton, Hampshire,
1789–98
Seven Bridges House, Bridge Street, Reading,
Berkshire, 1790
Union Fire Office, Surrey Street, Norwich,
Norfolk; additions, *c*. 1790
Wiston Hall, Wissington, Suffolk, 1791
Baronscourt, Newtownstewart, Co. Tyrone,
Ireland; remodelling, 1791–92 (altered later)
Wimpole Hall, Cambridgeshire; alterations,
1791–93
12–14 Lincoln's Inn Fields, Holborn, London,
1792
Piercefield Park, near Chepstow, Gwent, 1793
Lodge, Tyringham House, near Newport
Pagnell, Buckinghamshire, 1793
Tyringham House, near Newport Pagnell,
Buckinghamshire, 1793–97
Park Farm, in the grounds of Wimpole Hall,
near Cambridge, Cambridgeshire, 1794
Hyde Abbey House, Hyde Street, Winchester,
Hampshire; school room, 1795
936 Warwick Road, Solihull, West Midlands,
1798
Aynho Park, Northamptonshire, 1799–1804
(later remodelled and extended)
Pitzhanger Manor, Walpole Park, off Mattock
Lane, Ealing, London; enlargement for himself,
1800–02
Cairness House, near Fraserburgh, Grampian;
portico, *c*. 1800
Macartney House, Chesterfield Walk,
Greenwich, London; additions and internal
detailing, 1802
Simeon Monument, Market Place, Reading,
Berkshire, 1804
Port Eliot, St German's, Cornwall; remodelling,
1804–06
Ramsey Abbey, Cambridgeshire, 1804–07
Moggerhanger House (now Park Hospital), near
Sandy, Bedfordshire, 1809–11
Dulwich College Picture Gallery, Dulwich,
London, 1811–14
13 Lincoln's Inn Fields, Holborn, London, 1812
Ringwould House, Kent, 1813
Stables, Royal Hospital, Royal Hospital Road,
Chelsea, London, 1814
Butterton Grange, near Newcastle-under-Lyne,
Staffordshire, 1815
Marden Hill, near Tewin, Hertfordshire;
remodelling, 1818–19
Secretary's Offices, Royal Hospital, Royal
Hospital Road, Chelsea, London, 1818–19
Pelwall House, near Market Drayton,
Shropshire, 1822–28
St Peter's Church, Liverpool Grove, Walworth,
London, 1823–25
14 Lincoln's Inn Fields, Holborn, London; own
house, 1824

Above: *the John Soane Museum, 13 Lincoln's Inn Fields; and* below, *number 14*

Board of Trade, Whitehall, London, 1824–27 (remodelled 1844)
10 Downing Street, Whitehall, London; dining room, *c.* 1825
Holy Trinity, Marylebone Road, Marylebone, London, 1826–27
St John's Church, Cambridge Heath Road, London, 1826–28 (nave since remodelled)

Spiller, James (*d.* 1829)
St John the Baptist's Church, Mare Street, Hackney, London, 1792–97 (steeple added by Spiller 1812–13)

Spray, Matthew
St Mary Magdalene's Church, St Mary's Street, Woolwich, London, 1727–39 (thought to be by)

Stapleton
Belvedere House, Great Denmark Street, Dublin, Ireland, 1786

Star, W and **Collingwood, John** (*c.* 1760–1831)
Horton Road Hospital (formerly lunatic asylum), Gloucester, Gloucestershire, 1813–23

Stark, William (1770–1813)
St George's Church, Buchanan Street, Glasgow, Strathclyde, 1807
Court House, Gaol and Public Offices, Glasgow Green, Glasgow, Strathclyde, 1807–14 (rebuilt 1910)

Staveley, Christopher (1759–1827)
Leadenham House, Lincolnshire, 1790–96 (additions 1829)

Stephenson, David (1757–1819)
All Saints' Church, Newcastle-upon-Tyne, Tyne and Wear, 1786–96
Northumberland Arms Inn, North Shields, Tyne and Wear, 1806–17
Percy Tenantry Column, Alnwick, Northumberland, 1816

Steuart, George (*c.* 1730–1806)
Baronscourt, Newtownstewart, Co. Tyrone, Ireland; begun by Steuart *c.* 1780; completed and remodelled by Sir John Soane 1791 (altered later)
Attingham Hall, Shropshire, 1783–85
All Saints' Church, Wellington, Shropshire, 1788–1790
St Chad's Church, Shrewsbury, Shropshire, 1790–92
Blairuachdar (farm), near Pitlochry, Tayside, 1797
Court House, Ramsey, Isle of Man, *c.* 1798

Stevens, Alexander (*c.* 1730–96)
Dry Grange Bridge, Melrose, Borders, *c.* 1780
Bridge of Dun, Tayside, 1785
Raehills, near Moffat, Dumfries and Galloway, 1786 (enlarged 1829)
St Cuthbert's Church, Lothian Road, Edinburgh; tower and steeple, 1789

Stirling, William (1772–1838)
Home Farm, Doune Park, central Scotland, 1807–09
Athenaeum, King Street, Stirling, central Scotland, 1814–16
North Church, Airth, central Scotland, 1818
Lecropt Church, central Scotland, 1824–26

Stokoe, John (*c.* 1756–1836)
Moot Hall, Castle Garth, Newcastle-upon-Tyne, Tyne and Wear, 1810
Exchange, Sunderland, Tyne and Wear, 1812–14

Stone, Francis (1775–1834)
St Andrew's Hospital, Thorpe, Norfolk, 1811–14

Strahan, John (*d.* 1740)
A carpenter by training; his buildings show the influence of Vanbrugh and Campbell.
Painswick House, Painswick, near Stroud, Gloucestershire, *c.* 1725 (thought to be by)
66, 68, and 70 Prince Street, Bristol, Avon, *c.* 1725–30 (thought to be by)
Beauford Square, Bath, Avon, *c.* 1732 *right*
Redland Court, Redland, Bristol, Avon, *c.* 1735
Rosewell House, Kingsmead Square, Bath, Avon, 1736
with William Halfpenny
Redland Chapel, Redland Green, Bristol, Avon, 1740–43

Stratford, Ferdinando
Market Hall and Assembly Room,

Newtownards, Co. Down, Ireland, 1765

Strong, Sir Edward
Ivy House, 107 St Peter's Hill, St Albans, Hertfordshire, *c.* 1720

Stuart, James (1713–88)
He was known as 'Athenian' Stuart, and was one of the Scots who influenced English architecture. He educated himself as a draughtsman and by 1741 had gone to Rome, where he remained and worked for nine years, moving to Athens with Revett in 1751. In 1762, he published vol I of *The Antiquities of Athens*, being responsible himself for the landscape views while Revett prepared the measured drawings. His Doric temple of 1758 in the grounds of Hagley Hall was the first correctly Hellenic building in England
Hagley Hall, near Kidderminster, Hereford and Worcester; Temple of Theseus in the grounds, 1758
Shugborough, near Stafford, Staffordshire; Shepherds' Monument in the grounds, *c.* 1758
Dreadnought Hospital, Romney Road, Greenwich, London, 1763–64
Shugborough, near Stafford, Staffordshire; Tower of the Winds in the grounds, 1764
Shugborough, near Stafford, Staffordshire; Doric temple in the grounds, 1764
15 Duke of York Street, Westminster, London, 1764–66
Shugborough, near Stafford, Staffordshire; triumphal arch in the grounds, 1764–67
Shugborough, near Stafford, Staffordshire; Lanthorn of Demosthenes in the grounds, 1764–70
Greenwich Palace (now National Maritime Museum) and Royal Naval Hospital, Romney Road, Greenwich, London; south pavilion, King Charles block) 1769
Mount Stewart, Newtownards, Co. Down, Ireland; Temple of the Winds in the grounds, 1780
with the Earl of Harcourt
All Saints' Church, Nuneham Courtenay, Oxfordshire, 1764

Sweetman, John
St Mary's Pro-Cathedral, Marlborough Street, Dublin, Ireland, *c.* 1816 (thought to be by)

Sykes, Sir Christopher
Sledmere House, near Great Driffield, Humberside, 1781–88 (alterations and extensions thought to be by)

Tasker, John (*c.* 1738–1816)
St Mary's Roman Catholic Church, East Lulworth, Dorset, 1786
Spetchley Park, Hereford and Worcester, begun 1811

Tatham, Charles Heathcote (1772–1842)
He worked under Henry Holland and designed the decorations for Drury Lane Theatre. He published *Ancient Ornamented Architecture at Rome and in Italy* in 1799, exhibited at the Royal Academy, and was made warden of Holy Trinity Hospital, Greenwich

Castle Howard, near Malton, North Yorkshire;
sculpture gallery and museum, 1800–01
Roche Court, near Winterslow, Wiltshire,
c. 1805
Dropmore, Buckinghamshire; north and south
extensions, 1806–09
Trentham Hall, Staffordshire; mausoleum in the
grounds, 1807–08
Mausoleum, Ochtertyre, Tayside, 1809
Rookesbury, near Wickham, Hampshire,
1820–25

Tattersall, Richard (c. 1803–44)
Cumberland Infirmary, Newton Road, Carlisle,
1830–32 (remodelled 1870s)

Tawney, R D
The Master's Lodgings (formerly Canal House),
St Peter's College, Oxford, 1827–29

Taylor, James (c. 1765–1846)
St Edmund's Roman Catholic College, Old Hall
Green, Hertfordshire, 1795–99

Taylor, J H
St John's Church, Waltham Green, Fulham,
London, 1827–28

Taylor, Sir Robert (1714–88)
The leading figure of a new generation of
Palladian architects in London; by 1750
Burlington, Campbell, Leoni and Kent were all
dead or no longer practising. Flitcroft was
building only outside the capital and Gibbs, the
major survivor of the Wren tradition, was right
at the end of his career. Taylor, together with
James Paine, then held sway until the
emergence of Robert Adam. He was knighted
while Sheriff of London, 1782–83, and left the
bulk of his property for the teaching of modern
languages at Oxford.
Braxted Park near Witham, Essex; rebuilding,
1753–56
Harleyford Manor, near Marlow,
Buckinghamshire, 1755
Barlaston Hall, near Stoke-on-Trent,
Staffordshire, 1756–58
Chute Lodge, near Amesbury, Wiltshire, 1760
(thought to be by)
Asgill House, Old Palace Lane, Richmond-upon-
Thames, London, 1760–65
Danson Park, Welling, Bexley, London, 1760–65
Bank of England, Threadneedle Street, City of
London, 1766–74 (rebuilt in 1921–37)
Osney Bridge, Botley Road, Oxford,
Oxfordshire, 1767
33 Upper Brook Street, London, 1767–68 *right*
Mount Clare, Danebury Avenue, Roehampton,
London, 1770–73
Sharpham, near Totnes, Devon, c. 1770
3 The Terrace, Richmond Hill, Richmond-upon-
Thames, London, c. 1770 (thought to be by)
Swinford Bridge, Eynsham, Oxfordshire, c. 1770
(thought to be by)
3–6 Grafton Street, London, 1771–73
Ely House, 37 Dover Street, Piccadilly, London,
1772–76 (internal alterations 1909)
Bridge, Maidenhead, Berkshire, 1772–77
St Peter's Church, Wallingford, Oxfordshire;
spire, 1776
Belfast Bank Head Office (originally Market
House built in 1764), Belfast, Co. Antrim,
Ireland; conversion to Assembly Rooms, 1776
(exterior altered 1825, interior altered 1895)
Gorhambury, near St Albans, Hertfordshire,
c. 1777–84 (altered later)
Heveningham Hall, near Halesworth, Suffolk,
1779
with William Pilkington
Guildhall, Market Place, Salisbury, Wiltshire,
1788 (enlarged 1829)

Taylor, Thomas (c. 1778–1826)
Christ Church, Liversedge, West Yorkshire,
1812–16
Holy Trinity Church, Trinity Street,
Huddersfield, West Yorkshire, 1816–19

Holy Trinity Church, Littleborough, Greater
Manchester, 1818–20
St Laurence, Pudsey, West Yorkshire, 1821–24
St Mary, Quarry Hill, Leeds, West Yorkshire,
1823–26
Holy Trinity Church, Kirby Road, Ripon, North
Yorkshire, 1826–28 (altered 1874)

Teanby, William
Cobb's Brewery, Margate, Kent, 1807–08

Telford, Thomas (1757–1834)
Worked as a mason in Edinburgh in 1780 and
moved to London in 1782. He became surveyor
of public works for Shropshire and engineer of
the Ellesmere Canal in 1793, in which capacity
he built the remarkable aqueduct over the
Ceiriog Valley at Chirk, 1796–1801. He was
one of the founders, and the first president of,
the Institute of Civil Engineers in 1818
St Mary Magdalene's Church, Bridgnorth,
Shropshire, 1792–94
Tern Aqueduct (on Shropshire Union Canal),
Longdon-upon-Tern, Shropshire, 1793–94
St Michael's Church, Madeley, Shropshire,
1794–96 (chancel 1910)
Pontcysyllte Aqueduct, near Llangollen, Clwyd,
1794–1805
Bridge, Bewdley, Hereford and Worcester,
1795–99
Aquaduct, Chirk, Clwyd, 1796–1801
Tongland Bridge, near Kirkcudbright, Dumfries
and Galloway, 1805–06
Dunkeld Bridge, Tayside, 1806–09
Alford bridge, Grampian, 1810–11
Helmsdale Bridge, Highlands, 1811–12
Lovat Bridge, Highlands, 1811–14
Portarch Bridge, Grampian, 1811–15
Bridge, Craigellachie, Grampian, 1812–15
Waterloo Bridge, Betws-y-Coed, Gwynedd,
1815
Suspension Bridge, Menai Straits, Gwynedd,
1819–26
Cartland Crags Bridge, Strathclyde, 1821–22
Suspension Bridge, Conwy, Gwynedd, 1821–26
Mythe Bridge, Tewkesbury, Gloucestershire,
1823–26
Over Bridge, Gloucester, Gloucestershire 1825
Bridge (over River Avon), Hamilton,
Strathclyde, 1825
Don Bridge, near Aberdeen, Grampian,
1826–29

Thomas, William
Willersley Castle, Cromford, Derbyshire, 1789
Market Cross, Mountsorrel, Leicestershire, 1793

Thornhill, Sir James (1675–1734)
Employed by Queen Anne as a painter on
important works at Hampton Court,
Greenwich and Windsor, he designed the
paintings for the dome of St Paul's Cathedral,
London, decorated the Greenwich Hospital and
became sergeant-painter to George I. He was
knighted in 1720 and was MP for Melcombe
Regis from 1722–34
Moor Park, near Rickmansworth, Hertfordshire;
remodelling, 1725–27

Thornton, William
Beningborough Hall, near York, North
Yorkshire, c. 1712–1716

Thrubshaw, Richard
Pickhill Hall, near Wrexham, Clwyd, c. 1725

Timbrell, Benjamin
Grosvenor Chapel, South Audley Street,
London, c. 1730 *below*

Tite, Sir William (1798–1873)
President of the Architectural Society, MP for
Bath 1855–73, and knighted 1869
Mill Hill School, Ridgeway, Mill Hill, London,
1825–27

Tomkins, Benjamin
Stratton House, Bath Street, Abingdon,
Oxfordshire, 1722 *below*

Townesend, William
Shotover Park, near Oxford, Oxfordshire,
1714–18 (thought to be by)
Radley Hall, Radley College, Radley,
Oxfordshire, 1721–27

Tracy, C Hanbury
Toddington Manor, Gloucestershire, 1820–35

Traill, Sir John
Kilmainham Gaol (now museum), Kilmainham, Dublin, Ireland, c. 1796

Tuck, William
Gaol, Saturday Market, King's Lynn, Norfolk, 1784
with Thomas King
New Assembly Rooms, King's Lynn, Norfolk, 1766–68

Underwood, George Allen (c. 1793–1829)
Montpellier Pump Rooms and Rotunda, Cheltenham, Gloucestershire, 1817 (now Lloyds Bank)
Holy Trinity Church, Portland Street, Cheltenham, Gloucestershire, 1820–23
Masonic Hall, Portland Street, Cheltenham, Gloucestershire 1820–23

Vanbrugh, Sir John (1664–1726)
Dramatist, architect and herald; son of a London tradesman of Flemish descent whose family moved to Chester in 1666. He studied in France 1683–85, entered the army in 1686, and was imprisoned in France 1690–92. On returning to civilian life he was appointed Comptroller of the Board of Works, 1702–12, and again in 1715; manager of the Haymarket Theatre 1705–07, and was knighted in 1714. His work is of fundamental importance to the history of British architecture; along with Hawksmore, he is one of the two great originals of the English baroque period, and their work is like that of no other
Castle Howard, near Malton, North Yorkshire, 1700–26 (with help from Hawksmore) *below*

Blenheim Palace, Oxfordshire, 1705–16 (completed by Hawksmore)
Bladon Bridge, Blenheim Palace, Oxfordshire, c. 1710–16
King's Weston, Bristol, Avon, 1712–14 (altered internally 1763–68)
Town Hall, Morpeth, Northumberland, 1714 (rebuilt c. 1875)
Claremont, Esher, Surrey; belvedere in grounds, c. 1715
Royal Brass Foundry, Royal Arsenal, Woolwich, London, 1716 (thought to be by)
Vanbrugh Castle, Greenwich, London, 1717 (additions c. 1723)
St James's Palace, Westminster, London, 1717–18 (thought to be by)
Seaton Delaval Hall, near Blyth, Northumberland, 1717–29 (centre gutted 1822) *right*
Castle Howard, near Malton, North Yorkshire; Pyramid Gate, 1719
Stowe, near Buckingham, Buckinghamshire; Rotondo in grounds, 1719 (altered)
Lumley Castle, near Chester-le-Street, Durham; alterations, c. 1721
Grimsthorpe Castle, near Bourne, Lincolnshire; rebuilding of north front, 1722–26
Castle Howard, near Malton, North Yorkshire; Temple of the Four Winds, 1724

Vardy, John the Younger (d. 1765)
Clerk of works at the Horse Guards, London,

1751, at Kensington Palace and the Chelsea Hospital
7 Abingdon Street, Westminster Abbey, London, c. 1750 (thought to be by)
Spencer House, St James's Place, Westminster, London; side elevation, 1762–65
with Joseph Bonomi
7 Burlington Gardens (now Bank of Scotland), Piccadilly, London; alterations, 1785–89

Vesey, Agmondisham
Lucan House, Lucan, Co. Dublin, Ireland; own house, c. 1775

Vulliamy, Lewis (1791–1871)
A pupil of Sir Robert Smirke, he settled in London in 1822
St Bartholomew's Church, Westwood Hill, Sydenham, London, 1827–32
Corn Exchange, Bishops Stortford, Hertfordshire, 1828
St Barnabas' Church, Addison Road, Kensington, London, 1828
Leadenham House, Lincolnshire; additions, 1829

Wade, General
Wade's House, Abbey Churchyard, Bath, Avon, c. 1720
Bridge over River Tay, Aberfeldy, Tayside, 1733

Wakefield, William
A gentleman architect from Yorkshire whose buildings are clearly derived from Vanbrugh and Gibbs
Gilling Castle, near Thirsk, North Yorkshire; remodelling, c. 1725
Fountains Hospital, Linton, North Yorkshire, c. 1725 (thought to be by)

Wallace, Robert (c. 1790–1874)
St James's Church, St James's Road, Croydon, London, 1827–29

Wallis, Charles
St Swithin, Allington, Bridport, Dorset, 1826–27

Walpole, Horace (1678–1757)
with John Chute, Richard Bentley, Thomas Pitt, Robert Adam, James Wyatt and James Essex
Strawberry Hill, Twickenham, London, begun c. 1751

Walters, John (1782–1821)
St Paul's Church, The Highway, Whitechapel, London, 1820–21

Ware, Isaac (d. 1766)
He entered the Board of Works in 1728, serving as a draughtsman and published the *Complete Body of Architecture* in 1756. This volume gave information on all practical aspects, expressing the changing standards of the mid-century
Clifton Hill House, Clifton, Avon, 1746–50
Chicksands Priory, Bedfordshire; work on medieval remains, c. 1750
Wrotham Park, near Potters Bar, Hertfordshire, 1754 (interior gutted 1883)

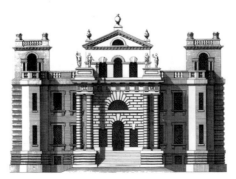

Ware, Samuel (1781–1860)
Burlington Arcade, Piccadilly, London, 1818–19 (partly rebuilt) *above*

Watson, Charles (c. 1770–1836)
St John's Church, St John's Square, Wakefield, West Yorkshire, 1791–95
Sessions House, North Bar Without, Beverley, Humberside, 1804–14
Court House, Pontefract, West Yorkshire, 1807–08
Saltmarshe Hall, Laxton, Humberside, 1818–28
with James Pigott Pritchett (1789–1868)
Friends' Meeting House, Clifford Street, York, 1816–19
Independent Chapel, Norfolk Street, Sheffield, South Yorkshire, 1827
Assembly Rooms, Blake Street, York; entrance front, 1828

Webb, John (c. 1754–1828)
The Vyne, near Basingstoke, Hampshire, 1754–56
Apley Park, near Bridgnorth, Shropshire, 1811
Warleigh House, near Bathford, Avon, 1814
Thrybergh Park, South Yorkshire, c. 1820

Webster, George (1797–1864)
Read Hall, Lancashire, 1818–25
Eshton Hall, near Skipton, North Yorkshire, 1825–27
Assembly Rooms (now Town Hall), Highgate, Kendal, Cumbria, 1725–27 (altered)
Underley Hall, near Kirkby Longsdale, Cumbria, 1825–28 (enlarged 1872)

Westbrook, Samuel
Brick Alley Almshouses, Abingdon, Oxfordshire 1718–20

Whichcord, John (1790–1860)
Royal Insurance (formerly Kent Fire) Offices, High Street, Maidstone, Kent, 1827
Oakwood Hospital, St Andrew's Road, Maidstone, Kent, 1830

White, Edward
Town Hall, Margate, Kent, 1821

White, John (c. 1747–1813)
Glevering Hall, Suffolk, 1792–94 (additions 1834)
St John the Baptist's Church, Buxton, Derbyshire, 1811

White, Thomas (1674–1748)
Mainly practised as a sculptor; he is thought to have been a pupil of Wren, from whose style his known buildings derive

Church of St Mary and St Margaret, Castle Bromwich, West Midlands, 1726 (thought to be by)
White Lodge (now the Royal Ballet School), Richmond Park, Richmond-upon-Thames, London; quadrant wings, begun *c.* 1755

Wickings, William (*c.* 1757–1841)
St Mary Magdalene's Church, Holloway Road, Islington, London, 1812–14

Wightwick, George (1802–72)
Entered the offices of Sir John Soane before establishing his own practice in Plymouth in 1829
Tregrehan House, St Blazey, Cornwall, *c.* 1804–05
Sussex Place, Plymouth, Devon, 1832–36

Wilds, Amon (*c.* 1762–1833)
1–4 Castle Place, Cowes, East Sussex, *c.* 1810
166 High Street, Lewes, East Sussex, *c.* 1810
Congregational Chapel, Union Street, Brighton, East Sussex, 1820
Park Crescent, Worthing, West Sussex, 1829

Wilds, Amon Henry
Son of Amon Wilds
Oriental Place, Brighton, East Sussex, 1825 *below*

Oriental Terrace, Brighton, East Sussex, 1825
Sillwood Place, Brighton, East Sussex, 1827 *below*
Western Pavilion, Western Terrace, Brighton, East Sussex; own house, *c.* 1827
Hanover Crescent, Brighton, East Sussex, *c.* 1827
Park Crescent, Brighton, East Sussex, 1829
Chestham Park, near Henfield, West Sussex, *c.* 1830 (thought to be by)
Milton Park Estate, Gravesend, Kent (including Berkeley Crescent) *c.* 1830

Wilkins, William the Elder (1751–1815)
Donington Hall, near Long Eaton, Leicestershire, 1790–93
Stanfield Hall, Wymondham, Norfolk, 1792 (altered 1830s)
Bracondale Lodge, Martineau Lane, Norwich, Norfolk, *c.* 1795
Prestwold Hall, Leicestershire; alterations, 1805 (later remodelled)
Dalmeny House, near Queensferry, Lothian, 1814–17

Wilkins, William the Younger (1778–1839)
Born in Norwich, he gained his BA from Caius College, Cambridge in 1800. His buildings are a central part of the achievement of the early nineteenth-century Greek revival in northern Europe, for he was the pre-eminent English scholar of that style. In Cambridge, where he built more than anyone else, he also designed in the gothic and Tudor styles
Bracondale Lodge, Martineau Lane, Norwich, Norfolk, *c.* 1795
Downing College, Cambridge, Cambridgeshire, 1804
The Grange, near New Alresford, Hampshire, 1804–09 (gutted 1972)
Osberton Hall, near Worksop, Nottinghamshire, *c.* 1805–06 (altered)
Haileybury College, near Ware, Hertfordshire, 1806–09
Dalmeny House, Lothian, 1814–17
Tregothnan, near Truro, Cornwall, 1816–18 (extended 1842)
Keswick Hall (now Training College), Norfolk, 1817–19 (enlarged 1951)
Nelson Column, Great Yarmouth, Norfolk, 1817–20
Friends' Meeting House (former Masonic Hall), York Street, Bath, Avon, 1819
Theatre Royal, Westgate Street, Bury St Edmunds, Suffolk, 1819
Trinity College New Court, Cambridge, Cambridgeshire, 1821–05
Shire Hall, Castle Meadow, Norwich, Norfolk, 1822–23 (refaced 1913)
Corpus Christi College New Court, Cambridge, Cambridgeshire 1823–27
Fellows' Buildings, King's College, Cambridge, Cambridgeshire; entrance screen, 1824–28
County Gaol (now Norwich Museum), Norwich, Norfolk, 1824–28
University College, Gower Street, Bloomsbury, London, 1827–29
Yorkshire Museum, York, Yorkshire, 1827–30
County Gaol (former), St Peter's Road, Huntingdon, Cambridgeshire; 1828 (pavilions and watchtower survive)
St George's Hospital (now the Lanesborough Hotel), Hyde Park Corner, London, 1828–29

Wilson, John (mason)
St Peter's Church, Sowerby, West Yorkshire, 1761–63

Wilson, John
St James's Church, St Peter Port, Guernsey, 1817–18
Market Hall, St Peter Port, Guernsey, 1822
Elizabeth College, St Peter Port, Guernsey, 1826

Wing, Edward
St Michael's Church, Aynho, Northamptonshire, 1723–25 (thought to be by)
Church, Gayhurst, Buckinghamshire, 1728 (thought to be by)

Wing, John the Elder
St Peter's Church, Galby, Leicestershire, 1741
St John the Baptist Church, King's Norton, Leicester, 1760–75

Wing, John the Younger (1756–1826)
House of Industry, Bedford, 1795–96
Gaol, Dame Alice Street, Bedford, 1801 (later additions)
Bridge, Bedford, 1811–13 (widened later)

Wishlade, Benjamin
Town Hall, Kingston, Hereford and Worcester, 1820

Wood, John the Elder (1704–54)
Known as Wood of Bath; he spent most of his career building in that city, after 1727 concentrating on plans to build a new town which was inaugurated with his Queen Square
Queen Square (north side), Bath, Avon, 1729
Balcombe Court, Bradford-on-Avon, Wiltshire, 1734
Prior Park, Combe Down, Avon, 1735–48
Frenchay Manor, Frenchay, Avon, 1736 (thought to be by)
General Infirmary (now Royal Mineral Water Hospital), Bath, Avon, 1738 *below*

North Parade, Bath, Avon, *c.* 1739–44
South Parade, Bath, Avon, *c.* 1739–44 *below*

Duke Street, Bath, Avon, *c.* 1739–44
Pierrepont Street, Bath, Avon, *c.* 1740 *below*

41 Gay Street, Bath, Avon, 1740
Exchange, Corn Street, Bristol, Avon, 1740–45

Exchange (now Town Hall), Liverpool,
 Merseyside, 1749–54 (damaged by fire 1795
 and rebuilt c. 1820)
with **John Wood the Younger**
The Circus, Bath, Avon, 1754–66 *above*
Palladian Bridge, Prior Park, Bath, Avon
 (thought to be to design of Wood the Elder),
 1755–56

Wood, John the Younger (*d.* 1782)
Helped to realise his father's grandiose schemes
 for Bath with the completion of the Circus and
 the addition of the Royal Crescent
Buckland House, near Faringdon, Oxfordshire,
 1755–57
All Saints' Church, Woolley, near Bath, Avon,
 1761

Trafalgar House (originally Standlynch), near
 Salisbury, Wiltshire; addition of wings, 1766
Royal Crescent, Bath, Avon, 1767 *below*
General Infirmary, Fisherton Street, Salisbury,
 Wiltshire, 1767–71
New Assembly Rooms, Bath, Avon, 1769–71
 (restored after bombing)
St Nicholas' Church, Hardenhuish, Wiltshire, 1779

Wimborne House, 22 Arlington Street, London;
  completion, 1750 (façade rebuilt 1983)
University Library, Cambridge,
  Cambridgeshire, 1754
Milton House, near Abingdon, Oxfordshire,
  1764–72 *below*

Bridge and garden buildings, Clumber House,
  near Worksop, Nottinghamshire, *c.* 1775

Wright, Thomas
Ragged Castle, Castle Barn, Root House and
  Thatched Cottage, Badminton House grounds,
  Avon, 1745–56

Wyatt, Benjamin
Swinfen Hall, near Lichfield, Staffordshire, 1759
  (now part of prison)
Royal Infirmary, Infirmary Road, Leicester,
  Leicestershire, 1771 (enlarged 1888–1929)
with William Wyatt
General Hospital, Foregate Street, Stafford,
  Staffordshire, 1769–72

Wyatt, Benjamin Dean (1775–*c.* 1855)
Eldest son of James Wyatt, he was educated at
  Westminster School and Christ Church,
  Oxford. He was appointed Surveyor of
  Westminster Abbey, 1813–27
Theatre Royal, Drury Lane, Covent Garden,
  London, 1810–12
Lancaster House, Westminster, London, 1825
Crockford's Club, Westminster, London, 1827
  (much altered)
with Philip Wyatt
Apsley House, Hyde Park Corner, London;
  portico, 1828–29

Wyatt, James (1746–1813)
Studied architecture in Rome and Venice; he
  was appointed Surveyor of Westminster Abbey
  in 1776; Surveyor-General to the Board of
  Works in 1796, and architect to the Board of
  Ordnance in 1806. Working at first in a
  Graeco-Italian style, he gradually turned his
  attention to the gothic and originated the
  revival of interest in that form of architecture
Erddig, near Wrexham, Clwyd; additions,
  c. 1770

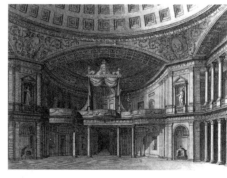

*The Pantheon, Oxford Street,
London 1769–72 by James
Wyatt (built as an entertainment
centre but destroyed in 1937)*

Woods, Joseph (1776–1864)
Clissold House, Clissold Park, Stoke
  Newington, London, *c.* 1800

Woodward, Edward
St Mary's Church, Preston on Stour,
  Warwickshire, 1753–54

Woodward, Thomas
Bedfont House, High Street, Chipping
  Campden, Gloucestershire, 1740
with Edward Woodward
St Nicholas's Church (body), Alcester,
  Warwickshire, 1729–30
St John the Baptist's Church, Northgate Street,
  Gloucester, Gloucestershire, 1732–34
St Swithun's Church, Church Street, Worcester,
  Hereford and Worcester, 1734–36
St Ann's Church, Bewdley, Hereford and
  Worcester, 1745–48

Worrall, Samuel
14, 17, 19 and 20 Princelet Street, Spitalfields,
  London, *c.* 1718–20
33A Fournier Street, Spitalfields, London; own
  house, *c.* 1721

Above: *the New Assembly
Rooms, Bath, originally designed
by John Wood the Younger*

8, 10 and 29–35 (odd) Fournier Street,
  Spitalfields, London, 1725–26
with John Worrall
Town House, Berwick-upon-Tweed,
  Northumberland, *c.* 1750–55

Worsley, Sir Thomas
Hovingham Hall, near Malton, North Yorkshire;
  own house, *c.* 1750

Wright, Nathaniel
St Botolph's Church, Aldersgate Street, City of
  London, 1788–91

Wright, Stephen (*d.* 1780)
The son of a bricklayer, and possibly clerk to
  William Kent; he found a patron in the Duke of
  Newcastle, for whom he designed the now-
  demolished Clumber, Nottinghamshire

Gunton Park, near North Walsham, Norfolk; wings, c. 1770 (gutted)

Dartrey (formerly Dawson Grove), Rockcorry, Co. Monaghan, Ireland; mausoleum in grounds of demolished house, c. 1770

Heaton Hall, Prestwich, Greater Manchester; rebuilding, 1772 (altered 1790 and 1806)

Radcliffe Observatory, Woodstock Road, Oxford, Oxfordshire; amended design, 1773

Shardeloes, near Beaconsfield, Buckinghamshire; library, c. 1775

Sheffield Place, near Haywards Heath, East Sussex, 1776–77 and 1789–90

Froebel Institute (originally Grove House), off Clarence Lane, Roehampton, London, 1777

Burton Constable Hall, near Kingston-upon-Hull, Humberside; ballroom, 1778

9 Conduit Street, Piccadilly, London, 1779

Heveningham Hall, near Halesworth, Suffolk; interior, 1780–84

Ragley Hall, near Stratford-upon-Avon, Warwickshire; portico, c. 1780

Orangery, Heveningham Hall, near Halesworth, Suffolk, 1780

Westport House, Westport, Co. Mayo, Ireland; completion of interior, 1781

Assembly Rooms, Chichester, West Sussex, 1781–83

Worcester College, Oxford, Oxfordshire; Hall, remodelled, 1784

Slane Castle, Slane, Co. Meath, Ireland, begun 1785

Goodwood House, near Chichester, West Sussex, 1787

White's Club, 37–38 St James's Street, Westminster, London, 1787–88 (refronted 1852)

Mausoleum, Brocklesby, near Grimsby, Lincolnshire, 1787–92

Guardroom, Royal Arsenal, Beresford Square, Woolwich, London, 1788

Aston Hall, near Oswestry, Shropshire, 1789–93

Worcester College, Oxford, Oxfordshire; Chapel, remodelled, c. 1790

Castle Coole, Enniskillen, Co. Fermanagh, Ireland; adopted from original plan by Richard Johnson, 1790–98

Dower House (Molecombe), near Chichester, West Sussex, c. 1790–1806

Broke Hall, Nacton, Suffolk; alterations, 1791–92

Balliol College, Oxford, Oxfordshire; alterations to former hall and library, 1792–94

Frogmore House, Home Park, Windsor, Berkshire; rebuilding, 1792–95

Stoke Park, Stoke Poges, Buckinghamshire; completion, c. 1793–97

Tower, Broadway Hill, near Evesham, Hereford and Worcester, 1794

Lasborough Park, near Nailsworth, Gloucestershire, 1794

Powderham Castle, near Dawlish, Devon; enlargements and alterations, 1794–96

Allestree Hall, Allestree, Derby, 1795

Bishop Auckland Castle, Bishop Auckland, Co. Durham; alterations, c. 1795

Plas Newydd, near Menai Bridge, Anglesey, Gwynedd; begun by Wyatt in 1795 and completed by Joseph Potter

Bishop's Palace, Bishop Auckland, Co. Durham; screen wall and inner gateway, 1796

Bowden House, near Chippenham, Wiltshire, 1796 right

Fonthill Abbey, near Shaftsbury, Wiltshire, 1796–1812 (only fragments remain)

Town Hall, Market Place, Ripon, North Yorkshire, 1798

Woodford Hall, Mellor, Lancashire, 1798–99 (thought to be by)

Dodington Park, near Bristol, Avon, 1798–1813

Norris Castle, East Cowes, Isle of Wight, 1799

Monument (to Thomas Gray, in the churchyard), Stoke Poges, Buckinghamshire, 1799

Pennsylvannia Castle, Isle of Portland, near Weymouth, Dorset, 1800

Bicton House, Devon, c. 1800 (remodelled 1908)

Church (Eglwys Newydd), Hafod, near Cardigan, Dyfed, c. 1800–03 (damaged 1932)

St Mary's Church, Dodington Park, near Bristol, Avon, 1800–05

White Lodge (Royal Ballet School), Richmond Park, London; porte-cochère on entrance front, 1801 (damaged 1932)

Wilton House, Wiltshire; north front and cloister, 1801–11

Lodges, Dodington Park, near Bristol, Avon, c. 1802

Wycombe Abbey, Marlow Hill, High Wycombe, Buckinghamshire; remodelling, 1803–04

West Dean Park, near Chichester, West Sussex, 1804 (much altered 1893)

(Old) Royal Military Academy, Academy Road, Woolwich, London, 1805–08

Ashridge Park, near Berkhamsted, Hertfordshire (completed by Wyatville), begun 1808–13

House, Acton Park, near Wrexham, Clwyd, 1810 (demolished)

Newark Park, near Ozleworth, Gloucestershire; remodelling, c. 1810

Chicksands Priory, Bedfordshire; alterations, 1813

with Benjamin Dean Wyatt, Matthew Cotes Wyatt and the Rev. J Thoroton

Belvoir Castle, Leicestershire; remodelling, 1801–c. 1830

Wyatt, Lewis William (1777–1853)

Wigginton Lodge, Staffordshire, 1804

Wonham Manor, Betchworth, Surrey; remodelling, c. 1805–10

Heaton Hall, Prestwich, Greater Manchester; alterations, 1806–24

Tatton Park, near Knutsford, Cheshire; completion and modifications, 1807–25

Rode Hall, Cheshire; alterations, 1810–12

Willey Hall, near Much Wenlock, Shropshire, 1813–15

Lyme Park, near New Mills, Cheshire; attic storey behind pediment only, 1814–17

Cuerden Hall, Lancashire; remodelling of earlier house, 1815

Mount Shannon, Castleconnell, Co. Limerick, Ireland, c. 1815 (ruin)

with Samuel Wyatt

Hackwood Park, near Basingstoke, Hampshire; rebuilding of earlier house, 1800–13

Wyatt, Philip William (d. 1835)

Conishead Priory, Cumbria, 1821–36

Wynyard Park, Co. Durham, 1822–30

Wyatt, Samuel (1737–1807)

Rectory, in the grounds of Kedleston, near Derby, Derbyshire, 1771

House, Baron Hill, near Beaumaris, Anglesey, Gwynedd, 1776 (ruin)

Doddington Hall, near Crewe, Cheshire, 1777–98

Admiralty House, Royal Dockyard, Portsmouth, Hampshire, 1784–86

Coton House, near Rugby, Warwickshire, 1785

Tatton Park, near Knutsford, Cheshire; begun by Samuel Wyatt 1785–91 and completed by Lewis William Wyatt 1807–25

Belmont Park, near Faversham, Kent, 1787–92

Heaton Hall, Prestwich, Greater Manchester; alterations, 1790

Shugborough near Stafford, Staffordshire; remodelling, 1790–98

Holkham Hall, near Wells-next-the-Sea, Norfolk; Great Barn, c. 1790

Trinity House, Tower Hill, City of London, 1792–94

Dropmore, Buckinghamshire, 1792–94 (extended 1806)

Somerley, Hampshire, 1792–95 (remodelled and extended 1869–74; partly demolished)

Stornoway House, Cleveland Row, St James's, Westminster, London, 1794–96 (altered externally)

Court Lodge (formerly Rectory), Wrotham, Kent 1801–02

Wyatville, Sir Jeffry (1766–1840)

Originally named Wyatt, he changed his name in 1824; he was the nephew of James Wyatt, with whom he worked between 1792–99, after which he established his own practice. He exhibited at the Royal Academy from 1786 and was knighted in 1828

Hillfield, Hillfield Lane, Aldenham, Hertfordshire, c. 1795 (originally known as Sly's Castle)

Bladon Castle, near Newton Solney, Derbyshire, 1799 (enlarged 1801)

Woolley Park, Brightwalton, Berkshire; remodelling, 1799

Nonsuch Park, near Ewell, Surrey, 1802–06

Hyde Hall, Hertfordshire, 1803–07

Gaol, Abingdon, Oxfordshire, 1805–11

Longleat, near Warminster, Wiltshire; internal remodelling, 1806–11

Rood Ashton House, West Ashton, Wiltshire, 1808 (altered 1836; ruin)

Lypiatt Park, near Stroud, Gloucestershire, 1809 (enlargement; altered 1876)

Tower, Nant-y-Belan, Wynnstay Park, Clwyd, 1810

Endsleigh, near Launceston, Devon, 1810–11

Philipps House, Dinton, Wiltshire, 1812–17

Stubton Hall (now school), Lincolnshire, 1813–14 (many additions; south front demolished)

Bretby Hall, Derbyshire, c. 1813–15

Ashridge Park, Hertfordshire, completion from 1813–18 (begun by J Wyatt)

Denford House, Berkshire, c. 1815 (later alterations and additions)

Bretton Hall, near Barnsley, West Yorkshire; remodelling, c. 1815

Townley Hall, Lancashire; alterations, 1817–19

Banner Cross, Eccleshall, Sheffield, South Yorkshire, 1817–21

Trebursey House, near Launceston, Cornwall, c. 1820

Claverton Manor, near Bath, Avon, c. 1820

Chatsworth House, Derbyshire; north wing extension, 1820–41

39 Lower Brook Street, London; own house, alterations and additions, 1821

Allendale House, Wimborne Minster, Dorset, 1823

Windsor Castle, Windsor, Berkshire; remodelling, 1824–40

'Temple of Augustus', Virginia Water, Berkshire, 1826–29

Lilleshall Hall, near Newport, Shropshire, 1826–33

Golden Grove, Pembroke, Dyfed, 1826–37

Fort Belvedere, Great Park, Windsor, Hampshire; extensions, 1827–30

with Jones & Clark of Birmingham

Camellia House, in grounds of Wollaton Hall, between Nottingham and Beeston, Nottinghamshire, 1823

Yenn, John (1750–1821)

Wargrave Manor, Berkshire, c. 1780–90

Peper Harrow, near Godalming, Surrey; alterations, 1791 (later altered)

Greenwich Palace (now National Maritime Museum) and Royal Naval Hospital, Romney Road, Greenwich, London; west front of King Charles block, 1811–14

Glossary

Abacus: a flat stone slab positioned underneath the entablature and forming the uppermost element of a classical capital. In Greek Doric, it is a square without chamfer or moulding; in Greek Ionic, thinner with ovolo moulding only; in Roman Ionic and Corinthian, the sides are hollowed or plain and have the angles cut off. The abacus is deeper in Romanesque, but projects less and is moulded with rounds and hollows, or chamfered on the lower edge. The circular or octagonal abacus was favoured in English gothic, while the square or octagonal abacus is a French feature.

Abutment: a mass of solid masonry at the meeting of an arch or vault, which resists the lateral pressure.

Acanthus: a stylised plant leaf motif, formally treated, with thick veins, frilled edges and sharp points. They are used to form the lower parts of the Corinthian capital, and represent one of the primary elements of classical architecture.

Acroteria: blocks resting on the apex and ends of the pediment, forming a plinth to support the statuary or ornaments. The term also applies to the statues.

Aedicule: now applied to the frames surrounding a classical doorway, window or niche, flanked by a pair of columns or colonnettes and topped by a pediment. It originated in the architectural treatment of the shrines of the classical period.

Aggregate: small stones added to a binding material. In modern architecture, it is used alone to describe concrete with an aggregate of stone chippings. The remains of demolished structures have traditionally been recycled as aggregate.

Aisles: lateral divisions running parallel with the nave in a basilica or church, and separated from it by arcades.

Alabaster: a very pale, fine-grained translucent gypseous mineral, used to a small extent as a building material in the ancient Middle East, Greece, Rome, the eastern empire of Byzantium and, in later times, by certain Victorian architects for its decorative qualities (and Biblical associations). A technique was evolved in Italy many centuries ago of treating alabaster to simulate marble; conversely, in the past marble was often mistakenly described as alabaster.

Alcove: a niche or recess in a room.

Almshouse: a group of dwellings which provided accommodation for the poor and needy. By the end of the seventeenth century they had evolved under royal patronage into new-style retirement homes for the armed forces.

Alure: an alley, walkway or passage; a gallery behind a parapet.

Ambo: a raised pulpit from which the Epistles and the Gospels were read.

Ambulatory: the cloister or covered passage or aisle, usually around the sanctuary or east end of a church, behind the high altar.

Amphitheatre: a circular or elliptical arena for sports, games and other spectacles.

Ancones: consoles on each side of a doorway, supporting a cornice. Also, projections left on blocks of stone, such as the drums of columns, for use in hoisting and setting in position.

Annulet: a small flat fillet or ring encircling a column. It is several times repeated under the **ovolo** or **echinus** of the Doric capital.

Anse de panier: basket arch.

Anta: a **pilaster**, the **base** and **capital** of which are different from the **order** used for the rest of the building; *in antis*, columns placed between such pilasters.

Antechamber: a room of lesser importance, which leads to a grander reception room.

Antefixae: ornamental blocks, fixed vertically and projecting at regular intervals along the lower edge of a roof, above a classical cornice; originally used to cover the ends of tiles.

Antiquarian: the phase in western European architecture, *c.* 1750–1830, when inspiration was sought from ancient Greek, Roman and medieval architecture. Its most notable manifestations were the Greek and gothic Revivals, both of which continued further into the nineteenth century.

Apophyge: the *cavetto* (concave sweep) at either end of the column shaft connecting it with the fillet.

Apartment house: the accommodation of a number of self-contained units of habitation behind a shared front door.

Apron: the raised panel below a window or at the base of a wall monument or tablet, sometimes shaped and decorated.

Apse: the semicircular or multi-angular termination of a church sanctuary, first applied to the magistrate's end of a Roman basilica. The apse is a continental feature, and contrasts with the square termination of English gothic churches.

Aqueduct: a channel or conduit built to convey water; usually an elevated bridge-like structure.

Arabesque: painted or carved surface decoration, light and fanciful in character, much used by Arabic artists. Applied also to the combination of flowing lines interwoven with flowers, fruit, and figures, as used by renaissance artists.

Arcade: a range of two or more arches supported on piers or columns, either attached to, or detached from, the wall.

Arch: a structure of cut, interlocking, wedge-shaped stone blocks over an opening, that hold together when supported only from the sides.

Architrave: the beam or lowest member of the classical entablature, which extends from column to column. The term is also applied to the moulded frame around a door or window.

Archivolt: the **architrave** mouldings on the face of an arch and following its contour.

Arcuated: a building, building system or style of architecture, which is dependent structurally on the use of the arch.

Arris: the sharp edge formed by the angle of meeting of two surfaces.

Art déco: a style of the twentieth-century interwar years, usually associated with leisure and entertainment in buildings, that delighted in bold shapes and smooth surfaces.

Art nouveau: a decorative movement in Europe, heralded in the 1880s and flourishing between 1893–1907. It attempted to find what was sometimes called a modern style, using natural, organic forms and decorative motifs rather than historically-derived architectural traits.

Arts and Crafts: galvanized by William Morris's (1834–96) disgust at what he perceived as the dehumanising tendencies of mass production and the factory system, a group of architects and designers attempted to revive the traditions of simple handicraft techniques in nineteenth-century Britain. In architecture they looked at the unselfconscious vernacular tradition of barns, mills and cottages as an inspiration, and at the aesthetics of the medieval period. Known as the Arts and Crafts movement, this design tendency initiated in 1867 spread across much of Europe to America and Australia.

Ashlar: masonry of smooth, squared, large blocks in regular courses, separated by the thinnest of joints.

Ashlar piece: a short vertical timber connecting an inner wall-plate or timber pad to a rafter above.

Astragal: a small semicircular moulding, often ornamented with a bead or reel. **Torus** is the name for larger mouldings of similar section.

Astylar: the treatment of a façade without columns or pilasters.

Atlantes: sculptured male figures serving as pillars, also called **telamones**.

Atrium: an inner court of a Roman villa, forming an entrance hall, and open to the sky in the centre;. in early Christian and later architecture, a forecourt. The word was adopted widely in the twentieth century to describe the dramatic enclosed glass-roofed indoor spaces associated with high-rise hotels and office buildings.

Far left: the Temple of Concord and Victory, Stowe, after recent restoration of the pediment sculpture and flanking columns. The design is ascribed to Kent, though there is no proof of his involvement; furthermore, although it was begun in 1747 and roofed in 1749, he died in 1748. It was originally known as the Grecian Temple, and its columns are of the Corinthian order. The Temple is not a copy of any known Greek or other ancient temple, and thus can justifiably be called the first English building of Greek intention

Attached column: *see* **engaged column**.

Attic: a term first applied in the renaissance period to the upper storey of a building above the main entablature of the facade; also applied to small rooms in a loft, especially with a slanting roof, of virtually any building.

Attic base: the most usual base to a classic column, so named by Vitruvius, formed of upper and lower **torus** and **scotia** joined by fillets.

Axis of honour: the formal symmetrical arrangement of the space within a building.

Back to back: a term used to describe urban housing of the late nineteenth and early twentieth centuries consisting of a row of terraced housing backing directly onto a similar row which faces in the opposite direction.

Bailey: the open area or court of a fortified castle around the motte.

Balcony: a projecting platform attached to an upper storey, enclosed by a railing or balustrade.

Baldacchino: a canopy supported by columns, generally placed over an altar or tomb; also known as a **ciborium**.

Ballflower: the ornament of Decorated gothic architecture, of three petals enclosing a small ball.

Baluster: a pillar or column of bellied form supporting a handrail or coping, in series forming a *balustrade*.

Baptistery: a separate building (or, sometimes, room) to contain a font, for the baptismal rite.

Barbican: a defending outwork of a medieval castle, the object of which was to protect a drawbridge or the entrance gate.

Bargeboard: a wooden panel fixed to the verge of a pitched roof, or beneath the eaves of a gable, to cover and protect the rafters from rainwater penetration.

Baroque: a term applied to design during the late renaissance period (1600–1760 in Italy), when architecture reached a characteristic, non-Roman expression of unprecedented elaboration.

Barrel vault: a continuous vault of semi-circular section, used at most periods and in many countries from Roman times to the present. Also called a tunnel, wagonhead, or wagon vault.

Bartizan: a small overhanging turret, square or round, and most often sited at a corner.

Bascule: the hinged part of a lifting bridge.

Base: the lower moulded portion of any structure or architectural feature.

Basement: the lower stage of a building; also a storey, either wholly or partly below ground level and below the main floor.

Basilica: a Roman public hall; hence an aisled building with a clerestory, most often a church.

Bas relief: carving in low or shallow relief.

Basse-cour or **base court:** a secondary court or service yard, generally at the rear of a house.

Bath house or **bathroom:** a building or room for the purpose of taking a bath, introduced into Britain by the Romans. The Victorians introduced the general provisions of a bathroom with elaborate showers and water jets.

Bath stone: oolite building stone, not confined to Bath, Somerset; used throughout English architectural history.

Batter: a wall with an inward-inclined face.

Battlement: a fortified parapet having a series of indentations or embrasures, between which are raised portions known as **merlons**.

Bauhaus: the architecture, design, craft and fine art school established by Walter Gropius in Weimar in 1919, transferred to Dessau in 1925, and finally moved to Berlin in 1932. It closed in 1933 under increasing political interference. Its influence was worldwide and enduring, providing the most coherent statement of architectural modernism, primarily through functionalist principles, of the twentieth century.

Baulk-tie: a tie-beam joining the wall-posts of a timber roof and preventing walls from spreading.

Bays: repetitive compartments into which the nave or roof of a building is divided.

Bay window: window of one or more storeys projecting from the face of a building at ground level, and either rectangular or polygonal in plan. A canted bay window has a straight front and angled sides; a bow window is curved, while an oriel window rests on corbels or brackets and does not start from the ground.

Bead: small round moulding often carved with an ornament resembling a string of beads.

Beakhead: a Norman enrichment consisting of a row of bird's or beast's heads with beak-like protrusions.

Beam: a horizontal load-bearing element that forms a principal part of a structure, usually of timber, steel or concrete.

Belfry: a term generally applied to the upper room in a tower in which the bells are hung, and thus often to the tower itself.

Bell capital: the solid part, core or drum of a capital, especially of the Corinthian and composite orders, or of a Corinthianesque character in French and English gothic. So-called bell capitals, moulded and without foliated ornament, occur frequently in the medieval ecclesiastical architecture of both countries.

Belvedere: a roofed but open-sided structure affording an extensive view, usually located on the rooftop of a dwelling but sometimes an independent building on an eminence in a landscape or formal garden.

Billet frieze: a Norman ornament consisting of small half-cylindrical or rectanglar blocks placed at regular intervals.

Blocked: term applied to columns that are interupted by regular projecting blocks; *see* **Gibbs surround**.

Blocking course: a plain course of masonry, on top of a cornice and crowning the wall.

Bolection moulding: curved moulding used to conceal the joint between two different planes and overlapping the higher as well as the lower one, used especially in the late seventeenth and early eighteenth centuries.

Bond: a term adopted to describe the various patterns used to lay bricks in order to give them maximum strength. It is an approach that has its origins in the period before the intervention of high-strength cement mortars, which made bonding of this kind unnecessary; but the patterns survive, now representing a cultural tradition rather than a functional necessity. English bond, for example, has been in use for 400 years, and is based on a mix of bricks laid end on, and side on, in such a way that the cross joints are regularly spaced. Other patterns include Flemish bond, heading, stretching, and American.

Boss: a carved stone at the intersection of the ribs of ceilings, whether vaulted or flat. The term is also applied to the carved ends of weather-mouldings of doors and windows.

Bowstring bridge: one which has the ribs of the bridge arch rising above the level of the road, which is suspended from them.

Box frame: timber-framed construction in which vertical and horizontal wall members support the roof. In modern architecture it has also come to mean a box-like form of concrete construction where the loads are taken on cross walls, suitable only for buildings consisting of repetitive small cells. This is also known as cross-wall construction.

Brace: in framed structures, a subsidiary member placed near and across the angleof two main members in order to strengthen them. It can be curved or straight.

Bracket: a small projecting member to support a weight; when carrying the upper members of a cornice, brackets are generally termed **modillions** or **consoles**.

Bracket moulding, *or* **brace** *or* **double ogee:** a late gothic moulding consisting of two ogee mouldings with convex faces adjoining, resembling a printer's {brace} or bracket.

Branch tracery: a form of tracery characteristic of German gothic, suggesting the branches of a tree.

Breaking joint *or* **imbrication:** the staggering of rows, as of overlapping tiles, like fish scales.

Bressumer: a big horizontal beam or lintel, usually set forward from the lower part of a building, supporting the wall above.

Brise-soleil: a fixed screen to break the glare of the sun upon windows. Such screens often take the form of louvres in recent architecture, and are used as an aesthetic element in their own right.

Brick: one of the oldest building materials, brick is based on a mixture of clay with silt and sand, pressed in moulds and then fired in a kiln, which gives the characteristic slightly glazed finish. Standard brick sizes vary from country to country and also have changed over the years. In mainland Europe, for example, bricks are often more slender than those commonly used in the USA and Britain.

Broach spire: an octagonal spire rising without a parapet above a square tower, with pyramidal forms at the angles of the tower, typical of Early English churches.

Brownstone: a brown sandstone found in New Jersey, Connecticut, Pennsylvania and elsewhere; a popular building material in the nineteenth century in New York and the eastern United States.

Brutalism: a short-lived architectural movement of the 1960s that set itself in opposition to the picturesque Scandinavian-influenced mainstream of the period, and instead advocated the brutally frank expression of the nature of modern materials, characterised by massive elements of unadorned concrete and the blunt detailing of joints and openings.

Bull's-eye window: a small round or oval window, originally set in the **tympanum**.

Buttress: the mass of masonry built vertically against a wall to resist the lateral thrust of an arch, roof, or vault. A flying buttress is an arch starting from a detached pier and abutting against a wall to take the thrust of the vaulting.

Cable: a Norman moulding, resembling a twisted rope.

Caen stone: a cream-coloured limestone building stone from Caen, Normandy; sometimes used in the construction of English medieval buildings, despite the difficulties of transport.

Camber: slight rise or upward curve of an otherwise horizontal line or plane.

Cames: slender lead strips, grooved at the sides for the reception of pieces of glass, in casement, stained glass and other types of window.

Campanile: the Italian name for a freestanding bell-tower.

Cancelli: low screen walls enclosing the choir in early Christian churches; hence 'chancel'.

Cantoria: a term generally used in the renaissance to denote a singers' gallery, often elaborately carved, in a major church.

Capital: the crowning feature of a column or pilaster.

Cartouche: a tablet with ornate frame, usually of elliptical shape and bearing a coat of arms or inscription.

Caryatid: a sculptured female figure used as a column or support, often flanking a doorway.

Casement: a concave moulding framing a window in gothic architecture; in military architecture, a vaulted chamber with embrasures for defence, whether built into the thickness of the wall of a castle or fortress or projecting from it.

Casement window: a window hinged at the side and which opens in the manner of a door.

Castellation: fortifying a house and providing it with battlements.

Cast iron: iron made into the required shape by pouring it into moulds. Cast iron was used to a rapidly increasing extent in building works from the late eighteenth century, until superseded by steel in the mid-nineteenth cnetury.

Caulicoli: the eight stalks supporting the volutes in the Corinthian capital.

Cavetto: a simple concave moulding of quarter-round section.

Cellar: a subterranean room or space, historically used for the storage of wine or fuel.

Celure or ceilure: enriched area of a roof above the rood or the altar.

Cenotaph: a sepulchral monument erected to commemorate a person buried elsewhere. It is not itself a burial place.

Centring: wooden support for the building of an arch or vault, removed after completion.

Chaînes: vertical strips of rusticated masonry rising between the horizontal string-mouldings and cornice of a building, and so dividing the façades into bays or panels. A popular mode of wall-ornamentation in French seventeenth-century domestic architecture.

Chamfer: the surface formed by cutting off a square edge, usually at an angle of 45 degrees; a hollow chamfer is the same but concave in form, like the *cavetto*.

Chancel: the space for clergy and choir at the eastern end of a church, separated by a screen from the body of the church; more usually referred to as the **choir**.

Chantry: a small chapel, usually attached to a church, endowed with lands or by other means, for the maintenance of priests to sing or say mass for whomever the donor directs.

Chapels: separate places of worship within a church, in honour of particular saints; sometimes erected as separate buildings.

Chapter house: the place of assembly for abbot, prior and members of a monastery, often reached from the cloisters. In England it was usually polygonal in plan, though sometimes oblong, with a vault resting on a central pillar.

Chevet: the French term for a circular or polygonal apse when surrounded by an ambulatory, with radiating chapels.

Chevron: a zigzag or V-shaped moulding, a feature of Norman architecture; so called from a pair of rafters, which gave this form.

Choir: the part of a church where services are sung. In monastic churches this can occupy the crossing and / or the easternmost bays of the nave; also used to describe, more loosely, the eastern arm of a cruciform church.

Ciborium: a fixed canopy of stone or wood over an altar, usually vaulted and supported on four columns; also referred to as the *baldacchino*.

Cimborio: the Spanish term for a lantern or raised structure above a roof, admitting light into the interior.

Cinquefoil: an arrangement of five foils or openings, terminating in cusps, in tracery.

Cladding: a lightweight outer veneer applied to a building façade; used especially on framed buildings and not carrying any weight.

Clapper bridge: one made of large slabs of stone, some making rough piers, with longer ones laid on top to make the roadway.

Classic: the defining achievement of a style.

Classicism: the architecture originating in ancient Greece and Rome, the rules and forms of which have shaped Western architecture ever since. It is characterised by a set of compositional rules and architectural elements, in particular columns and orders; largely revived during the Renaissance in Europe and elsewhere, it is a language that has continually reinvented itself, thus providing scope for successive generations to explore the fundamentals of design.

Claustra: sometimes used in the late nineteenth and early twentieth century to describe panels, pierced with geometrical designs, as employed by the French architect Auguste Perret in certain of his reinforced-concrete buildings.

Clear-storey, clere-story, clearstory or **clerestory**: an upper stage in a building with windows above adjacent roofs to bring light into the centre of the building; especially applied to this feature in churches.

Cloisters: covered passages round an open space, connecting the church to the chapter house, refectory, and other parts of the monastery. They were generally south of the nave and west of the transept, probably to secure sunlight and warmth.

Cluster block: a multi-storey building in which individual blocks of apartments cluster round a central service tower.

Coade stone: a weatherproof ceramic artificial stone made in Lambeth from 1769 to c. 1840 by Eleanor Coade (died 1821) and her associates.

Coffers: sunken panels, caissons or lacunaria formed in ceilings, vaults, and domes.

Cogging: *see* **dog-tooth**.

Colonnade: the range of columns supporting an entablature.

Colonnette: a small column or shaft, in medieval architecture.

Colossal order: any classical order, the columns of which extend in height through two or more storeys.

Column: a freestanding or self-supporting vertical structural element, generally consisting of a base, circular shaft, and spreading capital.

Competition: a means for selecting an architect for a significant commission. Architects are invited to take part in a competition, which can be either open to all comers or by invitation only. Open competition is regarded as an important way of discovering innovative new talent.

Compound pier: grouped shafts or a solid core surrounded by attached or detached shafts.

Conch: half-dome of an apse or niche, in the shape of a shell.

Concrete: a mixture of sand, water, stone and a binder (today generally Portland cement, which was available from 1824). The Romans used pozzolana in place of sand, and lime. Reinforced concrete, nowadays universally used, is concrete with a reinforcement of steel rods or mesh (often bamboo in eastern countries). Pre-stressed concrete is compressed in order to prevent cracking and to build in tensile force. Two principal methods are applied to achieve this, post-tensioning and pre-tensioning, both using bars or wires. Pre-stressed concrete is reliable and relatively economical for large spans. More recently pre-cast concrete, in which various concrete elements are cast on site or in a factory before assembly, has been much used in many building types. Board-marked concrete was made fashionable by Le Corbusier, its exposed surface retaining the marks of the wood shuttering. A roughened 'rusticated' appearance is attained with the aid of a bush-hammer, a mechanically operated percussive tool, in bush-hammering, which is another of the many other methods of treating a concrete surface.

Conservation: the art of the careful restoration and recycling of run-down and redundant buildings. It has become an increasingly sophisticated practice.

Conservatory: structure composed of glass panels set in a framework, usually of cast iron.

Console: an ornamented bracket of compound curved outline.

Constructivism: an avant-garde movement of the early twentieth century, that originated in revolutionary Russia with work by the sculptor Naum Gabo. It had a new sense of space, an imaginative understanding of geometry, and an enthusiasm for modern materials. Architectural adherents include the brothers Alexander and Vladimir Vesnin and Vladimir Tatlin, whose revolutionary but unbuilt tower commemorating the Third International Communist Congress (Moscow, 1921) remains an icon of the period.

Coping: the protective capping or covering of a wall with masonry or brickwork.

Corbel: a block of stone or timber, often elaborately carved or moulded, projecting from a wall to support the beams of a roof, floor, vault or other feature.

Corbelling: brick or masonry courses built out beyond one another like a series of corbels to support a chimneystack or window.

Corbel table: a plain piece of projecting wall, supported by a range of corbels and forming a parapet.

Corbie gable or **crow-step gable**: a gable with stepped sides.

Cornerstone: the stone in the projecting angle of a building.

Cornice: in classic or renaissance architecture, the highest member of the entablature, also used along the top of a building or feature as a crowning projection. A decorative moulding in the angle between wall and ceiling.

Corona: the square projection in the upper part of a cornice, having a deep vertical face, generally plain, and with its soffit or under-

surface recessed so as to form a drip, which prevents water from running down the building.

Corps de logis: that part of a substantial house which forms the main self-contained dwelling, i.e. without any service quarters, wings, stables or pavilions.

Cortile: the Italian name for the internal courtyard, surrounded by an arcade, of a palace or other edifice.

Cottage orné: an artfully rustic building, usually of asymmetrical plan, a product of the late eighteenth and early nineteenth-century picturesque.

Course: a continuous horizontal layer of stones or brick, for example in a wall.

Coving: a concave moulding that produces a large hollow, that forms part of an arch in section, and covers the joining of the walls and ceilings of a room. Often decorated with coffering or other enrichment.

Cradle roof: *see* **wagon roof**.

Crenelle: *see* **merlon**.

Cresting: a light repeated ornament, incised or perforated, carried along the top of a screen, for example.

Crocket: a projecting knob of stone carved with foilage to decorate the raking lines formed by angles of spires and canopies, in gothic architecture.

Crossing: the area at the intersection of nave, chancel and transepts, in a church.

Cross vault or **groined vault**: one characterised by arched diagonal **arrises** or groins, which are formed by the intersection of two barrel vaults.

Crown-post: a post standing upright on the tie-beam of a timber roof and giving support to a central collar-purlin and adjacent rafters by means of struts or braces, but not reaching the apex of the roof, as in the case of a king-post.

Crowsteps: squared stones set like steps, for example on a gable or gateway.

Crucks: pairs of timbers, usually curved, that are set at bay-length intervals, arched together and based near the ground, to form principals for the support of the roof and walls of timber-framed small houses. The individual cruck is known as a blade. They were in use in the western half of England until the sixteenth century or later.

Crypt: a space entirely or partly under a building; in churches generally beneath the chancel at the east end of a church. They were used for burial in early times.

Cupola: a spherical roof, especially a small dome, over a circular, square or multi-angular apartment; also used to crown a larger dome, roof or turret.

Curtail step: the lowest step of a staircase, of which the outer edge protrudes in a scroll-like shape.

Curtain wall: in modern buildings this is the logical outcome of skeleton-frame construction, in which the external walls serve no load-bearing purpose, but are suspended on the face of the building like a curtain. It must not be confused with the curtain wall of medieval military architecture, which was a defensive, usually outer, wall linking towers and gatehouses.

Cushion capital: a cubiform capital, the angles being progressively rounded off towards the lowest part.

Cusp: the projecting point formed by the intersection of the foils in gothic tracery.

Cyclopean masonry: built with large irregular polygonal stones, but smooth and finely jointed.

Cyma: a moulding with an outline of two contrary curves – either the *cyma recta* (concave part uppermost) or *cyma reversa* (convex part uppermost).

Cymatium: the crowning member of a cornice, generally in the form of a cyma.

Dado: the portion of a pedestal between its base and cornice; also used for the lower portions of walls when decorated separately. Traditionally these were timber panelled.

Dado rail: the moulding along the top of a dado.

Daïs: a raised platform at the end of a medieval hall, where the master dined apart from his retainers; now applied to any raised portion of an apartment.

Deconstructivism: an architectural fad of the 1980s, with its roots in a borrowing from the linguistic philosophers who purport to deconstruct meaning by looking at the structure of language. The idea was transplanted into design. An exhibition at the Museum of Modern Art, New York, promoted it, bringing together such architects as Zaha Hadid, Frank Gehry and Rem Koolhaas. In different ways their work reflects an architecture that is the product of unease with the idea of harmonious architectural composition, in a world in which such harmony is non-existent.

Decorated: the style of English gothic architecture of the period *c.* 1290–1350 and characterised by increasingly flamboyant ornamentation.

Demi-columns: engaged columns semi-sunk into a wall.

Dentils: tooth-like blocks in Ionic and Corinthian cornices; rarely used in Doric.

Diaconicon: the vestry, or sacristy, in early Christian churches.

Diaper: any small pattern, such as lozenges or squares, repeated continuously over the wall surface and which can be achieved in brickwork by using bricks of two colours.

Die: the part of a podium or pedestal between its cap-mould and base.

Diocletian window: a semicircular window with two mullions, so called because of its use in the Baths of Diocletian in Rome; also called a **Thermae window**.

Dog-tooth: an ornament resembling a row of teeth, especially occurring in Early English buildings; also known as **cogging**.

Dome: the custom in Italy was to erect cupolas over churches, and the word 'dome' has passed in English and French from the building (*duomo*) to this form of structural vault.

Dormer: a window in a sloping roof, usually that of a sleeping-apartment, hence the name.

Dovecote: a structure with nesting boxes, built to accommodate pigeons which provided a source of fresh meat.

Dripstone: in gothic architecture, the projecting moulding over the heads of doorways, windows and archways to throw off rain; also known as **hood moulding** or when rectangular, a **label**.

Drum: the cylindrical base on which a dome sits and in which windows might be placed to light the central areas of a building.

Dutch gable: a shaped gable surmounted by a pediment.

Early English: the style of English gothic architecture prevalent during the thirteenth century.

Eaves: the lower part of a roof projecting beyond the face of the wall.

Echinus: the convex or projecting moulding, resembling the shell of the sea-urchin, which supports the abacus of the Greek Doric capital; sometimes painted with egg and dart ornament.

Eclecticism: an architecture embracing a variety of sometimes conflicting stylistic inspirations rather than sticking to a single purist vision. It was first demonstrated in the late eighteenth century, when travellers from the grand tour brought back to Europe souvenirs of China, India, and the ancient classical world, which architects in western Europe used for free improvisations, mixing motifs from all of them. The word has been seen to imply negative connotations at various times.

Edwardian: an opulent and bombastic style of architecture which flourished during the reign of Edward VII (1901–10); it lasted until the outbreak of the First World War in 1914.

Egg and dart *or* **egg and tongue:** alternating ovoid and pointed motifs, originating in Greece, widely applied to mouldings during the renaissance.

Elizabethan: a term applied to early-renaissance English architecture of the period 1558–1603.

Embattled: furnished with battlements:

occasionally, an indented pattern on mouldings.

Embrasure: an opening in a parapet between two **merlons**; the inward splaying of a door or window.

Encaustic: the art of mural painting in any way in which heat is used to fix the colours; encaustic tiles are ornamental glazed tiles of different clays, producing colour patterns after burning. Used in the Middle Ages and revived in the nineteenth century, they were used mainly in paving.

En delit: stone shafts in gothic architecture, the grain of which runs vertically instead of horizontally, against normal building practice.

Enfilade: series of doors so aligned as to permit an unencumbered straight line of sight.

Engaged column: one that is partly merged into a wall or pier; also called an attached column.

Engineering bricks: dense bricks of uniform size, high crushing strength, and low porosity; originally used mostly for such structures as railway viaducts.

English bond: *see* **bond**.

Entablature: the upper horizontal part of an order of architecture, comprising the three horizontal members of **architrave**, **frieze** and **cornice**, supported by a colonnade.

Entasis: a very slight swelling or curving outwards along the outline of a column shaft, designed to counteract the optical illusion which gives a shaft bounded by straight lines the appearance of curving inwards.

Expressionism: an architectural movement, originating in Germany, that had its zenith between the two World Wars. It connected architecture and art, attempting to provide an aesthetic appropriate to contemporary technology and materials through the focus of an emotional perspective, rather than a functional one.

Extrados: the outer curved face of an arch or vault.

Entresol: a mezzanine storey within or above the ground storey.

Façade: the face or elevation of a building.

Fanlight: a glazed opening in an exterior wall above a door, usually semicircular.

Fan vault: vaulting peculiar to the Perpendicular period, in which all ribs have the same curve, and resemble the framework of a fan.

Fascia: a vertical face of little projection, usually found in the **architrave** of an order and, later on, a shop front. The architrave of the Ionic and Corinthian orders is divided into two or more such bands. Also, a board or plate covering the end of roof rafters.

Fenestration: the arrangement of window openings in a building, to create an architectural pattern.

Fibreglass *or* **GRP** (**glass-reinforced polyester**): a synthetic resin reinforced with glass fibre, formed in moulds, often simulating the appearance of traditional materials. **GRC** (**glass-reinforced concrete**) is also formed in moulds and used for components (such as cladding) in industrialised building.

Fielded panels: the surface of which projects in front of the enclosing frame.

Fillet: a narrow flat band between mouldings or flutes of a column, to separate them from each other; also the uppermost member of a cornice.

Finial: the decorative uppermost portion of a pinnacle, bench end or other architectural feature.

Flamboyant: tracery in which the bars of stonework form long flowing curves like flames.

Flèche: a slender wooden spire rising from a roof, also called a **spirelet**.

Flemish bond: *see* **bond**; alternate headers and stretchers in the same course.

Fleuron: a decorative carved flower or leaf, often rectilinear.

Flushwork: flint, used decoratively in conjunction with dressed stone, so as to form patterns of tracery or initials.

Fluting: the vertical channelling on the shaft of a column. Their common edges can be sharp (**arris**), or blunt (**fillet**).

Foil: the small arc openings in gothic tracery

separated by cusps. Trefoil (three), quatrefoil (four), cinquefoil (five), and so on, express the number of foils in a shape.

Folded slab: a development of the reinforced concrete thin slab, which has both aethetic and structural advantages in spanning large halls and buildings of similar type, while also facilitating the provision of good natural and artificial lighting; so called because the resultant ribbed roof assumes the form of pleats or folds, in section.

Foliate: decorated, especially carved, with leaves.

Formwork: a temporary casing of woodwork, within which concrete is moulded to cast complex and self supporting structures; commonly called **shuttering**.

Free plan: one of the key elements of architectural modernism was the so-called free plan. Traditionally, massive load-bearing structures made structure a primary element in any floor plan. The use of structural steel and concrete and curtain walls changed all this and allowed for an architectural plan free of such constraints. It allowed for large, open interiors, rather than for massive walls and cellular spaces.

Framed building: where the framework (of steel, reinforced concrete, or timber) carries the structure instead of load-bearing walls.

Freestone: stone that is cut, or can be cut, in all directions, usually fine-grained sandstone or limestone.

Fresco: originally painting on a wall while the plaster was wet, but often used for any wall painting not in oil colours. Painting onto dry plaster was more common in Britain.

Fret: an ornament in classic or renaissance architecture, consisting of an assemblage of straight lines intersecting at right angles, and of various patterns; sometimes called the key pattern.

Frieze: the middle division of the classical entablature. Also a broad band, either plain or decorated with a pattern, running along the upper part of a wall immediately below the cornice.

Functionalism: modernism was based on a philosophy that saw a direct relationship between functional requirements and form, the former dictating the latter. In the 1920s and 1930s, this view set aside emotional or symbolic elements in architecture.

Frontispiece: the central feature of doorway and windows above it linked in one composition, in sixteenth and seventeenth-century buildings.

Futurism: a movement originating in Italy in the early years of the twentieth century, involving architects, painters and writers. It embraced the intoxicating quality of the avalanche of change brought about by the early period of the industrial revolution – iron, steel, electricity, steam engines, aircraft – and to find an appropriate aesthetic for architecture and city planning in this context. It celebrated the danger and sense of risk implicit in modernity, rather than looking back to the past for security.

Gable: the triangular area of a wall between the enclosing lines of a hipped roof. In classic architecture it is called a pediment.

Gadroon: one of a series of convex curves, like inverted fluting, used as an ornamental border.

Galilee: a large porch used as a chapel, often for penitents, in some medieval churches; usually at the west end of a church.

Galleting: the decorative use of small stones in a mortar course.

Gallery: a communicating passage or wide corridor, often used for pictures and statues, it was an internal or external feature in medieval buildings; an upper mezzanine storey or balcony, often with seats, in a church and overlooking the main interior space.

Gargoyle: a projecting water spout, grotesquely carved, to throw off water from the roof.

Gauged brickwork: soft brick sawn roughly, then rubbed to a smooth, precise (gauged) surface with a stone or another brick; mostly used for door or window openings, and also called **rubbed brickwork**.

Gazebo: a raised summerhouse or garden pavilion.

Geometric: a historical division of English gothic architecture, covering the period *c.* 1250–90.

Georgian: English late renaissance architecture of the period 1714–1830.

Gibbs surround: an eighteenth-century treatment of a door or window surround, seen especially in the work of James Gibbs (1682–1754).

Girder: a large beam of various forms; **box girder**, of hollow-box section; **bowed girder**, with its top rising in a curve; **plate girder**, of I section, made from iron or steel plates; **lattice girder**, with braced framework.

Glasgow style: the late nineteenth-century style related to *art nouveau*, pioneered by the architect Charles Rennie Mackintosh (1868–1928).

Glazing bars: wooden bars arranged vertically and horizontally to retain window panes.

Glyph: a carved vertical channel.

Gothic: the name generally given to the pointed style of medieval architecture prevalent in western Europe from the thirteenth to the fifteenth century. It was a physical expression of spirtual values, suffused with Christian symbolism.

Gothic Revival: a manifestation first evident in the late eighteenth century, but belonging principally to the nineteenth; the countries most affected were England, France and Germany and, less strongly, the USA. It was identified with the evangelical revival, being a visible assertion of Christian values.

Greek cross: a plan form based on a cross with arms of equal length.

Greek Revival: like the Gothic Revival, this had its beginnings in the late eighteenth century. In England it culminated in the 1820s and had concluded by 1840 (later in Scotland), while similarly in France it was at its most evident in the early nineteenth century. In Germany it endured to the mid-nineteenth century. It was the especial characteristic of the architecture of the period 1815–60 in the USA. It led to a significant shift away from the classical language of Palladianism, towards a more simplified architectural vocabulary.

GRC (glass-reinforced concrete): *see* **fibreglass**.

GRP (glass-reinforced polyester): *see* **fibreglass**.

Groin: the curved sharp edge (**arris**) formed by the intersection of vaulting surfaces.

Guilloche: a classical running ornament of interlaced bands that form a plait.

Guttae: small cones under the **triglyphs** and **mutules** of the Doric entablature.

Hagioscope: an oblique opening in a medieval church wall giving a view of the altar, sometimes known as a **squint** or **leper's squint**.

Half-timber building: a building of timber posts, rails and struts, with the interstices filled with brick or other material, and sometimes plastered. Half-timbering is sometimes used for non-structural decorative timberwork, for example in gables of the late nineteenth century.

Hall church: a church in which the nave and aisles are of, or approximate to, equal height.

Hammerbeam: a late gothic form of timber roof without a direct tie.

Hammerpost: a vertical timber set on the inner end of a hammerbeam to support a purlin; it is braced to a collar-beam above.

Helix: one of the 16 small volutes (helices) under the abacus of a Corinthian capital.

Helm roof: a type of roof in which four faces rest diagonally between the gables and converge at the top; most commonly found in Germany.

Hemicycle buttress: a half-moon-shaped buttress, sometimes very large, often masked by other masonry or designed to perform utilitarian tasks additional to its purely structural purpose.

Herringbone work: masonry or brickwork in zigzag courses.

High-tech: an architectural style with its origins in England, that boomed in the 1980s. It took the elements of architectural engineering from its beginnings with the Crystal Palace, where structural elements were visible, and made them into the basis of a decorative style. The most celebrated examples are the Pompidou Centre in Paris of 1976, designed by Richard Rogers and Renzo Piano, and the Lloyds Building in London, 1986, also by Rogers.

Hip: the junction point between two roofs.

Hipped roof: a roof with sloped instead of vertical ends.

Historicism: the idea that architecture could take account of its own past came to seem increasingly significant in the nineteenth century. Architects took a scholarly interest in the past, using it as a pattern book for their own work.

Hood mould: a projecting moulding above an arch or lintel to throw off rainwater; when the moulding is rectangular it is often called a **label**.

Hoop-tie principle a method developed during the renaissance period, by which a pierced ring of timber, a metal chain, or hoop, binds the lower part of a dome or cupola to prevent splitting outwards or minimises the burden on external buttresses having a similar purpose.

Hyperbolic paraboloid: a double curved shell roof form, particularly characteristic of the 1950s onward, made either from poured concrete or from laminated timber.

Hypotrachelion: the channels or grooves beneath the **trachelion** at the junction of the capital and shaft of a column.

Imbrication: *see* breaking joint.

Impost: the horizontal member, usually formed of mouldings, at the springing of an arch.

In antis: see **anta**.

Incrustation: the facing of a wall surface, generally marble, with a decorative overlay; an Italian, predominantly Venetian, craft.

Indent: a shape chiselled out of a stone to match and receive a brass.

Indented moulding: one cut in the form of zigzag pointed notches.

Industrialised building: the use of a mass-production system of manufactured units assembled on site. One of the most popular is the Consortium Local Authorities Special Programme (CLASP) system of light steel framing, suitable for schools, for example.

Inglenook: a recess for a hearth with provision for seating.

Interlace: relief decoration simulating woven or entwined stems or bands.

International style: the name first used by American architect Philip Johnson for the white, purist architecture of the 1920s, to suggest that the modern movement had produced an architecture that was defined not by national boundaries but by its universality.

Intrados: the inner curve of an arch.

Jack arch: a shallow segmental vault springing from beams, used for fireproof floors, bridge decks and so on.

Jacobean: English early renaissance architecture of the period 1603–25.

Jambs: the sides of doors and windows; the part exposed outside the window-frame is the reveal.

Jetty: in a timber-framed building, the projection of an upper storey beyond the storey below, made by the beams and joists of the lower storey oversailing the external wall. On their outer ends is placed the sill of the walling for the storey above. Buildings can be jettied on several sides, in which case a dragon beam is set diagonally at the corner to carry the joists to either side.

Jib door: a concealed door which is disguised to match the wallpaper or other decoration.

Joggle: mason's term for joining two stones to prevent them slipping or sliding, by means of a groove in one and a corresponding projection in the other.

Joists: parallel timbers laid horizontally to support the floorboards of a room.

Jubé: the French equivalent of the English rood-screen between nave and chancel.

Jugendstil: the movement in Germany contemporay to *art nouveau*.

Keel moulding: a moulding like the keel of a ship formed of two ogee curves meeting in a sharp **arris**; used, rounded in form, during the fifteenth century. The word keel is also applied to the ogee form of arch.

Keystone: the central stone of a semicircular arch or a vault, sometimes sculptured.

King-post: a vertical post extending from the ridge to the centre of the tie-beam below.

Knapped flint: a traditional East-Anglian craft of splitting flints, so that they present a smoooth black surface on a wall face. The arrangement of knapped flints in patterns is sometimes called **flushwork**; *see above*.

Kneeler: a horizontal projecting stone at the base of each side of a gable, on which the inclined coping stones rest; also known as a padstone.

Label: *see* **dripstone** *or* **hood mould**.

Laced windows: windows visually pulled together by strips of brickwork, usually of a different colour, which continue vertically the lines of the vertical parts of the window surround; typical of the early eighteenth century.

Lacing course: of one or more bricks serving as a horizontal reinforcement to walls of flint or stones.

Lamination: a structural technique involving gluing leaves of timber together to create strong, load-bearing but free-form members.

Lancet arch: a tall, sharply-pointed arch or window, chiefly in use during the Early English period.

Lantern: a circular or polygonal construction such as a tower at the crossing of a church, rising above the neighbouring roofs and glazed at the sides.

Lath: a thin strip of wood used for anchoring slates or tiles on a roof; used in combination with plaster to form a lath and plaster wall or ceiling.

Leaded light: a window comprised of of small panes of glass (**lights**) held together by lead **cames** in lieu of glazing bars.

Leaf and tongue: a conventional motif of the *cyma reversa* in Greek architectural ornament.

Lean-to roof: a roof with one slope only, built against a vertical wall; also used for the part of the building such as roof covers.

Lesene: an undecorated pilaster without base or capital.

Lich or lych gate: a covered gateway to a churchyard, forming a resting place for a coffin where part of the burial surface is often read.

Lierne: a short intermediate rib in gothic vaulting which does not rise from the impost and is not a ridge rib.

Light: the compartment of a window defined by the mullions.

Linenfold: a type of relief ornament, imitating folded linen, carved on the face of individual timber panels; popular in the late fifteenth and sixteenth centuries.

Lintel: the horizontal timber or stone beam used to bridge an opening such as a doorway, also known as the **architrave**.

Loggia: a gallery behind an open arcade or colonnade.

Long and short work: a method of laying the **quoins** or angles in Anglo-Saxon buildings, in which the stone slabs are laid vertically and horizontally in alternate courses.

Louvre: a series of inclined slats in a vertical frame, allowing ventilation without admitting rain or direct sunlight; a roof ventilator embodying this principal; sometimes applied to roof ventilators in general.

Lucarne: a window with a sloping roof.

Lunette: a semicircular window or wall panel let into the inner base of a concave vault or dome.

Machicolations: in medieval military architecture, a series of openings through which missiles can be dropped, under a projecting parapet between corbels that support it.

Mall: used to describe outdoor spaces as well as interiors; in the former, a formal boulevard lined by civic structures. Its use is now more common in connection with the out-of-town shopping centre, where 'mall' has become a generic description.

Mannerism: the characteristic output of Italian renaissance architects of the period 1530–1600.

Manometer *or* **standpipe tower:** contains a column of water to regulate pressure in water mains.

Mansard roof: a roof with steep lower slope and flatter upper portion, named after the French architect François Mansart.

Marquise: a projecting canopy over an entrance door, often of metal and glass.

Mason's mitre: the treatment in masonry, and sometimes joinery, for mouldings meeting at right angles when the diagonal mitre thus formed does not coincide with the joint, but is worked on the face of one piece which is carried straight through and simply butts on the other.

Mathematical tiles: brick tiles designed to imitate facing bricks; they are nailed externally to a wall through a concealed flange.

Mausoleum: a monumental building or chamber, usually intended for the burial of members of one family.

Meander: running ornament in the form of a fret or key pattern.

Medieval: a term taken to comprehend the romanesque and gothic periods of architectural development.

Merlon: the upstanding part of an embattled parapet, between two **crenelles** or embrasure openings.

Metabolism: the name coined by a group of Japanese architects in the 1960s to describe their approach to design, based on the idea that architecture could usefully be compared to a biological process.

Metope*:* a square space between two triglyphs of a Doric frieze, often adorned with carved work.

Mezzanine: an intermediate floor formed within a lofty storey, usually between the ground and the first floor.

Mitre: the term applied, especially in joinery, to the diagonal joint formed by the meeting of two mouldings at right angles.

Modernism: originally a pejorative description of the work of those followers of the modern movement who reduced its philosophy to a set of stylistic mannerisms, the machine aesthetic, without any real content. Modernity has also come to be seen as a historical period influencing the design of many commercial buildings of the 1950s and 1960s.

Modillion: a small bracket, usually in a series, supporting the top element of the cornice in an entablature in classical architecture.

Module: a measure of proportion, by which the parts of a classic order or building are regulated, being usually the semi-diameter of a column immediately above its base, which is divided into thirty parts or minutes.

Mortar: a compound of cement, sand, and lime, used for laying bricks and stone.

Mosaic: a decorative surface formed by small cubes of stone, glass and marble; much used in Hellenistic, Roman and later times for floors and wall decoration.

Mouldings: the contours given to projecting members.

Mullions: vertical members dividing windows into different numbers of smaller **lights**.

Multi-storey: a modern term, denoting five or more storeys.

Mushroom construction: a system of reinforced-concrete construction without beams, in which the floor-slabs are directly supported by columns flared at the top.

Mutules: projecting inclined blocks in Doric cornices, derived from the ends of wooden beams.

Narthex: a long arcaded antechamber to a Christian basilican church, originally appropriate to penitents.

Nautilus shell: a decorative motif used by the Greeks, especially for the spiral of the Ionic volute.

Nave: the main western limb of a church, as distinct from the choir; also the central aisle of the basilican, medieval, or renaissance church.

Necking: the space between the **astragal** of the shaft and the commencement of the capital proper in the Roman Doric.

Neoclassicism: there have been many revivals of the elements of classical architecture during the past millennium. The earliest was the romanesque; the renaissance period saw a self-conscious rediscovery of the lost elements of classical architecture. Neoclassicism, however, defines a very particular, archaeologically accurate use, especially of the Greek orders during the nineteenth century.

Newel: the central post of a circular staircase. It is also applied to the post into which the handrail is framed.

Niche: a small vertical recess in a wall, hollowed like a shell, for a statue or ornament.

Night stair: the stair by which monks entered the transept of their church from their dormitory to celebrate night services.

Norman: the style, also termed English romanesque, of the eleventh and twelfth centuries.

Nosing: the projection of the tread of a step; a bottle nosing is half-round in section.

Nymphaeum: a building for plants, flowers and running water, ornamented with statues, in classic architecture.

Obelisk: a tall slender pillar of square section tapering upwards and ending in a pyramid.

Oculus: a circular opening in a wall or roof, such as that in the roof of the Pantheon in Rome.

Odeion: a building, resembling a Greek theatre, designed for musical contests.

Ogee: a moulding made up of a convex and a concave curve; also an arch of similar shape.

Ogival: the traditional term in France, no longer in common usage, for gothic architecture.

Opus alexandrinum: mosaics inlaid in a stone or marble paving.

Order: an order in architecture comprises a column, with base (usually), shaft, and capital, the whole supporting an entablature. The Greeks recognised three orders: Doric, Ionic and Corinthian. The Romans added the Tuscan and the Composite (also known as the Roman), while using the Greek orders in modified form.
* The **Doric** order is unique in having no base to the column. The capital is plain; the shaft fluted.
* The **Ionic** order is lighter and more elegant than the Doric, with slim columns, generally fluted. It is principally distinguished by the volutes of its capital.
* The **Corinthian** order has a bell-shaped capital, from which eight acanthus stalks (**caulicoli**) emerge to support the modest volutes. The shaft is generally fluted.
* The **Tuscan** order resembles the Doric in all but its very plain entablature. The shaft is properly unfluted.
* The **Composite**, or **Roman**, order combines the prominent volutes of the Ionic with the acanthus of the Corinthian on its capital, and is thus the most decorative. The shaft may be fluted or plain.

Ordinates: parallel chords of conic section (in relation to the bisecting diameter) describing an ellipse; a principle followed by renaissance builders to adjust cross-vaults of equal height, but unequal span.

Ordonnance: the disposition of the parts of a building.

Oriel: a projecting upper-storey window.

Orthostats: courses of large squared stones at the base of a wall.

Overthrow: a decorative fixed arch between two gate piers or above a wrought-iron gate.

Ovolo: a wide convex moulding much used in classic and renaissance architecture, often carved with egg and dart or egg and tongue decoration.

Palladian motif: an arched opening flanked by two smaller, square-headed openings.

Palladianism: one of the most influential architects of the sixteenth century was Andrea Palladio (1508–80). His restrained plans and his use of symmetrical façades with such recurring elements as the Palladian (or Venetian) window inspired followers, especially in England and America, where he became a model for such Palladians as Inigo Jones, Robert Adam, and Thomas Jefferson.

Palmette: classical ornament, like a symmetrical palm shoot.

Palm vaulting: similar to fan vaulting.

Panel: a compartment, sunk or raised, in walls, ceilings, doors, or wainscoting.

Pantile: a roof tile of curved S-shaped section.

Parabolic vaulting: a thin shell covering, normally reinforced concrete, of parabolic section (ie a shape made by cutting a cone parallel to one edge). Such structures are comparatively light, and not subject to tensional stresses under conditions of uniform loading.

Parapet: the portion of wall above the roof-gutter, sometimes battlemented; also applied to the same feature, rising breast-high, in balconies, platforms and bridges.

Parclose: a screen enclosing a chapel as a shelter from draughts, or to prevent the distraction of worshippers; also the screen around a tomb or shrine.

Pargetting (*also* **pargeting** *or* **parging**)**:** external ornamental plasterwork in low relief on timber-framed buildings, having raised, indented or tooled patterns; used from Tudor times onwards, chiefly in East Anglia and the south-east of England.

Parlour: in a monastery, a room where monks were permitted to talk to visitors.

Parpen: a block of masonry which passes through the full thickness of a wall.

Parterre: a level space in a garden laid out with low, formal beds of plants; also, the ground floor of a theatre auditorium behind the orchestra.

Patera: round or oval ornament in shallow relief, especially in classical architecture.

Patio: a Spanish arcaded or colonnaded courtyard.

Pavilion: a prominent structure, generally distinctive in character, marking the ends and centre of the façade of a major building; a similarly distinctive building linked by a wing to a main block; an ornamental structure for occasional use in a garden.

Pavimentum: a pavement formed by pieces of tile, marble, stone, flints or other material set in cement and consolidated by beating down with a rammer.

Pedestal: a support for a column, statue or vase. It usually consists of a base, die (or dado) and cornice or cap-mould.

Pediment: in classical architecture, a triangular piece of wall above the entablature, enclosed by raking cornices; used for any roof end in renaissance architecture, whether triangular, broken or semicircular. In gothic, such features are known as gables.

Pele (or Peel) tower: a small square tower of massive construction, built in the border country of England and Scotland until the late Middle Ages.

Pendant: an elongated boss used as a decorative feature, projecting downwards or suspended from a ceiling or roof.

Pendentive: the triangular curved overhanging surface that supports a dome over a square or polygonal compartment.

Penthouse: an ancillary structure with a lean-to roof; in modern architecture, a separately-roofed structure on top of a multi-storey block.

Peristyle: in classical architecture, a range of columns all round a building such as a temple, or an interior space such as a courtyard.

Perpendicular: a later period of English gothic evolved from the Decorated style, and prevalent during the fifteenth and sixteenth centries; characterised by large squared-off window openings. The name is derived from these upright tracery panels.

Perron: a landing or platform outside the portal of a domestic or public building, approached in a dignified way by a single or double flight of steps.

Piano nobile: the Italian term for the principal

floor of a classical building on which the major rooms are concentrated, usually with a ground floor or basement underneath and a lesser storey overhead. Its importance is signalled by its height and the ornamentation around the windows.

Piazza: a public open space surrounded by buildings: they vary in shape and in civic purpose.

Picturesque: the romantic taste, developed in the late eighteenth and early nineteenth centuries, for buildings to be sited in contrived and controlled landscape settings.

Pier: a mass of masonry, as distinct from a column, from which an arch springs in an arcade or bridge; also applied to the wall between doors and windows, or sometimes used for a pillar in gothic arhitecture.

Pietra dura: ornamental or pictorial inlay by means of thin slabs of stone.

Pilaster: a pier in the shape of a column, but projecting only about one-sixth of its breadth from the wall, and of the same design as the order with which it is used.

Pile: a row of rooms; most commonly used as double pile, describing a house that is two rows thick.

Pillar: the freestanding upright member of any section, not conforming to one of the Orders.

Piloti: a post on an unenclosed ground floor carrying a raised building; characteristic of the architecture of Le Corbusier.

Pinnacle: in gothic architecture, a tall turret-like termination on the top of buttresses, parapets, or elsewhere, often ornamented with bunches of foliage called **crockets**.

Plaisance: summerhouse or pleasure house belonging to a mansion.

Plateresque: an intricate style of the early Spanish architecture of the later fifteenth and early sixteenth centuries, named after its likeness to silverwork.

Plinth: the lowest square member of the base of a column; also applied to the projecting stepped or moulded base of any building.

Plough-share twist: the irregular or winding surface in a vault, where the wall ribs, owing to the position of the clerestory windows, start at a higher level than the other ribs.

Podium: a continuous pedestal platform or base; used more recently to describe an artificial ground level or a relatively low block forming the base of a high-rise structure. Also, the enclosing platform of the arena in an auditorium.

Point block: a high block of housing, in which the apartments fan out from a central core of lifts or staircases.

Pointing: the joint between bricks or masonry blocks are customarily filled with mortar, a process known as pointing. This a utilitarian feature has considerable aesthetic qualities.

Polychromy: originally applied to the art of decorative painting in many colours, extended to the colouring of sculpture to enhance naturalism; very loosely used in an architectural context to describe the application of variegated materials to achieve brilliant or striking effects. As such, it is a characteristic of the high Victorian phase.

Poppy-head: the ornamental termination of a bench-end, frequently carved with fleurs-de-lys, animals or figures.

Porch: a covered projecting entrance to a building.

Portal frame: a single-storey frame comprising two uprights rigidly connected to a beam or pair of rafters, particularly to support a roof.

Portcullis: a defensive gate, constructed of a heavy lattice grille of timber or iron, sliding in vertical grooves in the jambs of a portal.

Porte-cochère: a covered porch to provide shelter for cars (originally for horse-drawn traffic) at the entrance to a building.

Portico: a colonnaded space forming an entrance or vestibule, with a roof supported on at least one side by columns.

Porticus: a shallow side chamber off the nave of a Saxon church.

Postern: a small gateway at the rear of a building.

Postmodernism: a term borrowed from twentieth-century literary theory, applied to architecture in the 1970s to describe a reaction against the prevailing school of modernism. It was an argument based on complexity rather than simplification, and the symbolic content rather than purely functional.

Prefabrication: conventional building practice is to assemble components and process raw materials on-site. Prefabrication, by contrast, is based on assembling complete buildings, or substantial elements of buildings, in factory conditions, possibly entirely remote from the building site, and then shipping them to the required destination in as complete a form as possible. This allows for the most delicate tasks to be done under cover, well away from weather and mud, thus speeding up the construction process, reducing costs, and improving quality control.

Presbytery: the space at the eastern end of a church for the clergy, but often applied to the whole sanctuary.

Principals: the pair of inclined lateral timbers of a truss which carry common rafters. Usually they support side purlins and their position corresponds to the main bay division of the space below.

Propylaeum: an important entrance gateway or vestibule, in front of a sacred enclosure.

Proscenium: in classical architecture, the stage of a theatre; in modern terminology it denotes the part of a theatre between the curtain and the orchestra, or the stage arch facing the auditorium.

Prostyle: with a freestanding row of columns in front.

Pudding stone: a building stone of coarse texture, composed mostly of an amalgam of sandstone fragments that has been smoothed by the passage of water.

Pulpit: a raised and enclosed platform used for the preaching of sermons.

Pulpitum: a stone gallery or rood loft over the entrance to the choir of a cathedral or church.

Pulvinated: describes a frieze, the face of which is convex in profile.

Pumice: igneous rock derived from volcanic lava. It was used by the Romans as a building stone, and, later, is present in Byzantine and romanesque work. It had the advantage of extreme lightness.

Purlin: a horizontal beam in a roof, resting on the principal rafters and supporting the common rafters and roof covering.

Putholes or putlock holes: holes created in a wall to receive putlocks, the horizontal timbers on which scaffolding boards rest. They are often not filled in after construction is complete.

Quadrangle: a broad enclosure or inner court, defined by buildings.

Quadripartite vaulting: a vault in which each bay is divided by intersecting diagonal ribs into four parts.

Quarries: square or diamond-shaped panes of glass supported by lead strips which are called **cames**; also used to describe square floor-slabs or tiles.

Quatrefoil: in tracery, a panel divided by cusps into four openings.

Queen-posts: a pair of vertical, or near-vertical, timbers placed symmetrically on a tie-beam and supporting side purlins.

Quirk: a sharp V-shaped groove to one side of a convex moulding, for example beside a roll moulding, which is then said to be quirked.

Quoin: a term generally applied to the dressed cornerstones at the angles of buildings and hence to the angle itself.

Radiating vaults: those springing from a central column.

Rafter: an inclined lateral timber sloping from wall-top to apex and supporting the roof covering.

Raggle: a recess or groove cut in masonry, especially to receive the edge of glass or roof covering.

Rampart: a defensive (originally earthen) bank surrounding a castle, fortress or fortified town; it may have a stone parapet.

Rationalism: an Italian strand of the modern movement, associated with the authoritarianism of the Mussolini period. Unlike other totalitarian societies, Italy was prepared to countenance architecture stripped of overt historical references.

Rebate: a rectangular sinking, channel or groove cut longitudinally in a piece of timber to receive the edge of another, or a recess in the jambs of an opening to receive a door or window.

Reeding: a series of convex mouldings of equal width, side by side: the inverse of fluting. The fluting of the lower third of column shafts was sometimes filled in with reeds to strengthen them.

Refectory: the dining-hall in a monastry, convent or college.

Regency: the architectural style that provided the transition between Georgian and Victorian. The name derived from the regency of the Prince of Wales, 1811–20. He later reigned as King George IV.

Regula: the short band, under the **triglyphs**, beneath the **tenia** of the Doric entablature, and to which the **guttae** are attached.

Relieving arch: designed to relieve the weight pressing down on another arch or opening.

Renaissance: the reintroduction of classic architecture all over Europe but more particularly with the cultural flowering of Florence, in the fifteenth and sixteenth centuries.

Rendering: a uniform covering or skin of plaster or **stucco** applied to an external wall; internally, a first coat of plaster. Cement rendering is a cheaper and more recent substitute for stucco, usually with a grainy texture and often left unpainted. The wall surface may be roughly lime-plastered and then whitewashed in more simple buildings, or covered with a plaster mixed with a coarse aggregate such as gravel, known as roughcast. A variant fashionable in the early twentieth century, in which the stones of the aggregate were kept separate and thrown at the wet plastered wall to create a textured effect was known as pebbledashing.

Repoussé work: ornamental metalwork, hammered into relief from the reverse side.

Reredos: the screen, or ornamental work, rising behind the altar. The Spanish retablo is a sumptuously ornate form of reredos.

Respond: a half-pillar at the end of an arcade.

Retable: a framework of decorative panels, normally sited behind the altar.

Retro-choir: the parts of a large church behind the high altar.

Reveal: the surface at right angles to the face of a wall, especially applied to the part outside the window or door frame; known as a **splay** when cut diagonally.

Revetment: the retaining wall of an embankment, or the decorative facing of a wall.

Rib: a projecting band on a ceiling vault or elsewhere.

Ridge: the apex of a sloping roof, running from end to end.

Riser: the vertical face of a step.

Rock-faced: masonry which is cleft to produce a natural rugged appearance.

Rococo: a type of renaissance ornament in which rock-like forms, fantastic scrolls and shells are worked together in a profusion and confusion of detail, often without organic coherence, but presenting a lavish display of decoration. It was the latest phase of the baroque style current throughout Europe between c. 1720 and c. 1760

Roll moulding: a plain round moulding; in medieval architecture, sometimes known as the bowtell.

Romanesque: the style, founded on Roman architecture, prevalent in Western Europe from the ninth to the twelfth century.

Rood loft: a raised gallery over the *rood screen*, a name given to the chancel screen when it supports the *rood* (large cross) erected in many churches in medieval times. It was reached by stairs in the chancel wall and also used as a gallery for minstrels and singers on festival days.

Roof, single-framed: constructed with no main trusses. The rafters may be fixed to a wall-plate or ridge, or longitudinal timbers may be absent altogether. A common rafter roof is one in which pairs of rafters are not connected by a collar-beam. A coupled rafter roof is one in which the rafters are connected by collar-beams. **Double-framed:** constructed with longitudinal members such as purlins. Generally there are principals, principal rafters supporting the longitudinal members and dividing the length of the roofs into bays.

Rostrum: (pl *rostra*) originally the raised platform in the *forum Romanum* from which orators addressed the people; *cf* **tribune**.

Rose window *see* **wheel window**.

Rotunda: a round building.

Rubbed brickwork: *see* **gauged brickwork**.

Rubble: stone walling of rough, undressed stones.

Rustication: a method of forming stonework to have roughened surfaces and recessed joints, principally employed in renaissance buildings to create the impression of strength.

Sacristy: a room in a church for storing sacred vessels and vestments.

Saddleback roof: a normal pitched roof, sited over a tower.

Sanctuary: a holy or consecrated place; the most sacred part of a church.

Sash window: a double-hung, usually wooden, glazed frame (the sash), designed to slide up and down in grooves by means of pulleys.

Säteri roof: a form of hipped roof, interrupted by a smaller vertical part sometimes provided with windows. This low perpendicular break forms the middle portion between the lower part of the roof and its considerably smaller continuation above the break. It is characteristic of the great houses of the Swedish nobility and gentry of the seventeenth and eighteenth centuries.

Saxo-Norman: transitional romanesque style combining Anglo-Saxon and Norman features, current *c.* 1060–1100.

Scagliola: a composition imitating marble, made from gypsum, sand, lime, fragments of marble and cement.

Scissor arch: a strainer arch consisting of an inverted arch on top of a supporting arch.

Scotia: the concave moulding between the two **torus** mouldings in the base of a column, throwing a deep shadow.

Screen: a partition or enclosure of iron, stone or wood, often carved; when separating the choir from the nave, it is termed the choir screen.

Scroll moulding: one resembling a scroll of paper, the end of which projects over the other part.

Section: the representation of a building cut by a vertical plane, so as to show the construction.

Segmental: a curved element that is less than a semi-circle.

Semi-detached: a pair of houses which share a party wall, and usually, a common roof.

Severy: a compartment or bay of a vault.

Sgraffito: a method of decoration by which a top coat of stucco is partially cut away to expose a dark undercoat and so form a design.

Shaft: the portion of a column between base and capital; in medieval architecture also applied to a small column, as in a clustered pier, supporting a vaulting rib.

Shell vaulting: a thin curved plate-like form of roofing, generally of reinforced concrete and often of striking elegance, widely used in recent times for spanning large halls.

Shingle style: the cladding of external walls with the wooden tiles, known as shingles, over a timber frame.

Shuttering: *see* **formwork**.

Sill: a horizontal member at the bottom of a window or door frame. Also used to describe the horizontal member at the base of a timber-framed wall into which the posts and studs are tenoned.

Skirting: wooden board used to protect the base of an internal wall.

Slab block: a rectangular multi-storey block of housing or offices.

Slate-hanging: a covering of overlapping slates on a wall, which is then said to be slate-hung; similar to tile-hung.

Sleepers: beams which support joists.

Slype: a covered way or passage, especially in a cathedral or monastic church, leading east from the cloisters between the transept and chapter house.

Soffit: the ceiling or underside of any architectural member.

Solar: the upper living room or withdrawing room of a medieval house, accessible from the high table end of the hall.

Solar gain: the increasing use of glass as a primary material in the twentieth century has brought with it some initially unexpected side effects. The use of a structural steel skeleton has made lightweight glass walls structurally possible, but massive stone walls have other advantages that glass does not have: they change the thermal performance of a building. Massive stone makes a building slow to heat up, and in winter slow to lose that heat. Glass produces a greenhouse effect: it makes a building heat up quickly, and then lose that heat equally quickly. For a building to be kept at a comfortable temperature, it is necessary either to use large amounts of artificial energy to counteract solar gain, or else to take measures such as shading or double glazing and insulation to counteract the effects of solar gain.

Sopraporta: a painting or relief above the door of a room, usual in the seventeenth and eighteenth centuries.

Sounding-board: *see* **tester**.

Space frame: a frame which is three-dimensional and stable in all directions; it is a means of carrying structural load with a minimum of material.

Span: the distance between the supports of an arch, roof or beam.

Spandrel: the triangular space enclosed by the curve of an arch, a vertical line from its springing, and a horizontal line through its apex. In modern architecture, an infill panel below a window frame in a curtain wall.

Specus: the duct or channel of a Roman aqueduct, usually rectangular in section and lined with a waterproofing of successive coatings of hydraulic cement, and covered by stone slabs or arched vaults.

Spere: a fixed timber screen, sometimes elaborately carved, shielding the entrances of medieval houses and large halls. When directly attached to a roof-principal, the resultant structure became a spere-truss.

Spina: the spine wall down the centre of an ancient hippodrome or circus.

Spire: the tapering termination of a tower in gothic or renaissance architecture, which was the result of elongating an ordinary pyramidal or conical roof.

Splay: the diagonal surface formed by the cutting away of a wall, as when an opening is wider inside than out, or conversely.

Springer: the lowest unit of the **voussoir** of an arch, occurring just above the springing line; the stone that rests on the impost.

Sprocket: a short timber placed on the back and at the foot of a rafter to form projecting eaves.

Squince: a small arch, bracket or similar device built across each angle of a square or polygonal structure to form an octagon or other appropriate base for a dome or spire; sometimes known as a squinch arch.

Stairs:
- **dog-leg** parallel flights rising alternately in opposite directions, without an open well;
- **flying** cantilevered from the wall of a stairwell, without newels;
- **geometric** a flying stair, the inner edge of which describes a curve;
- **newel** ascending round a central supporting newel; called a *spiral* stair or *vice* when in a circular shaft;
- **perron:** an external stair leading to a doorway, usually of double-curved plan;
- **well:** any stair contained within an open well, but generally one that climbs up three sides of a well with corner landings. The timber-framed newel stair was common from the seventeenth century onwards.

Stalls: divisions with fixed seats for the clergy and choir, often elaborately carved, with projecting elbows, misericords and canopies.

Stanchion: a vertical steel support. Cast iron was used until relatively cheap steel became available.

Starling: the pointed mass of masonry projecting from the pier of a bridge for breaking the force of the water, hence known as a cutwater.

Steel frame: a framework of horizontal and vertical girders that replaced reliance on loadbearing walls in the construction of high-rise buildings.

Steeple: a tower crowned by a spire.

Stellar vault: a vault in which the ribs compose a star-shaped pattern.

Stepped gable: a gable with stepped sides, especially characteristic of the Netherlands.

Stereobate: in classical architecture, the base of a wall or colonnade.

Stijl, de: a short-lived geometric-abstract movement in the Netherlands (1917–31), which had a lasting influence on the development of modern architecture and of industrial design.

Stilted arch: an arch having its springing line higher than the line of impost mouldings, to which it is connected by vertical pieces of walling or stilts.

Stop: plain or decorated blocks terminating mouldings or chamfers in stone or wood, or at the end of labels, hood moulds, or string courses.

Storey: the space between two floors.

Strapwork: a type of relief ornament or surface decoration resembling studded leather straps, arranged in geometrical and sometimes interlaced patterns; much used in the early renaissance architecture of England and the Low Countries.

String: the sloping edge of a staircase which supports the treads of the individual steps.

String course: a moulding or projecting course running horizontally along the face of a building.

Strings: two sloping members which carry the ends of the treads and risers of a staircase. Closed strings enclose the treads and risers; in the latter open string staircase the steps project above the strings.

Stud: a subsidiary vertical timber of a timber-framed wall or partition.

Strut: a vertical or inclined timber which runs between two members of a roof truss but does not directly support longitudinal timbers.

Stuart: late-renaissance English architecture of the period 1625–1702.

Stucco: a fine smooth quality of lime plaster, much used in Roman and renaissance architecture for ornamental modelling work in low relief. It was extensively employed in England in the late eighteenth and early nineteenth centuries as an economical medium for the modelling of external features in lieu of stone, and is usually painted.

Stylobate: in classical architecture, the top step forming a platform on which a colonnade is placed. Collectively, the three steps of a Greek Doric temple constitute a *crepidoma*.

Suspension bridge: a bridge suspended from cables or chains draped from towers.

Tabby: a form of concrete made from oyster shells.

Tabernacle: a canopied structure, especially on a small scale, to contain the reserved sacrament or a relic. Also, an architectural frame for example of a statue on a wall or freestanding, with flanking orders; in classical architecture, also called an **aedicule**.

Tablet-flower: a variation of the ball-flower

ornament of Decorated gothic architecture in the form of a four-panelled open flower.

Tenia: the flat projecting band capping the **architrave** of a Doric entablature.

Tas-de-change: the lower courses of a vault or arch laid horizontally.

Tempietto: a small temple. The term is usually reserved for Renaissance and later buildings of an ornamental character, compact circular or temple-like structures erected in the parks and gardens of country houses, although the most famous instance is Bramante's chapel in the cloisters of S Pietro in Montorio, Rome.

Tenement: urban housing consisting of a multi-storey dwelling with many apartments and access by a common stair.

Terminal figure: pedestal or pilaster which tapers towards the bottom, usually with the upper part of a human figure rising from it; also called a *termo* herm.

Terracotta: earth baked or burnt in moulds for use in construction and decoration, harder in quality than brick.

Tessera: a small cube of stone, glass or marble, used in making mosaics.

Tester: a flat canopy over a tomb or especially over a pulpit, where it is also called a sounding-board.

Thermae window: *see* **Diocletian window.**

Tholos: the dome (cupola) of a circular building, hence the building itself.

Thrust: the force exerted by inclined rafters or beams against a wall, or obliquely by the weight of an arch, vault or dome.

Tie-bar: a beam, bar or rod which ties parts of a building together, and is subjected to tensile strain; sometimes of wood, but usually of metal. Tie-bars are especially notable in Byzantine, Italian gothic and renaissance architecture to stiffen arcades or to contain the outward thrust of vaults.

Tie-beam: normally the lowest member of a roof truss, extending from wall-plate to wall-plate and primarily intended to prevent the walls from spreading. A secondary function may be to carry a king-post or crown-post.

Tierceron: an intermediate rib between the main ribs of a gothic vault.

Timber-framing: method of construction where walls are built of interlocking vertical and horizontal timbers. The spaces are filled with non-structural walling of wattle and daub, lath and plaster, brickwork (known as nogging), and so on. Sometimes the timber is covered over by plaster, boarding laid horizontally (weather-boarding), or tiles.

Torus: a large convex moulding, used principally in the bases of columns.

Tourelle: a turret corbelled out from the wall.

Tower house: a compact medieval fortified house with the main hall raised above the ground and at least one more storey above it. The type survives in odd examples into the sixteenth and seventeenth centuries.

Trabeated: a style of architecture which uses only horizontal and vertical structural elements.

Tracery: the ornamental patternwork in stone, filling the upper part of a gothic window; it may be either plate or bar tracery.

Plate tracery is the earliest and simplest form, where the shape appears to be cut out of the stone spandrel between two lancet windows.

Bar tracery was introduced into England *c.* 1250, and was designed principally for the pleasing forms produced by combinations of geometrical figures. It is also applied to work of the same character in wood panelling. Types of bar tracery include: geometrical, consisting chiefly of circles or foiled circles; Y-shape, consisting of a mullion which branches into two to form a Y-shape, typical of *c.* 1300; intersecting, in which each mullion of a window branches out into two curved bars in such a way that every one of them is drawn with the same radius from a different centre; reticulated, typical of the early fourteenth century, consisting entirely of circles drawn at top and bottom into

ogee shapes so that a net-like appearance results; panel, perpendicular tracery which is formed of upright straight-sided panels above the lights of a window; dagger, a decorated tracery motif; Kentish, a cusp split into a fork, and also known as split cusp tracery, and mouchette, a curved version of the dagger form, and popular in the early fourteenth century.

Trachelion: the neck of a Greek Doric column, between the **annulets** and the grooves or **hypotrachelion.**

Transept: that part of a cruciform church which projects at right angles to the main building.

Transitional: a transitional phase between two styles, most often used for the phase between romanesque and early English (*c.* 1175–1200).

Transom: the horizontal division or cross-bar of a window.

Transverse rib: a rib which extends at right angles to the wall across a bay or other vaulted space.

Tread: the horizontal part of the step of a staircase. The tread end may be carved.

Triangulation: the principle of the design of a roof truss, in which every panel or space enclosed by its members is triangular.

Tribune: the gallery of a church, the presiding seat in the apse of a basilica, or the platform on which that seat is placed.

Triforium: the space between the sloping roof over the aisle and the aisle vaulting. The term was first applied to the Norman arcades at Canterbury which have triple openings towards the nave, and was afterwards used for any passages and galleries in this position. It occurs in large churches only, and, because it has no windows to the open air, is often called a blind storey.

Triglyphs: blocks with vertical channels which form a distinguishing feature in the frieze of the Doric entablature.

Trussed-rafter roof: a form of roof composed of pairs of rafters, closely spaced and without a ridge-piece. To contain the outward thrust, the rafters were joined by collars and further stiffened by braces.

Trumeau: the central stone mullion supporting the tympanum of a wide doorway. A **trumeau figure** is a carved figure attached to a trumeau.

Tudor: late-gothic English architecture of the period 1485–1558.

Tufa: a building stone of rough or cellular texture, of volcanic or other origin.

Tumbling *or* **tumbling-in:** courses of brickwork laid at right angles to the slope of a gable and forming triangles by tapering into horizontal courses.

Turrets: small towers, often containing stairs, and forming special features in medieval buildings.

Tympanum: the triangular surface bounded by the sloping and horizontal cornices of a pediment; also the space between the lintel and the arch of a medieval doorway.

Undercroft: in medieval architecture, vaulted chambers upon which the principal rooms are sometimes raised.

Unité d'habitation: Le Corbusier's name for an ideal housing type, the multi-story block including social facilities, shops, and play space contained within a single building, arranged around what he called streets in the sky. Realised by Le Corbusier himself most famously in Marseilles, but also in Berlin and at the new town of Firminy, the *Unité* was to prove hugely influential, if far from universally socially successful.

Vault: an arched covering over any building, usually in stone or brick, and reinforced when necessary by ribs.

Vaulting-shaft: the shaft leading up to the springer of a vault.

Venetian window: a triple window, the use of which was popularised by Palladio, composed of a central arched opening flanked on each side by two smaller openings.

Veranda: a shelter or gallery against a building,

its roof supported by thin vertical members.

Vernacular: the unselfconscious building tradition of a culture or a community, rather than its high architecture. Generally it is expressed by more modest buildings such as houses and agricultural buildings and relies on precedent and tradition rather than innovation, on the slow evolution of characteristic elements over time.

Vestibule: an anteroom to a larger apartment of a building.

Villa: originally a Romano-British farm or country house. Now widely used to describe a wide spectrum of sites, ranging from humble farmsteads to sumptuous mansions associated with large estates. Various architectural traditions, including both classical and vernacular, are evident in villas, but all display some pretensions towards fundamental Roman standards.

The sixteenth-century Venetian type with office wings, derived from Roman models and made grander by Palladio's varied application of a central portico. It became an important type in eighteenth-century Britain.

Vitrified: bricks or tiles which have been fired in such a way as to produce a darkened glassy surface.

Vitruvian opening: a door or window which diminishes towards the top, as advocated by Vitruvius.

Vitruvian scroll: classical running ornament of curly waves.

Volute: the scroll or spiral occuring in Ionic, Corinthian and Composite capitals.

Voussoirs: the truncated wedge-shaped blocks forming an arch.

Wagon roof: one in which closely-set rafters with arched braces give the appearance of the inside of a canvas tilt over a wagon. Wagon roofs can be panelled or plastered (ceiled) or left uncovered; also called **cradle roof.**

Wall-plate: a timber laid longitudinally on the top of a wall to receive the ends of the rafters. In a timber-framed building the posts and studs of the wall below are tenoned into it.

Water wheel: water mills were originally used for grinding corn and are described by the way the water is fed on to the wheel:
- **overshot** over the top;
- **pitchback** on to the top but falling backwards;
- **breastshot** mid-height, falling and passing beneath;
- **undershot** where the wheel is turned by the momentum of the water passing beneath;
- **water turbine** water fed under pressure through a vaned wheel within a casing.

Wattle and daub: a wall construction that consists of a loose structure of branches (wattles) covered with mud or clay (daub) mixed with straw.

Wealden house: a medieval timber-framed house of distinctive form. It has a central open hall flanked by bays of two storeys. The end bays are jettied to the front, but a single roof covers the whole building, thus producing an exceptionally wide overhang to the eaves in front of the hall.

Weatherboarding: overlapping horizontal boards, covering a timber-framed wall, most common after the mid-eighteenth century.

Weathering: the slope, to throw off rain, given to offsets to buttresses; also applied to the upper surface of cornices and mouldings.

Wheel window: a circular window, the mullions of which converge like the spokes of a wheel.

Winder: an individual step of a staircase which is wider at the outside edge. Several winders together will form a right-angled turn, and if continued with, a spiral staircase.

Wrought iron: iron forged into decorative patterns, or forged and rolled into bars, joists and so on; it is ductile and high in tensile strength.

Index

Far left: Serle's House, Southgate Street, Winchester, Hampshire c. 1710–20, since 1796 belonging to the Ministry of Defence but at the time of writing under threat of sale. Presently it houses the regimental museum of

the Princess of Wales's Royal Regiment, and in its memorial garden are scattered the ashes of many soldiers who died in the world wars. Widely attributed to Thomas Archer, the house has giant Doric pilasters with swelling

capitals rising at the corners of the building and emphasizing the centre bay, which projects by means of single-bay quadrant corners. Inside there is a round entrance hall, behind which is a staircase starting double and returning single